"*The Savings Solution* uses a light-hearted conversation to make managing finances and building wealth simple and easy to understand. An enjoyable read that will keep you turning the pages to find your pot of gold at the end of the book."

—ARKADI KUHLMANN, CHAIRMAN AND PRESIDENT OF ING DIRECT USA, AKA THE CEO OF SAVINGS

"From the simple stuff like strawberries and sneakers to the big stuff like retirement savings, *The Savings Solution* tackles it all, demonstrating each of us has the ability to create a more secure financial future. Michael shows us how—with a little forethought—we can live for today even as we prepare for a more prosperous future. Unlike most financial "How To's", *The Savings Solution* is refreshingly entertaining and straightforward. Whether you're blue collar, white collar, or no collar at all, Michael's entertaining and informative book is sure to help you set the course for a more financially secure future."

—BEN NORQUIST, PRESIDENT AND CEO, CONVERGENT RETIREMENT PLAN SOLUTIONS

Also by Michael B. Rubin

Praise for *Beyond Paycheck to Paycheck: A Conversation
About Income, Wealth, and the Steps in Between*

"A comprehensive book that will help anyone struggling to make ends meet … It's easy to read and funny."
—CAREERBUILDER.COM, IN NAMING *BEYOND PAYCHECK TO PAYCHECK*
ONE OF FIVE BOOKS TO HELP YOUR CAREER

"The most straightforward financial planning book you'll find. Understandable by the financially clueless yet extremely beneficial to those who have already begun. Unique conversational format. Unbelievable glossary!"
—ARTHUR F. VON DER LINDEN, JR., CFP®, FOUNDER AND
PRINCIPAL, WINGATE FINANCIAL GROUP, INC.

"I wish I could've read *Beyond Paycheck to Paycheck* when I was first starting out. But I can't wait to share Michael Rubin's wisdom with my daughters as soon as they join the workforce themselves. If you have any doubts whether this concise, cogent, and compelling book is for you (or your children), just read the preface. Now."
—B. JOSEPH PINE II, CO-AUTHOR, *THE EXPERIENCE ECONOMY:
WORK IS THEATRE & EVERY BUSINESS A STAGE*

"*Beyond Paycheck to Paycheck* is the perfect gift for every new college graduate. Rubin discusses debt, taxes, investments, insurance and other financial topics, using humor and a hypothetical dialogue to effectively illustrate his lessons."
—ELAINE MORGILLO, CFP®, PRESIDENT OF MORGILLO FINANCIAL MANAGEMENT INC.

"Michael Rubin has provided and delivered an effective roadmap to navigate the increasingly complex landscape of personal financial security. *Beyond Paycheck to Paycheck* disperses uncommonly good sense in an interesting and easily understandable way. Bravo!"
—DANIEL N. HEBERT, PRESIDENT, NEW HAMPSHIRE JUMP$TART COALITION

"From managing your debt to investing for your future, *Beyond Paycheck to Paycheck* provides you with the tools and motivation necessary to intelligently pursue your financial dreams."
—CARL LEHMANN, ENTREPRENEUR, FORMER PRESIDENT,
TRAVELERS CHEQUE GROUP WORLDWIDE, AMERICAN EXPRESS COMPANY

"What really stands out is the conversational approach. You almost get the feeling that you're sitting down and talking with Michael directly. I think this approach has many advantages over more conventional books that can come off as a bit preachy … goes a long way in making sure that people who read it actually go on to take action."
—JEREMY VOHINKLE, *GENERATION X FINANCE*

THE
SAVINGS
SOLUTION

A Conversation
About Living for Today
While Saving for Tomorrow

"The Savings Solution uses a lighthearted conversation to make managing finances and building wealth simple and easy to understand."

Arkadi Kulmann
Chairman and President of ING Direct USA

Michael B. Rubin

Second in a series from Total Candor

W&M
WACHTEL & MARTIN

Published by Wachtel & Martin LLC
Portsmouth, New Hampshire
www.wachtelandmartin.com

Printed in the United States of America

For information on bulk purchases of *The Savings Solution,* including significant discount opportunities, please contact *bulksales@wachtelandmartin.com.*

For author availability for a specific date to lead a workplace event or university workshops, or for a calendar of public seminars, please contact *info@totalcandor.com* or visit *www.totalcandor.com.*

Publisher's Cataloging-in-Publication
(Provided by Quality Books, Inc.)

Rubin, Michael B.
    The savings solution : a conversation about living
for today while saving for tomorrow / by Michael B.
Rubin.
    p. cm. — (Total candor ; 2)
    LCCN 2011938041
    ISBN-13: 978-0-9787927-7-0
    ISBN-10: 0-9787927-7-7

    1. Finance, Personal. 2. Saving and investment.
3. Budgets, Personal.   I. Title. II. Series: Total
candor ; 2.

HG179.R83 2012   332.024'01
                        QBI11-600183

SUMMARY TABLE OF CONTENTS

DETAILED TABLE OF CONTENTS

For Hannah, Allyson, and the little one on the way,
You're my ultimate free stuff—
And worth every penny.

ACKNOWLEDGMENTS

I remain blessed by not only the unending support of my beautiful wife Laura, but also the zest for life (and all things edible) of my two very sweet daughters, Hannah and Ally.

Nearly five years have passed since I wrote *Beyond Paycheck to Paycheck* to sales levels exceeding any reasonable expectation, launching my speaking career along the way. Not surprisingly, the efforts of others truly enabled my passion for financial literacy to reach the masses. While the list of people to whom I am indebted is long, I must specifically thank Todd Sandler of ING DIRECT, Dan Hebert of the Jump$tart Coalition for Personal Financial Literacy, as well as Matt Herek and Aspasia Apostolakis of Northwestern University.

In addition, thank you to my prized assistant Brittany Drew and to my original financial planning mentor—and fellow obsessive Red Sox fan—Stephen P. Ahern. Each of you has greatly facilitated *The Savings Solution* moving from concept to reality.

And, of course, a very large thank you goes to *You:*

Bruce Mitchell:
A Man With A Problem

My caller ID displayed an unexpected name: BRUCE MITCHELL I immediately recalled our only conversation, more than five months earlier. For an initial phone call, Bruce had been extremely open and honest.

"I've never been very good with money," Bruce began.

"A lot of people don't understand basic personal finance, Bruce," I told him.

"I know, but I'm in trouble and I need your help."

"Okay. Tell me what's going on, Bruce."

"Over the years, my wife Ann and I have borrowed extensively. We've always been able to repay our debt but find ourselves in the same spot a few months later."

"What do you think causes the problem? Any health or employment issues?" I asked.

"No. Fortunately, we're good there. Everyone's healthy. Ann and I have never been let go. On the income side, we're fine. Honestly, we do *very* well," Bruce concluded.

"So what do you think the problem is?" I asked.

Bruce paused a few seconds to collect his thoughts. "We moved out of the city a couple of years ago," he said. "When we did, we sold our apartment for a profit—a huge profit. We used the money gained on the sale as a down payment on a suburban home."

So far so good, I thought to myself.

"Despite the large down payment, we took a big mortgage because homes in the suburbs aren't cheap. Then, we spent a ton of money improving the home."

"Okay," I said listening intently. "Tell me more about the home improvements."

"Looking back, we probably spent too much on the remodel," Bruce confided. "To make it worse, the contractor went bankrupt at a time when we had paid for more work than had been completed. We got royally screwed; we were unable to get any money back. As a result, I had to borrow money from my family to complete the renovation. I still owe most of that money."

"Well, a contractor's bankruptcy is a tough break—one which would financially harm most people. Still, you *were* able to borrow money from your family and complete the remodel. Since you haven't paid your family back yet, your ongoing financial problems don't seem to be entirely due to the contractor's bankruptcy."

"You're right, Michael. A few other things happened since we bought the home," Bruce confessed.

"Such as?" I inquired.

"First, our property taxes doubled," Bruce disclosed.

"Doubled? This must have been some renovation!" I said, shocked.

"It was, but I still never expected my property tax to double. That's ridiculous, right?" Bruce asked.

"It does seem absurd, Bruce," I told him.

"I'm fighting the increase, but in the meantime I have to pay those illogical taxes. Plus, our monthly credit card bills are very high," Bruce told me.

"Are they higher than before you moved out of the city?" I asked.

"Yes, there's all this stuff with the new home: landscaping, heating oil, electricity, and so on. All of those costs are out of sight. You can see why

I'm so frustrated, right? I have to heat the house. I can't turn the lights off. You get where I'm coming from, don't you?"

"Sure, I do. But there's one thing I still don't understand," I told Bruce. "It appears you spend more than you make."

"We definitely spend more than we make," Bruce readily admitted.

"And you've been doing so for a very long time. The only way anyone can spend more than they make for an extended period is by continually raiding their savings or by taking on additional new debt. Besides your family, who else have you borrowed from?"

"We have big credit card balances. We've used all of our home equity. In prior years, I've taken advances on my bonus," Bruce explained matter-of-factly.

"How were you able to do that?" I asked.

"It's a family-owned company and I'm family, so I asked for help," Bruce replied.

"That was fortunate," I pointed out.

"It was," Bruce conceded. "Ann and I have also borrowed from our 401(k) plans. Most recently, we found some additional money we could borrow from our life insurance policies. But at this point, we have no money left."

"None?" I asked.

"None. I get paid on Friday but right now we have only $75 in the checking account and I have a few thousand dollars of past due bills. There's no money, Michael" Bruce told me with exasperation in his voice.

Just as I was about to respond, Bruce continued.

"It's embarrassing," he said.

"Of course it is," I told him. "On the other hand, you're still employed, your wife is still employed, and you're both healthy. You *can* fix this."

"I hope so," Bruce said. "You know, I finally came clean with Ann about this last night."

"Your wife didn't know your financial situation?" I asked.

"No, not really. I take care of all the bills," Bruce explained.

"How did she react?"

"Well, she was shocked, of course. But she was also very supportive and confident we'd be able to make the changes necessary to get back on track. She wants to do whatever we can to keep our house. We really don't want to lose our home."

"Okay, I hear you," I told Bruce.

In explaining how I would help him, I outlined Bruce's responsibilities including summarizing their debts, assets, income, and monthly expenses. I told Bruce we'd move quickly before things became worse.

"Good. One more thing, though, Michael," Bruce replied.

"Sure."

"I'm having heart surgery next week."

"I'm sorry you have to go through that—sounds serious," I said empathetically.

"It is. My mother passed away due to a heart problem years ago. I've been periodically tested since then and the doctors recently found something to address. I'll be fine. Honestly, the financial stuff is stressing me out far more. Send the paperwork you need me to complete and I'll be back to you after the heart surgery, likely in about two weeks."

"Sounds good, Bruce," I responded. "Good luck with the surgery."

"Thanks, Michael."

"Goodbye, Bruce."

"Goodbye."

That was five months ago.

When I didn't hear from Bruce a few weeks later, I feared something went wrong with his surgery. Fortunately, a mutual acquaintance assured me Bruce was in good health. Relieved, I hoped Bruce had resolved his financial problems and no longer needed my assistance.

THIS MORNING

"Good morning. This is Michael," I answered the phone.

"Hi, Michael. This is Bruce Mitchell. We spoke a few months ago."

"How are you Bruce?" I responded.

"Oh good, you remember me."

"Of course I do, Bruce," I assured him.

"Sorry I didn't get back to you until now," Bruce apologized.

"No worries," I told him. "I heard your heart surgery went well."

"Fortunately, yes. I heard you checked in on me—thank you. I'm sure you're busy. Are you still willing to work with me?" Bruce asked.

"Sure, Bruce."

"Great" he said, sounding somewhat relieved.

But I had to ask. So I did. "Well, what's happened since February, Bruce? At the time, you appeared to be at the end of your financial rope."

"We were," Bruce admitted.

"So how have you been doing these last few months?" I inquired.

"We got lucky and unexpectedly ran into some money. With the extra money, we were able to get current with our credit cards and our mortgage. But here we are, just a few months later in even worse shape than we were in February.

"Michael, we love our home. We don't want to lose it, but we don't know if we can afford to keep it. Our home is the number one priority."

"Do you think you're at risk of losing your home now?" I asked.

"We're two months behind on the mortgage," Bruce stated.

"Gotcha," I acknowledged.

"That's not all. AmEx has cut us off. So now we have to pay cash for everything—or use Ann's Visa. And the banks we owe money to? They're calling all day long. Evenings too. It's gotten to the point where we can't even answer our home phone.

"After we got the unexpected money I just told you about," Bruce continued, "we noted our good fortune and tried to be especially careful with our spending."

"What happened?" I asked.

"It was one thing after another. First, the dog got sick and so we had some crazy vet bills. Am I supposed to say, 'Put the dog down,' because we can't afford to pay for the operation? How do I say that to my children?

Then it was time for summer camp. Do I not send my kids to camp when all their friends are going and it's the same camp they went to last year? Maybe I have to. I just don't know. Michael, I'm desperate."

"I understand," I told him.

"I'm willing to make changes, Michael. You just gotta help me keep my house—I have three kids," Bruce pleaded.

"I hear you. We will do everything we can to save your home," I said, not knowing if we'd be able to do so.

ARE BRUCE AND ANN MITCHELL NORMAL?

In many ways, Bruce and Ann are no different from a typical American family. They're struggling to pay their bills, have no idea how to save, but don't feel they're living beyond what they deserve. They don't the see opportunities right in front of them. They also don't admit the implications of previous decisions.

On the other hand, Bruce and Ann are quite different from the typical American household. Combined, Bruce and Ann earn over $600,000 per year.

You: Dude, I think you put in an extra zero up there. It now reads $600,000, not $60,000. You should have hired a proofreader.

It's right. Ann and Bruce make over $600,000 a year.

You: And they might lose their home?

Yes.

You: On $600,000 a year?

Yes.

You: Holy shit.

Your words, not mine. (But I agree.)

· · · · · · · · · · · · · · ·

CHAPTER 1

Saving Gives You Options

"Two roads diverged in a wood, and I—
I took the one less traveled by,
And that has made all the difference."
—Robert Frost, *The Road Not Taken*

"Look to the left. Look to the right. One of you will not be here at the end."

Such is the highlight of a dean's otherwise unremarkable self-congratulatory welcoming at countless universities each fall. The implication is clear: one out of three freshmen won't make it to graduation.

Don't worry—you will make it through *The Savings Solution*. Still, humor me and look at a person near you.

You: Excuse me?

Go ahead, but be quick and subtle. If you can look but not leer, odds are the person won't notice.

You: What if you're wrong?

Tell the individual *I* said to do it and you're not going to do it again. Show them this page if you must.

You: This is weird, but okay . . .

· · · · · · · · · · ·

Thank you. Between you and the person you were just checking out, one of you—statistically speaking—is living paycheck to paycheck.

You: How do you know?

One in two Americans are currently only *one* missed payday from significant financial hardship. In other words, half of all Americans live paycheck to paycheck.[1] Consequently, if you live from one paycheck to the next, you are not alone. Far from it.

THE TYPICAL EXPLANATION

I always take questions at the end of my financial education workshops. Since some people do not feel comfortable speaking in front of a large group, I also answer questions privately at the end of the event. With one glaring exception, I have found no pattern between questions asked publicly and those asked privately.

You: What is the exception?

The person sharing his particular explanation of his paycheck to paycheck lifestyle does so *only* in private. Since he is certain his situation is unique, he does not embarrass himself or others by discussing it publicly. So with great irony, I hear his rationale repeatedly:

"Michael, the problem isn't with my *spending*, it's with my *income*."

I nod my head, knowing what comes next.

"If I only made a few hundred dollars more a month," he inevitably continues, "I wouldn't struggle. Heck, if I pulled in *close* to what my boss makes, I'd have no financial problems at all. None."

You: Although I haven't said those exact words, many of my financial problems would be eliminated if I made a bit more money.

Wrong.

You: Excuse me?

You're wrong.

You: How do you know?

---

[1] Before the "Great Recession" which began in 2008, about 50 percent of Americans were living paycheck to paycheck. Subsequent studies show more than 60 percent live paycheck to paycheck (CareerBuilder.com, 2009) today. No matter the precise statistic, ample evidence demonstrates the majority of people struggle to make ends meet, no matter the economic environment.

Thirty percent of people who make more than $100,000 a year still live paycheck to paycheck.[2]

You: Get out of here.

It's true. Yet today's high-income earners once made entry level salaries. Back then, when they thought of their ideal future, they never expected to struggle on a $100,000 per year income. They assumed if their income doubled, tripled, or quadrupled, their money worries would disappear. But that's not what happened.

You: Why not?

Because just as soon as people make enough money to live comfortably, they want to live extravagantly. Some people call this "Keeping up with the Joneses." Others refer to the trend as the new "American way." The media often describes the phenomenon as our "insatiable desire for instant gratification." No matter what you call it, things formerly considered *wants* are now *needs*.

You: Really?

Yes, and it takes more "stuff" to make us happy. Worse, as our income changes, so do our peer groups.

You: I don't think so. At least not for me.

Think about it. Shortly after starting your career, places you recently frequented as a student are now "dumps." Once the typical person earns her first promotion, she doesn't lunch at the same places—or with the same people—as she did only weeks earlier.

Most executives eat with other executives, middle managers spend time with other middle managers, and so on. Not surprisingly, the typical person promoted from an entry level to management position quickly increases their lunch spending.

You: Still, you're ranting about lunch. We're not talking big bucks here.

Lunch is just an example. It goes much further. Remember Ann and Bruce Mitchell, who I profile during the introduction?

You: The couple struggling on a $600,000 income? I don't think I'm going to forget them for a while.

---

[2] CareerBuilder.com, 2009.

Good. Let me partially defend the Mitchells.

You: Seriously?

I said "partially." First, neither Ann nor Bruce has a finance background. Second, they live in one of the most expensive parts of the country.

You: Are those supposed to be excuses?

No, they're not—and the Mitchells would be the first to say they shouldn't struggle. I mention those facts only to highlight the differences between the Mitchells and the Violas.

You: Who are the Violas?

Back in 1994, I helped Ned Viola. Even then, Ned's income was already over $400,000. Unlike the Mitchells, Ned and his wife lived in the comparably affordable Midwest. Still, Ned was struggling to pay his family's bills.

Take a guess as to Ned's occupation.

You: Let me think. He was making nearly half a million dollars in the Midwest during the mid-nineties. Was he a young professional athlete?

Good reasoning, but not quite. The guy was a Certified Public Accountant!

You: And he couldn't pay his bills on several hundred thousand dollars a year? A freaking accountant?

And a darn good one—hence the high salary.

You: That's crazy. A well paid accountant living paycheck to paycheck. Wow.

Indeed, the phenomenon knows no occupational or income boundaries. While the Violas and Mitchells obviously represent extreme cases, they are far from unique.

You: After all, 30 percent of those making six figures continue to live paycheck to paycheck.

Well said. The moral of the story: **If you live paycheck to paycheck, it is not because of the income you make. It is because of the decisions you make.**

HOW DOES ONE SAVE?

How much money will you make during the next three months?

You: I'm not going to tell you that. We just met.

Fair enough. Instead, tell me: could you figure out how much money you'll make in the next 90 days?

You: Sure.

How would you calculate your expected earnings?

You: I'd look at my last paycheck and multiply it by the number of paydays I'll have during the next three months.

Makes sense. What if I asked you to determine how much you were going to *spend* during the next three months?

You: That would be much harder to estimate.

Why?

You: Too many categories! Plus, I spend money on everyday things like coffee and lunch and on weekly things like groceries.

Don't forget your rent, mortgage, and any other monthly bills like car payments. Plus, be sure to include a portion of annual expenses such as insurance premiums and auto registrations.

You: With all that, I could only muster a guess in an attempt to answer your spending question.

Another approach might help. For example, if you live paycheck to paycheck—

You: No comment.

None needed. But *if* you live paycheck to paycheck, you can easily calculate your anticipated spending over the next three months by reminding yourself of your expected income over the period. Since you're effectively spending everything you make, your spending equals your income.

You: What if I am not living paycheck to paycheck?

Are you?

You: No comment.

No problem. Say you save $300 each month. To determine your savings, just subtract $900 ($300 x 3 months) from the total you expect to earn.

DO YOU CONTROL YOUR INCOME?

Let me ask you another question. When you get to work tomorrow, can you give yourself a raise?

You: Pardon?

Can you log on to your computer, enter a few passwords, and give yourself a raise?

You: Not if I still wanted a job at the end of the day!

Exactly. In the short-term, you have virtually no ability to affect your income. Your income over the next several months is determined by the decisions and effort you have made in the past. It is based on choices such as how much education you pursued, your grades, your effort at work, your performance at work, your relationship with your boss—

You: Excuse me?

Not *that* kind of relationship. Calm down there, tiger.[3]

You: I knew that.

All those previous choices affect your pay during the next three months. Over the long-term, your current and future effort should affect your compensation. In addition, the general economy and external forces shaping your industry may dramatically affect your annual compensation 10 years from now. But not now. Not today. Your income is relatively fixed in the short-term.

You: So it is.

THE SAVINGS FORMULA

Here is an incredibly simple formula:

> Your Income – Your Spending = Your Saving

The savings formula above demonstrates only two factors influence your ability to save: your income and your spending. Yet you've just concluded you don't control one of them—your income—in the short-term. What does that mean?

You: The only way I can save more is if I spend less.

Precisely.

You: Not exactly inspiring, Michael.

Not the kind of thing which will get me on the cover of *Money Magazine*, that's for sure.

---

[3] Note I say "tiger," not "Tiger."

You: I can see the headline now: "Genius says you must spend less to save more!"

That'll be fine. I've always said basic personal finance is remarkably simple. The savings formula helps prove it.

You: But what if I don't want to spend less?

Do you want to save more?

You: I think I have to.

Unless you can suddenly earn more, you must spend less to save more.

You: That stinks. I think I'll get a different book.

Even if you pursue the strategies put forth by a "Get Rich Quick" book, you're still going to need something to begin.

You: What?

Money!

You: But isn't making money the whole point of a "Get Rich Quick" book?

Yes, but you still need money to start. You can only make your money grow if you have some money in the first place.

You: Argh.

Don't fear spending less.

You: But I've never been good at doing without.

Neither are most people.

You: So how do I get past this?

When you are no longer afraid of being cheap but eagerly anticipate becoming fiscally responsible, saving is achievable.

You: There's a difference between being cheap and fiscally responsible?

A huge difference! I'm sure you know cheap people.

You: Alex. Gosh, Alex is so cheap, he squeaks.

No need to name names.

You: Oh, right.

Would you describe Alex as fiscally responsible?

You: No, not really. He spends big money on himself.

Okay, so you see the difference. One can be cheap and fiscally irresponsible. I've also encountered many fiscally responsible individuals who are among the most generous people I know, especially when it comes to their charitable donations.

You: Now I get the distinction. I'd much rather be fiscally responsible than cheap.

Me too.

You: But can I be fiscally responsible and still like my life?

Absolutely. Chapters 3 through 12 are dedicated to demonstrating exactly how. But first I want to talk about Sandra, Paula, and Debbie.

You: Don't you mean Peter, Paul, and Mary?

I do not.

You: Okay.

THE OPEN SECRET OF SAVING AND SPENDING

Are you reading *The Savings Solution* to learn how to become poorer?

You: Excuse me?

Are you looking for the secret to a life of misery, despair, and poverty?

You: Of course not.

Good, but I'm going to tell you anyway.

You: I'm on the edge of my seat. Go ahead, spill the "secret."

Spend more than you make.

You: That'll do it, huh?

Absolutely. Not only that, it's 100 percent guaranteed.

Gary: 'It's 100 percent guaranteed?' Hey—that's my line!

You again?

Gary: Yeah, so?

You: What's going on here?

You don't know Gary?

You: I don't believe so.

Gary: Sure you do! I'm Gary!

You: Like I said, I don't—

Gary: We met in the last book.

You: The last book?

Gary: Sure, Beyond Paycheck to Paycheck.

You: Oh, Beyond Paycheck to Paycheck. Now you're starting to ring a bell.

Good.

Gary: Uh-oh.

You: Aren't you the dude who is—

Gary: Intelligent, connected, experienced, charming—

You: Annoying?

Gary: No.

You: Yes.

Gary: No.

You: Actually, that confirms it. Indeed, I remember. You were the irritating, commission-obsessed, and me-first financial salesman in **Beyond Paycheck to Paycheck.**

Bye, Gary.

Gary: For now.

Be skeptical whenever you hear "guaranteed" from a financial professional, especially if the topic is investing. Still, given I'm currently explaining how to lose money, cut me some slack on my guarantee.

You: Fair enough.

By definition, if you spend more than you make, your net worth must go down.

You: My net worth? What does that mean again?

The definition of your net worth is:

Your Assets – Your Liabilities = Net Worth

You: What does that mean?

What You Own – What You Owe = Net Worth

You: Got it. Why does my net worth decrease if I spend more than I make?

Only two ways exist to spend more than you make. The first is to borrow. Whether by using a credit card or tapping Chappy down the street, taking a loan allows you to spend money you don't have. When you borrow you create a debt (i.e., a liability). Since you must pay it back, it is something you now owe. The formula above shows how adding new debt lowers your net worth, making you poorer.

The other way to spend more than you make is to withdraw money from an asset like a savings account. By doing so, you reduce the value of the asset (i.e., the thing you own) which—like borrowing—decreases your net worth. With me?

You: Clear enough, but I told you I wasn't here to learn how to become poorer.

But you follow how this works, right? You understand how spending more than you make is **guaranteed** to make you poorer, correct?

*You: Yes, but I don't want to become poorer! I want to become richer. How can I do **that**?!*

Just do the opposite.

You: Just do the opposite?

Yes. Spend *less* than you make. The secret is that simple. It is the *only* guaranteed way to become richer. Hoping for some silver bullet to make you suddenly affluent is impractical, especially when an alternative certain to succeed is readily available: spend less than you earn.

You: I've heard that refrain before.

Did you know "spending less than you earn" goes by another name, one easier to recall?

You: What's the other name?

Saving. Get to it.

THREE FRIENDS WITH TWO DIFFERENT STORIES

Although Sandra, Paula, and Debbie have not formed a folk band, they have formed the following saving habits:

➤ Sandra spends less than she makes.

➤ Paula spends everything she makes.

➤ Debbie spends more than she makes.

You: I admire Sandra and understand Paula's habits. But how does Debbie pull off her routine?

Easily.

You: Easily?

Sure, she just borrows.

You: Right. Credit cards.

Probably, but she might also have car or home equity loans.

Are your saving habits most similar to Sandra's, Paula's, or Debbie's?

You: Ah—

If you're not sure, welcome to homework assignment number one. If you don't know where you are today, you'll find it difficult to improve tomorrow.

Other than their financial habits, the three women have much in common.

You: Such as?

For starters, they wear their hair the same way.

You: Why does that matter?

It doesn't. More importantly, they work at the same company on the same floor in cubicles next to each another. They have the same job title at work and have identical salaries.

You: But—

I never said they made different amounts. I only stated each spent differently compared to the amount earned.

You: Right.

The three women also live in the same town and get along famously. So, when Sandra suggested car-pooling to work several months ago, Paula and Debbie eagerly agreed.

Recently, the three women were driving to work when the radio station they always listen to went to its usual newsbreak. But rather than drone on about the performance of the Dow Jones Industrial Average, the business reporter noted, "Before the market opened today, locally operated PDR

Corporation announced it was acquired by its former European competitor JS Incorporated for $26.75 per share."

Since the three women worked at PDR, Paula said out loud what Debbie and Sandra were already thinking. "I wonder what that's going to mean for our jobs."

At 4PM they found out.

All three were let go.

For several hours afterwards, each was numb. None had a hint of prior warning and each genuinely enjoyed their job as well as the income it provided. A day or two later, reality began to set in.

Pop quiz! Who was in the best position, financially speaking, to handle this unexpected adversity?

You: Sandra.

Right. Why?

You: Because she has been saving.

Meaning?

You: She can go to the bank and get some money.

Correct. But there are two more reasons why Sandra is in the best shape to get through her sudden job loss.

You: Go on.

First, she doesn't need as much money as Debbie or Paula.

You: Why not? All three women lost their jobs making the same income.

Let's say each woman earned $3,000 per month ($36,000 annually). If Sandra was saving 10 percent ($300) of her net pay, she was only spending $2,700 ($3,000–$300) monthly. So, while Paula is short the full $3,000 required for her ordinary monthly expenses and Debbie lives on an even greater amount, Sandra needs only $2,700 to close her gap.

You: Because you wouldn't expect Sandra to save when she has no job.

I wouldn't expect anyone to save when they are unemployed—for two reasons. First, recall the savings formula.

You: Your income minus your spending equals your savings.

Right. So if your income is zero, it's not possible to save.

You: No, it isn't. What's the other reason?

Why does one save in the first place?

You: Huh?

What's the purpose of saving?

You: Because it's good for you?

Yes, but why?

You: So you can get stuff later?

Right.

You: Really?

Yes. "Stuff" might include an iPhone, a comfortable retirement, a nice car, or a home. It certainly includes food when you have no job.

When you begin saving, one of the first things you should save for is a rainy day. Financial professionals call such savings an "emergency fund." What you call the money is irrelevant, but it's critical to prepare for what most people eventually and suddenly face—an unexpected negative financial event.

Such an event could include the layoff we're talking about or it could be something more mundane like damage to your car or an expensive home repair. Other possibilities include serious illness and disability. Regardless, always be prepared by establishing an emergency fund of three to six months of living expenses.

Back to Sandra, who has saved for exactly this moment. Not only can she spend her savings during her financial emergency, she should. It's why she has her emergency fund in the first place.

Sandra is also in better shape than Paula and Debbie because Sandra has the right habits.

You: The right habits?

Sandra was already spending less than she earned when she did *not* face an immediate crisis. She consciously saved during the good times. Compare this to Paula, whose attitude was, "If I have it, I spend it" or to Debbie's mantra, "I don't need it to spend it."

We must have faith Sandra, now suddenly unemployed, will find a way to spend even less than before. Heck, she was probably already thinking about ways to cut back before she left the building.

On the other hand, Paula and Debbie have their work cut out for them. Paula's wondering how she's going to be able to spend with no money coming in while Debbie is quickly calculating how much more she can borrow.

If you suddenly lost your job, how would you fare? Don't like your answer? Be like Sandra.

SAVING GIVES YOU OPTIONS

A few weeks pass and the company, realizing it has fired too many workers, offers Sandra, Paula, and Debbie their previous jobs.

You: Great news!

At 80 cents on the dollar.

You: Meaning?

They have to take a 20 percent pay cut if they want their old jobs back.

You: That's a raw deal.

No doubt, but it's an unfortunate reality in many similar cases. Guess what happens?

You: They take it.

Probably. Debbie will certainly take it because she needs money yesterday. Creditors are already calling her to ask why she hasn't made her minimum required payments. Other lenders pressure her for a timeline of when she will resume paying. Paula's situation is only slightly better. Her bills are piling up too.

While Sandra isn't living the high life, her savings have allowed her to avoid a state of panic. If she's feeling good about her employment prospects elsewhere—say she's had two interviews for a job paying her more money—Sandra may decide to hold out, rather than take the pay cut offered by her old employer. At a minimum, she's in a better position to negotiate with her old employer for her old salary.

You: Why?

She has alternatives.

You: The other job possibility?

Yes. Sandra's savings provide her the option to wait. Paula and Debbie simply don't have any flexibility.

Remember, saving gives you options.

Even if you never lose a job, an emergency fund is critical.

You: Why?

Many people incorrectly conclude their exceptional job security implies they do not need an emergency fund.

You: Hard to believe, especially given the unemployment rate.

But some people really do have job security for life.

You: Like who?

Supreme Court Justices.

You: Okay, that's like nine people in America. What about the other 300 million of us?

Many government workers, particularly those in education who receive tenure, have very strong job security.

You: Oh.

Some people work for businesses where the owner is Mom or Dad. Short of little Napoleon lighting the factory on fire, he's pretty much always going to have a job. Yet even those people should have an emergency fund.

You: But why?

Possible financial emergencies include far more than job losses. Here's how I addressed this issue on my *Beyond Paycheck to Paycheck* blog.

MORE THAN A JOB LOSS

Adapted from a post to the *Beyond Paycheck to Paycheck* blog, January 23, 2009

My wife and I are going to receive a hefty income tax refund. We have been saving aggressively but are still four months short of a six-month emergency fund. I also have a student loan and a Roth IRA I haven't funded in a long time. Meanwhile, Wall Street is having a huge sale.

My wife's job is very secure, so I don't believe the emergency fund is as crucial for us as for some people right now. After I get done with grad school, I am going to teach in the Philadelphia public school district.

So, what do I do with my tax refund?

—Jeffrey R., Pennsylvania

Short Answer: No one ever expects an emergency. If you did, it wouldn't be an emergency.

Detailed explanation: Jeff, it's great you're viewing your finances broadly. Your long-term holistic view will be a key ingredient in your ultimate financial success. Your question is one of financial priorities. While you and your wife have strong job security as teachers, events other than sudden job loss cause financial emergencies. Such possibilities include car accidents, health issues, and expensive unplanned home repairs. While job security reduces one key concern, it does not eliminate all of them.

I, along with most financial planners, recommend a minimum of three months of living expenses for an emergency fund. Those people who are self-employed are better served by having a year's worth set aside. Most employed individuals can be comfortable with about three to six months.

Keep in mind the number of months included in the emergency fund is *necessary living expenses, not income.* In a true financial emergency, you won't spend money on discretionary items, so include only rent/mortgage, car payment, groceries, utilities, child-care, and other monthly payments you can't change in the short-term.

Your sizable tax return may instantly give you the ability to get your emergency fund to an appropriate level.

Good luck, Jeff, and thank you for submitting your question!

MORE THAN AN EMERGENCY FUND

Saving gives you options far beyond a rainy day stash. For example, if two years from now Sandra, Paula, and Debbie decide they've had it at work and wish to start their own businesses, who has the best shot at taking the plunge?

You: Sandra?

Yes. Why?

You: She went to business school?

Hardly. She is the most likely to be able to start her own business because of—wait for it—her savings.

You: Why do her savings matter when starting a business?

Most businesses don't make money right away. In fact, to get started, most businesses require the owner to spend money for things like computers, office supplies, a web site, and so on. How would you get a business off the ground with no money?

You: A loan.

Possibly, but banks are going to want collateral,[4] likely including your home. If you haven't saved enough to buy a home and have no alternative collateral, you're less likely to get a loan.

You: Sandra wins again.

Savings give her options in numerous potential scenarios. Let's say all three women get pregnant at the exact same time.

You: Really?

I'll rephrase. Say all three women are pregnant at the same time.

You: Nice clean-up work.

Who can afford to stay at home, if she chooses, with the baby the longest?

You: Let me guess: Sandra.

Right again, because Sandra—

You: Has savings.

Precisely. And savings give her—

You: Options.

Correct again. The same way savings give Sandra options, your savings will give you options too.

> **No matter how you choose to use your money, saving today gives you options tomorrow.**

---

[4] Collateral is something you'd have to give to the bank if you didn't pay your debt back.

To take advantage, you merely need to free up some cash flow. When you do, you'll begin taking advantage of the miracle of compounding interest.

You: Free up some cash flow? Miracles? What are you talking about?
Stay tuned.

CASE STUDIES

THE 45-CENT STRAWBERRY:
ARE ORGANIC FOODS WORTH IT?

Adapted from a post to the *Beyond Paycheck to Paycheck* blog, February 25, 2008

Does the title above lead you to expect me to rant about how costly and irresponsible purchasing organic food is?

You: Pretty much.

Not going to happen.

You: So you bless spending $75.16 at "Whole Paycheck" for two small bags of groceries?

Not quite. Like with all financial and life matters, balance is key. Some organic foods have clearly demonstrated health benefits, but so do fitness and smoking cessation. Yet, many people avoid exercise and continue to smoke. Furthermore, the value of some organic foods is questionable.

Of course, stores don't indicate which foods fall into the "worth it" vs. the "it isn't going to hurt you any, but will make us good money" categories. So **you** must assess the relative importance of buying organic in the context of your financial priorities.

You: But how do I find out which foods are in either category?

Go to the web, do some research, and carry a list.

You: Fair enough.

While my wife and I typically follow the consensus guidelines when choosing whether to buy organic, shopping responsibly can still be painful at times.

You: Ugh. Such as?

Such as when my older daughter eats $3.00 of blueberries before I can take a bite of my 15-cent bowl of cereal and looks at me with her big puppy dog eyes and says, "More strawberries puh-lease Daddy?" (Keep in mind there's an additional $1.75 worth of blueberries on the floor next to her high-chair and 35 cents of organic milk on her lap.)

Indeed, being nutritionally responsible isn't easy. Of course, if you can't afford or don't choose to spend on organic blueberries and instead eat <gasp!> regular blueberries—as virtually everyone now older than 20 did through their entire youth—everything will probably be just fine.

Personally, I struggle with the organic vs. non-organic decision. Except with cauliflower. Reports suggest the vegetable isn't worth spending the organic premium on and, quite frankly, I dislike cauliflower in all forms.

Key lesson: You'll never live *Beyond Paycheck to Paycheck* if you're spending money on things you don't value. Even if they happen to be vegetables.

COULD YOU GET BY ON HALF A MILLION A YEAR?

Adapted from a post to the *Beyond Paycheck to Paycheck* blog, February 10, 2009

The *New York Times* published a story[5] explaining why earning a $500,000 salary might not be sufficient for New York City living.

You: Why half a million?

Such was the proposed salary limit from President Obama for executives working for companies which receive significant governmental assistance.

You: Why New York City?

Many potentially affected executives work in New York.

You: Half a million a year seems like a lot, even in New York.

It is. While $500,000 clearly doesn't go as far in New York City, the exclusive suburbs of Long Island, Westchester, or New Jersey as it does in the rest of America, earning half a million a year is more than merely survivable.

---

[5] You Try to Live on 500K in This Town, The New York Times, February 6, 2009.

Yet the article paints a very different picture:

> "A modest three-bedroom apartment . . . which was purchased for $1.5 million, not the top of the market at all, carries a monthly mortgage of about $8,000 and a co-op maintenance fee of $8,000 a month. Total [annual] cost: $192,000. A summer house in Southampton that cost $4 million, again not the top of the market, carries annual mortgage payments of $240,000."

Hello? Who says you're entitled to *a second home* valued at *eight times* your annual income? Does it matter if it isn't "top of the market?" Are you implying this is frugal or even modest living? And who is defining "top of the market" in the first place? Of course you're going to struggle on annual housing payments of $432,000. But this isn't poverty. This isn't even struggling. Let's be clear: we're talking about a second home in one of the world's most exclusive areas, even if their neighbor's house—owned by Mr. and Mrs. Jones—is worth $6 million.

It gets worse:

> "A chauffeur's pay is between $75,000 and $125,000 a year."

Oh please. Take a taxi. At one point in your life, a taxi was a luxury over taking the subway—as most New York City mortals do proudly. A taxi provides point-to-point transportation with little waiting.

Truth be known, the article states the problem well:

> "As hard as it is to believe, bankers who are living on the Upper East Side making $2 or $3 million a year have set up a life for themselves in which they are also at zero at the end of the year with credit cards

and mortgage bills that are inescapable," said Holly Peterson, the author of an Upper East Side novel of manners, "The Manny," . . ."

So there you have it. Proof positive what I've been telling everyone for years: if you spend everything you make, you're living paycheck to paycheck. With a slight hiccup, you'll struggle to maintain your lifestyle—even on a *measly* $500,000 a year.

HOW SAVING IS LIKE FOOTBALL

Adapted from a post to the *Beyond Paycheck to Paycheck* blog, September 3, 2008

In honor of the football season kick-off, here are five ways saving is similar to football:

1. **Like rooting for a loser, saving is about the future.**

Rather than a singular focus on today, rooting for a bad team and choosing to save are about loyalty to your principles. By sticking to your convictions, you will enjoy the benefits even more when "it" finally happens, whether it's a Super Bowl Championship (at last!) or the achievement of genuine financial independence.

2. **Never throw good money in after bad.**

The front-office of a lousy (but wise) football team makes moves explicitly designed *not* to maximize this year's performance. Rather, they trade higher-priced older players for inexpensive younger players likely to be at their peak when the team is competitive with the league's best.

Smart savers don't buy dessert at a restaurant where the main course didn't meet expectations hoping the experience improves. Instead, they get ice cream elsewhere. In doing so, they probably save a few bucks and, at the same time, get a new venue.

3. Don't play a game you can't win.

Lousy football teams don't play the game the same way good football teams do. Poor teams know they can't compete straight-up, so they're more likely to attempt trick plays and gimmicks.

When you have friends with substantially more financial resources (or at least *appear* to), don't readily agree to meet them at a very expensive restaurant of their choosing. Instead, play a different game. Meet for dessert, a movie, or simply invite them to your place.

4. Focus on value received, not on dollars spent.

The best team in the league often does not have the highest payroll. Instead, it gets the most value from the dollars it spends. It puts together the best combination of players—not the most expensive group of individual players.[6]

To save effectively, you make conscious decisions to maximize the value you receive from every dollar you spend. By doing so, you're not being cheap, you're being fiscally responsible.

5. It can suck to be new.

Expansion teams almost always finish last. The odds are against them, as their teams are comprised primarily of other teams' cast-offs. Yet for the players who would otherwise not be in the league and the fans who root for a new team in their city, excitement is real.

Likewise, when you start your first real job and start to make money, you are—and should be—thrilled. But the amount of money can seem small in comparison to your desires. But being

---

[6] To do this, some elite players accept less money from good teams than they would earn from inferior teams. For example, Tom Brady and Randy Moss accepted less than top-dollar contracts for 2007 in order to play for the highly touted New England Patriots. (Of course, other players choose to leave competitive teams to pursue the biggest contract possible. Though richer, many appear miserable by the third quarter of their first game. We talk about balance in later chapters.)

new isn't forever. Hang in there; good long-term decisions are typically rewarded richly and sometimes sooner than you'd expect. The
Jacksonville Jaguars made it to the Conference Championship in only
their second year.

Now if we could only get Hank Williams Jr. to sing "Are you
ready for some saving?!"

CHAPTER 2

Size Matters (and so Does Timing): Save More Today for an Incredible Tomorrow

"People do not lack strength, they lack will."
—Victor Hugo

"People do not lack income, they lack wealth."
—Michael B. Rubin

I received the most valuable lesson of my entire college education during a tax class.

You: A tax class?

Indeed. Rather than demonstrating how to complete another Schedule M-1[1], Professor Griffin devoted part of the last class to "Lessons Learned." In doing so, he changed my life.

You: That's a pretty big statement. How did he do it?

He illustrated the miracle of compounding interest. I was dumbstruck.

You: Dumbstruck?

---

[1] The ever enjoyable "Reconciliation of Income (Loss) per Books With Income per Return" schedule.

Awed. Blown away. Shaking my head in disbelief. Totally floored. Yeah, I was dumbstruck by the miracle of compounding interest.

You: Sounds powerful.

It's critical. In fact, understanding and taking advantage of the miracle of compounding interest will be the most important contributor in your eventual financial success. Such is the reason why I discuss the miracle in *Beyond Paycheck to Paycheck*, and again, albeit differently, here.

You: But what is it? What is the miracle of compounding interest?

Let's take it one word at a time, in reverse. First, interest. **Interest** is what savers get paid for saving. As an example, if you keep $600 in a savings account earning 2 percent interest for one month, you earn $1.00 of interest every month.

You: A buck? Big deal.

It actually is a big deal.

You: No, it's actually a buck. Even a Taco Bell® $2 Meal Deal costs twice as much.

The absolute numbers aren't important yet—I'm just showing an example. Hang with me for two minutes.

You: Proceed.

The next word is **compounding**. Compounding is the frequency at which interest is calculated and paid. As a saver, you like frequent compounding.

You: Why?

Because you get paid quicker and more often.

You: That does sound nice. Show me how.

Let's say your $600 is compounded daily, instead of monthly as I assumed earlier. Consequently, you'll be credited with $612.12 of interest after a year—not $612.11, as would be the case with annual compounding.

You: So the compounding element gets me a penny?

Yes, in this particular case, it gets you a penny.

You: I don't even pick up pennies anymore.

My two minutes isn't up. Now for the miracle.

You: So far this conversation has got me one cent, so this "miracle" better be good.

Let's say you save $300 a month.

You: Excuse me?

Let's say you save $300 a month.

*You: Now **that** would be a miracle! Jeez, that's a lot of saving, Michael!*

Three hundred dollars a month is only ten dollars a day.

You: You're starting to sound like a "Feed a hungry child" commercial. I don't have that kind of money.

Anyone employed can save ten dollars a day following the simple saving strategies outlined throughout this book.

You: Then why haven't we discussed them yet?

Because I want you to be *very* motivated when we get there.

You: But I am motivated—I'm reading The Savings Solution, *for crying out loud.*

You're motivated, yes. But after my demonstration of the miracle of compounding interest, you'll be *very* motivated.

THE MIRACLE OF COMPOUNDING INTEREST

Let's assume you can take that $300 a month you'll be saving soon and earn an 8 percent rate of return.

You: What does rate of return mean?

Mathematically speaking, it's like interest. Think about it like that.

You: But there aren't any savings accounts paying 8 percent interest!

No there aren't—not today, anyway.[2]

You: So why use such a ridiculous example?

I wasn't thinking in terms of savings accounts, so 8 percent isn't ridiculous.

You: Where can I get an 8 percent rate of return or interest or whatever you call it on my money?

Although it is not guaranteed, the long-term historical average of the stock market is 8 percent.

---

[2] Circa 2010. In a few years, we may laugh at how some banks take advantage of lazy customers by paying them such a low 8 percent interest rate. Higher interest rates will inevitably return. A little historical perspective: in the mid nineties, savings accounts routinely paid in the 4–6 percent range. During the late seventies and early eighties, you could have earned double-digit returns just by parking your money in an ordinary savings account.

You: Why would I put my savings in the stock market? I could lose money in the stock market.

You absolutely could lose money in the stock market. But the best way to demonstrate the miracle of compounding interest is over the long-term. Since the stock market is where most mainstream financial advisors recommend investing the bulk of your long-term savings, we'll assume it's what you would do too.[3]

You: Okay, so here I am saving $300 a month and earning 8 percent a year in the stock market.

Earning 8 percent a year in the stock market on average.

You: Why did you add "on average?"

Because you won't earn 8 percent every year. Rather, you can reasonably expect, over the long-term, your gains and losses—some very far from 8 percent—to average to an 8 percent gain per year.

You: That's quite a little caveat. Are you afraid I'm going to sue you?

Of course not, but I want you prepared for reality—your money will not grow in a straight line. Still, the miracle of compounding interest is powerful.

You: How powerful?

You're going to tell me.

You: I am?

Yes. Let's say you save $300 every month between now and when you turn 65. How much money will you have then?

You: I don't know—you're the CPA.

Take a guess.

You: I wouldn't know how to begin.

How old are you?

You: None of your business.

Fine. Keep your age to yourself, but subtract it from 65. The difference is the number of years you will save $300 a month.

You: Okay.

---

[3] This is *not* a book about investing. But if you refer to Chapter 8 of *Beyond Paycheck to Paycheck,* you'll learn everything you need to know about introductory investing. Or read any number of beginning investing books for similar information presented in a significantly more boring and confusing way. Your call.

Remember you'll be saving $300 a month. To convert $300 a month into an annual figure, simply multiply $300 by 12 for a total of $3,600 in yearly saving. To get the amount you'll have by age 65—

You: I'd multiply the number of years I'd save by the $3,600 saved per year.

Yes, but don't forget to add in the interest you'll earn. Got your final number?

[Take a minute to create a ballpark estimate. To calculate the amount you'll save, get a calculator and multiply $3,600 by the number of years you have before you reach age 65. Then, add your estimate of the interest you'll earn over the years to approximate what you'll have available to you at retirement.]

Got your number?

You: I have a decent guess.

Look below.

You: At my feet?

No! At the table.

You: How do you know what's on my table? And, hey, it's usually cleaned up by now.

Not your kitchen table, the table on this page—Figure 2-1.

Figure 2-1

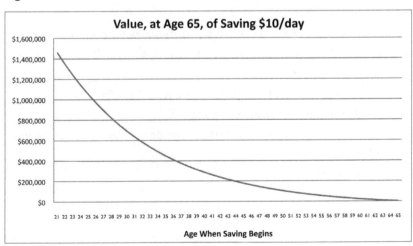

You: I knew that. What's going on there?

Find your age underneath the lowest horizontal line. Then look up until you find the thicker line. From that point, look to the left for an estimate of the amount of money you'll have at age 65.

You: Whoa, are you sure?

Yup.

You: For just $300 a month?

Or ten bucks a day.

You: That's a lot of money.

Ten bucks?

You: No, the amount of money I'd have at retirement, if I only saved ten bucks a day.

Now *that's* what I'm talking about. Furthermore, I've assumed you have nothing saved today. If you already have savings, that money should grow significantly too.

You: Cool.

Look back at the graph again.

You: I still haven't taken my eyes off it.

What else do you notice about the line?

You: It's black.

Profound, but I was thinking something a bit more relevant.

You: Oh. It slopes downward.

True. Why?

You: Because every year you wait to begin saving means another year you haven't saved. Since you're saving less, you'll clearly end up with less.

Mr. Gambini, that is a lucid, intelligent, well thought-out—

You: Are you quoting "My Cousin Vinny"?

It happens. Anyway, you're right. What else do you notice about the line?

You: I'm not sure.

Is the line straight?

You: Excuse me? It's a line, what does its sexual orientation have to do with anything?!

I'm asking whether the line is straight or curved, not if it is straight or homosexual.

You: Right—of course you are. The line curves.

Indeed it does. The curve is the most important part of the graph.

You: Really?

Yes, the curve illustrates the miracle of compounding interest.

You: How so?

The line, steepest at the left, flattens as it proceeds to the right.

You: What's the implication?

The steeper the line, the greater the loss from not saving.

You: Implying?

Your younger years are the most valuable. Specifically, your twenties mean the most.

You: Still not following you.

Each point on the line corresponds to 1) an age when you start saving $10 a day and 2) the resulting wealth from your daily $10 when you reach age 65. If you move your finger along the line from age 21 to 25 or 31, you'll see the decrease is dramatic. But the decline from 41 to 51 is much less severe.

You: True. Also depressing.

Why is it depressing?

You: What about people who aren't in their twenties? Don't you think this information could be counter-productive?

Now *I'm* not following *you*.

You: What about a 40-year old who looks at Figure 2-1 and ponders the $1,4000,000 she could have achieved by retirement, if she had started saving 20 years earlier. Wouldn't that be depressing for her?

Sure. But the implication of starting sooner doesn't change no matter your age. Take a look at Figure 2-2 which, like Figure 2-1, shows the value of your savings at age 65. What do you notice about the line in Figure 2-2?

Figure 2-2

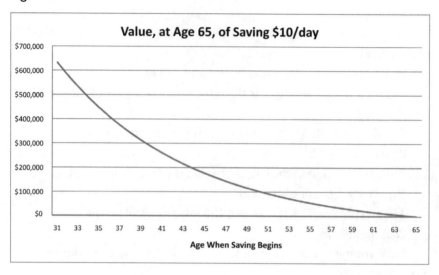

Value, at Age 65, of Saving $10/day

You: It looks similar to the line in Figure 2-1.

It does. But look at the starting age.

You: Hey! Before it was 21 and now it's 31. What's going on here?

Compare the numbers alongside each figure's vertical axis. Do you see how the ending amounts changed?

You: Yes.

Effectively, Figure 2-2 is just a magnification of all but the extreme left side of Figure 2-1. Take a look at the Figure 2-3 and Figure 2-4 on the next page. See how the starting ages change dramatically while affecting the curved line only slightly?

Figure 2-3

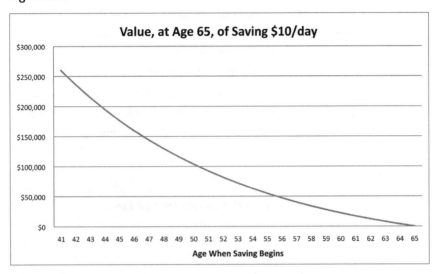

Figure 2-4

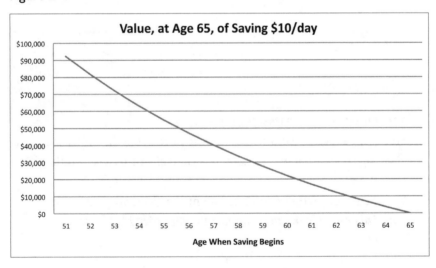

You: Yes, the lines look similar to one another.

Find the starting age that is closest to yours. (For a customized report of your potential future savings, visit totalcandor.com/motivation)

The implication is clear. **No matter your age, this is the most important year of your life to save.** In no future year could a single dollar saved—let alone ten dollars—be worth as much simply because of *when* you saved it.

You: Even though you don't know how old I am?

I don't need to know your age. As the previous charts show, saving immediately is critical if you're approaching retirement. Younger folks still searching for motivation should take a good look at Figure 2-5, which demonstrates the interest forfeited at each year you do not save.

Figure 2-5

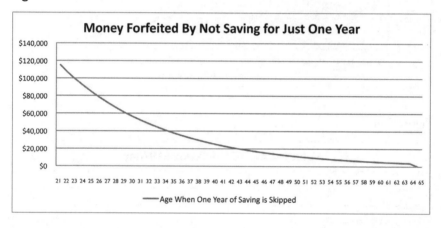

You: Can you explain this graph?

Someone at age 25 who decides not to save $10 a day until she turns 26 gets to age 65 with about $84,000 less than she otherwise would have.

You: Wow.

You are never further from retirement than you are right now.

You: This really is the most important year of my life to save.

Indeed.

TIME IS YOUR MOST VALUABLE ASSET

Let's compare Ginger, who starts saving when she's 21, to Trish, who begins at age 31.

You: Obviously, Ginger reaches retirement with more money than Trish.

But the difference is striking.

You: I saw that already in Figure 2-1.

Look again.

You: Done.

How much money does Trish have in retirement?

You: More than $600,000.

Yes, she has about $632,000.

You: A pretty good sum of money.

Indeed, proving those who don't take financial advantage of their twenties can still accumulate significant sums.

You: Good.

Still, how much will Ginger have in retirement?

You: Nearly $1.5 million. That's a lot of dough.

It sure is—about $825,000 more than Trish ends up with.

You: Wow.

How much less did Trish save?

You: Pardon?

Compared to Ginger, who began saving at age 21, how much less did Trish, who began at age 31, save?

You: Ten years worth.

Exactly. How much money is that?

You: Three hundred dollars per month multiplied by 12 months per year is $3,600 per year. Over 10 years, Trish saves $36,000 less than what Ginger saves.

Correct, because from the point Ginger and Trish reach age 31, they save the same monthly amount. The only difference in their respective savings pattern is their savings during their twenties.

You: Hold on a minute.

Yes?

You: I just realized something.

Here it comes.

You: The difference in what they save is $36,000 but the difference in what they wind up with is more than $800,000?

Yes indeed, about $825,000.

You: How's that possible?

The miracle of compounding interest makes it possible.

You: I call BS!

What?

You: Excuse me, but c'mon! Is this for real?

As real as the taxes in New York and California.

The $36,000 Ginger saves during her twenties grows to $825,000 by age 65.

Figure 2-6

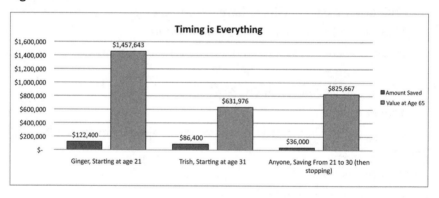

You: That chart above is incredible. So someone who saves from ages 21 to 30 and stops—never to save again—reaches age 65 with more money than someone who saves from age 31 to 65?

Indeed. Furthermore, **the early saver saves only 42 percent of what the later saver saved ($36,000 vs. $86,400) and reaches age 65 with 31 percent more ($825,667 vs. $631,976).**

You: Incredible.

You said that already.

You: I know.

MAKE UP THE DIFFERENCE LATER?

Many twenty-somethings think it will be easier to save in the future.

You: Because they'll presumably make more money?

So the thinking goes.

You: True, no?

Although most people will earn higher salaries later in their careers than during their twenties, many do not find it easier to save. Like I say in Chapter 1, 30 percent of people earning six figures live paycheck to paycheck. Sadly, a higher income alone does not cause savings.

You: So when should I begin saving?

Ideally, you would start saving when you start working. Unfortunately, few actually pull it off.

You: Why not?

First off, you might have been working for years already. In that case—

You: I don't want to talk about it.

Right. Furthermore, many young people are either still in school or have yet to land their first "real" job. Such folks have a very difficult time saving right away. Rather than pretend you'll start saving as soon as you reach a certain salary level, begin as soon as possible.

You: But could I begin later and make up for lost time?

Technically, of course.

You: Technically? Why do you say it like that?

Let's say you want to reach age 65 with a million dollars. How late could you wait to begin saving and still achieve your million-dollar goal?

You: I'm not sure.

Technically, you could save $1,000,000 the day before your retirement party and, presto, you'd have a million dollars at age 65.

You: Not very realistic.

No, not remotely. But it's technically possible to wait just about forever. The real question is when does it become, for practical purposes, impossible to make up for lost time.

Let's say your goal is to reach age 65 with the same amount you could have had if you began squirreling away $10 a day at age 21. In other words, your goal is to reach 65 with the $1,457,643 demonstrated in Figure 2-6.

You: That's a very specific goal.
It is but you get the point.
You: I do.

Figure 2-7

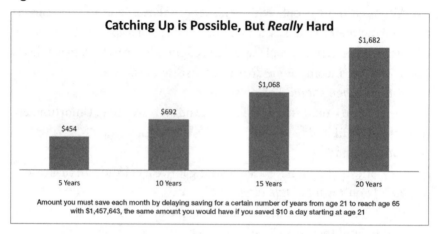

Catching Up is Possible, But *Really* Hard

$454	$692	$1,068	$1,682
5 Years	10 Years	15 Years	20 Years

Amount you must save each month by delaying saving for a certain number of years from age 21 to reach age 65 with $1,457,643, the same amount you would have if you saved $10 a day starting at age 21

As Figure 2-7 shows, if you wait until age 26 (five years after age 21) to begin saving and wish to reach retirement with the same money you would have had beginning at age 21, you'd need to save $454 per month.

You: Versus $300? That doesn't seem like much of a difference.
At first, I thought the same thing.
You: But then?
I changed my mind.
You: Now you think it's a big difference?
It is—saving $454 instead of $300 is an increase of more than 50 percent per month.
You: Say again?
By waiting five years, the amount you must save each month ($454) is 50 percent higher than had you started at age 21 ($300). Furthermore, you must save the additional 50 percent every month for forty years. That's 480 consecutive months!
You: That doesn't seem fair.
I agree, but that's the math.

But you're still talking about delaying saving vs. a start date of age 21 and, like you said, almost no one starts at age 21.

So far, yes. But, as Figures 2-8 and 2-9 demonstrate, delaying is always very costly. **Procrastination is simply not a strategy—motivation matters.**

Figure 2-8

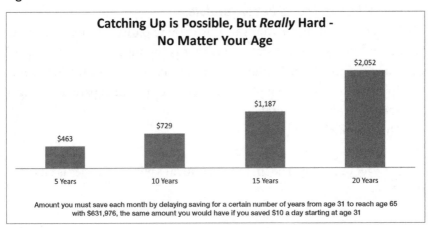

Catching Up is Possible, But *Really* Hard -
No Matter Your Age

$2,052
$1,187
$729
$463

5 Years   10 Years   15 Years   20 Years

Amount you must save each month by delaying saving for a certain number of years from age 31 to reach age 65 with $631,976, the same amount you would have if you saved $10 a day starting at age 31

Figure 2-9

Catching Up is Possible, But *Really* Hard -
No Matter Your Age

$2,052
$1,187
$729
$463

5 Years   10 Years   15 Years   20 Years

Amount you must save each month by delaying saving for a certain number of years from age 41 to reach age 65 with $259,994, the same amount you would have if you saved $10 a day starting at age 41

Compared to a five year delay, waiting 10 or 15 years means you must save even more—much more. By the time 20 years pass, the monthly saving amounts required to match an earlier start might be impossible to achieve.

You: So what happens then?

You lower your expectations.

You: Meaning?

You'll no longer seek to reach retirement with nearly $1.5 million in savings, as an example, you could have achieved starting with $10/day at age 21. Instead, you'll try to achieve a comparably more modest retirement.

You: Which still could be comfortable.

Certainly. But not if you wait until you're 64 to commence saving. Sooner or later, you must start. *This year* is the most important year of your life to begin. As such, I hope you're sufficiently motivated to become fiscally responsible—not cheap—and find your personal path to saving.

You: I'm definitely motivated.

That's almost what I was looking for.

You: Right. I'm very motivated.

Let's get to it then. The first of ten critical saving strategies is an emotional one.

CASE STUDIES

FIVE REASONS NOT TO COUNT ON AN INHERITANCE

Adapted from a post to the *Beyond Paycheck to Paycheck* blog, July 17, 2009

Counting on a future inheritance, some people minimize the importance of their low or non-existent savings rate. That's unfortunate.

You: Maybe for you, but my parents still love me.

It has nothing to do with love.

You: Sure it does. Blood is thicker than water. Heck, I wouldn't let two-thirds of my relatives in my house if they weren't family.

That's not a good ratio.

You: Tell me about it.

Still, it's a mistake to count on an inheritance.

You: Even a little bit?

Even a little.

You: Why?

Five reasons:

Reason 1: Your Parents Might Not Have as Much Money as You Think

You: My folks have a lot of money.

Is that a fact or are you assuming it based on how your parents live?

You: What do you mean?

Have your parents told you how much money they have or do you merely believe they are affluent because they have earned a lot of money, live in a very nice house, drive nice cars, and go on upscale vacations?

You: More of the latter, I suppose.

Meaning you actually know nothing.

You: Excuse me?

Although your parents are still your parents, if you haven't talked to them about money—their money—you're flying blind. It's no different than your utter lack of understanding of your neighbors' or co-workers' true financial picture; just because they might drive a nice car doesn't mean they don't also have credit card debt up to their eyeballs.

Reason # 2: Your Parents Might Have Much Less Money Than They Used To

Many retirees and pre-retirees got crushed, like the rest of us, when the stock market tanked during the late 2000s. Unlike their children and grandchildren however, they have little time to make up their losses via a combination of additional savings and investment gains. While many have adjusted to a lesser retirement, others have purchased annuities. In doing so, parents will take a big portion of their wealth with them when they pass away.

You: Why? How? What?

A typical immediate annuity purchased near or during retirement is an exchange of a large single payment by the purchaser (i.e., the annuitant) in return for a series of smaller payments back. When the annuitant or annuitants die, payments typically cease. Said another way, a standard annuity pays no additional money to the descendants of the annuitant (i.e., you).

Reason # 3: Your Parents May Live a Lot Longer

Your parents' longevity is another reason you shouldn't count on an inheritance. Studies show if you have two parents who live to age 65, at least one is likely to live until age 90. Not only is an additional 25 years a huge drain on their wealth, but you won't actually get an inheritance until they pass away. How old will you be when Mom turns 90? What if she lives a few years longer? Is that when you want to begin retirement?

Reason # 4: Your Parents May Grow Old

One or both of your parents may require assisted living one day. If, like most, they lack top-notch long-term care insurance, your potential inheritance—even a large one—could disappear quickly. The cost of a nursing home is tremendous[4] and, absent insurance, they'll be paying for all of it. Medicaid only steps in when your parents are financially wiped out, leaving them with virtually nothing to pass on to you.

Reason # 5: You Have Siblings

Have a brother or sister? Whatever you think of them, they're likely to get an equal cut of whatever is left too. So divide your parents' potential wealth by two, three, or more.

Counting on an inheritance is not wise. It is not financial planning. Creating financial independence and wealth takes savings—your savings.

Start today.

TEN STUPID AND CARELESS WAYS TO WASTE MONEY

Adapted from a post to the *Beyond Paycheck to Paycheck* blog, May 17, 2010

After a very successful trip to Annapolis to speak at the University of Maryland's Personal Finance Seminar for Professionals, I returned to an enormous box on my desk.

I approached it cautiously.

You: Did you fear it was a bomb?

Of course not, why?

You: It's possible.

I think you're watching too much TV.

---

[4] $80,000 a year for care isn't cheap.

You: What does that have to do with anything?

Nothing, just an independent observation.

You: So what did you do with the box?

I picked it up.

You: And?

I almost threw it to the ceiling!

You: Because you thought it was a bomb! I was right!

No, because the box weighed a LOT less than I thought it was going to weigh. When I opened and searched the approximately 30" x 18" box, it contained exactly one 6" x 9" book.

You: That's it?

No.

You: What else?

A ton of packing material.

You: Was it at least a good book?

Yes, it was *Beyond Paycheck to Paycheck*, but that's not the point.

You: Now who would return Beyond Paycheck to Paycheck?

Better question. One distributor returns books from time to time if a book was damaged in transit. Anyway, shipping one book in a box big enough for two toasters is a total waste of money.

You: I agree.

So this got me thinking . . . what other stupid and careless ways exist to waste money? Here's my list.

1. Playing the lottery.
2. Printing your airline boarding passes in color.
3. Not recycling ink cartridges at Staples®.(Receive payment for something which would otherwise wind up in a landfill? Works for me.)
4. Paying to park in a lot when free street parking is readily available nearby.

5. Skipping the complimentary breakfast at a hotel.[5]

6. Ignoring routine maintenance (e.g., car, house, spouse) in the short-term so it costs you much more (e.g., engine overhaul, new furnace, jewelry) in the long-term.

7. Putting way too many stamps on an envelope.

8. Buying an enormous package of a perishable item at a warehouse club because it's SO much less per serving . . . then throwing half the jar out after you realize you have enough mayonnaise to eat said condiment hourly for six months.

9. Paying sticker price for a car to avoid the inherent conflict and uncomfortable situations sure to arise by saying, "What would it take for you to sell me this car for less than invoice today?"

10. Saying "yes" to the $4.00 extended warranty on a $15.00 set of workout gloves (I was actually offered this yesterday.).

FIVE NONSENSICAL REASONS TO DELAY SAVING

Adapted from a post to the *Beyond Paycheck to Paycheck* blog, April 9, 2008

1. My house is my IRA; I don't need to save.

Oh c'mon! Open a newspaper. Counting on home price appreciation was crazy before 2008, but now, finally, most people get it. Sadly, there's still a few who act as if the change to housing prices is temporary and the price of their house will once again skyrocket annually. Sure it will. As soon as pets.com, etoys.com, and webvan shoot back to the moon.

---

[5] Assuming you're staying at the hotel. If you're just driving by on the interstate, your breakfast isn't complimentary.

2. All those computer programs assume an 8 percent rate of return for my investments. That's pathetic. When I get around to investing again, I'll get at least double that. Heck, I got 30 percent in 9 months back in 1999!

Anyone can earn huge returns in a bull market, but doing so doesn't make you a better investor anymore than banking a three-pointer makes you a good outside shooter.[6] In fact, if I lined up 100 people just like you, your average return would be . . . average! If you invest appropriately for the long term, it's reasonable to expect about 8 percent a year—on average. As I've said before, some years you will do much better. At other times, you will do far worse.

But here's the fundamental question: why would you want to *rely* on doing much better than the market? Wouldn't it be far better to have your "phenomenal" returns—I'll dream with you for a moment—simply make you more comfortable as opposed to needing spectacular performance to barely make it? Do you really want your long-term financial security dependent on luck instead of solid planning?

3. I already save in my 401(k) plan up to the level my employer matches. I'm doing better than most people.

Like eating vegetables is a great start to *health*, contributing to your 401(k) plan is a great start to *saving*. But if you smoke like a chimney and haven't worked out since the Reagan administration, an annual taste of asparagus alone will not turn you into an impressive physical specimen. Same thing with saving; contributing up to the match is wise, but it's going to take much more to achieve your financial goals.

---

[6] Even if you call it.

4. I have student loans. I'll save when they're paid off.

Sorry. I had them once myself, so I know your pain. Hopefully, many of those loans are at relatively low interest rates. And while your student loans represent one financial challenge, do not allow them to overwhelm your other monetary goals. Instead, find ways to save while paying down your debt, especially if interest rates are low. The remainder of *The Savings Solution* shows you dozens of ways to save.

5. I'm going to inherit a bunch of money one day. That'll take care of me.

As I demonstrate in the previous sidebar, don't count on others to fund your retirement. Pardon the pun, but that's your job now.

CHAPTER 3

. . . .

Saving Strategy # 1:
Stay Emotionally Connected
to Your Money

"I gotta dollar!"
—You, Age 5

I t's 11 AM Saturday morning and Uncle Robert has just pulled his car onto your driveway. Your brother excitedly wonders if the visitor will have any new toys with him.

For you, the suspense is minimal. Even as a kindergartener, you know which relatives bring you new toys—entertaining you nonstop for nearly 20 minutes—and those family members, like Uncle Robert, who greet you with a hug and a kiss only. Disappointed, you retreat to your room, forced to play with the same old stuff you got yesterday. (One of the joys of being five years old is such behavior is nearly excusable; adults acting similarly often require therapy.)

Tomorrow, Aunt Esther will visit and it will be a whole different story. Rather than give you a toy or arrive empty-handed, she will give you money. It won't be much, but it will be yours—totally yours.

\#   \#   \#

Perhaps you recall receiving money as a present from certain people when you were a child? If so, you probably remember which relatives did so and the amount they gave. On the other hand, you likely cannot recollect more than a handful of all the toys your extended family gave you during your childhood.

You: Why not?

Your emotional connection to money was much stronger than it was to new toys. As a child, you knew exactly what you were going to do with your money—you had plans![1] If you were going to spend it, you knew how: maybe you'd get Milk Duds®, a doll, or some baseball cards. Maybe you'd use it at a vending machine, pay for a ride outside on one of those toys outside the grocery store, or purchase stickers. If, on the other hand, you were going to save your money, you also knew how you were going to do that, whether by putting it in your wallet, your desk drawer, your piggy bank, or your purse with a princess on it.

If upon waking up the morning after Aunt Esther's visit, you discovered your money wasn't exactly where you left it, you'd go into your brother's room and start pummeling him. After all, he *must* have taken it—no way you could have "just spent" your new money as many do today with far greater sums.

When you were five years old, you could account for every single dollar. As an adult, things are quite different.

You: Tell me about it.

A Typical Friday Afternoon?

Your Boss: Hey there. Just wanted to let you know I really appreciate all your hard work. In particular, you did a great job taking care of that situation with Brian. It could have been a lot worse but, thanks to you, we're all set now. Thanks.

You: No problem, boss. You know me—always trying to help.

[At this point, your boss starts counting out twenties for your week's pay.]

---

[1] A psychologist might say "Your strong emotional connection to this gift of money is caused by the time spent processing its possibilities. The more time spent thinking about something, the more likely you are to remember it." A psychologist married to a personal finance author looking to support his theories would definitely say it.

Does that scenario sound familiar?

You: No, that never happens to me. I don't get paid in cash. (Come to think of it, I don't receive compliments at work either, but that's another story.)

Few people are paid in cash.[2] Do you receive a paycheck—a real paper check—you take to the bank instead?

You: No, I am paid by direct deposit.

Most people are. Direct deposit is a good thing; it's cheaper for your company and saves you the time and hassle of depositing your paycheck at the bank. Plus, many banks waive minimum balance requirements or offer other small perks for establishing a direct deposit relationship with them.

But for all the advantages of direct deposit, one big negative looms: direct deposit emotionally separates you from your income. While you may visit your bank's web site on payday to be sure your *first* paycheck arrives, it's unlikely you bother to verify each subsequent deposit. I bet you're incredibly busy.

You: Swamped. It's one reason I haven't managed to get my financial house in order yet.

I understand completely. You have neither the time nor the desire to verify something which has worked 38 consecutive times will work the 39th. So when it comes to direct deposit, you simply trust your money is there—which is okay, because the money *is* there.

You: Right.

But because you're not seeing and touching your money, you're emotionally separated from it. Now, your disconnection isn't from some toy bought at a drugstore, it's from your entire paycheck—hundreds or thousands of dollars. Worse, the same emotional separation happens on the way out.

You: On the way out?

Your money often goes out of your bank account shortly after your paycheck goes in. Such withdrawals include automatic payments such as rent/mortgage, heat, electric, phone, Netflix™, gym membership, and so

---

[2] Legally.

on. Those are all bills *you* previously authorized to be paid with money in *your* checking account.

You: But it's convenient to automate.

Yes, it is. I pay many of my bills the same way. But remember the cost.

You: What cost? I don't pay anything to automate my payments—why do you? Maybe I should I write a book.

I'm not talking about service fees or other charges banks sometimes assess for automatic payments; I'm speaking of the cost of your emotional separation. Between direct deposit and automatic payments, you're completely emotionally isolated from your income and your biggest monthly expenses. Undoubtedly, you're in a very different world than when you were five years old and thoroughly planned the future of a small gift of money.

Today, most of your spending results from *previous* decisions. **The emotional separation created by convenient automation prevents many people,** *including those who aggressively reduce their daily spending,* **from achieving meaningful savings.**

DAILY SPENDING

Your day-to-day spending can also be affected by a lack of emotional connection to your money.

You: But you can't automate your daily spending.

True, but automation is not the sole cause of emotional separation.

You: What do you mean?

How much money do you have in your wallet?

You: Me?

Yes, you.

You: In my wallet?

Yes.

You: Right now?

Yup.

You: About twenty bucks.

Now go check your wallet.

You: Right now?

Yes, go check. See how close you came.

You: Okay, I checked. I was pretty close.

When I do this exercise in large groups, here are the results.[3]

➤ 35 percent know exactly how much money they have

➤ 20 percent are wrong, but are within $10 of the right amount

➤ 30 percent are off by more than $10

➤ 15 percent have no idea and don't bother to guess

Many people don't have a clue how much cash they have in their wallets until they're at some random place which doesn't accept credit cards. Then, they're embarrassed because they need to hit the ATM in order to pay the measly six bucks they owe.

You: I've seen that happen at the pizzeria. Why?

It's not the pizza. People caught without cash typically don't use much of it in the first place—they primarily spend using credit cards.

You: So?

To emotionally reconnect with your money, you've got to use cash.

You: What if I pay my credit card balance off every month?

Do you?

You: Sometimes.

Even if you avoid interest charges by paying your entire balance every month, you're still better off using cash for everyday expenses.

You: C'mon. Who cares if I charge everyday expenses I pay off right away?

You care.

You: But why?

FEEL THE PAIN

When you use a credit card, you spend more money and you spend more often. Even those who promptly pay their entire balances each month still face the real cost of emotional separation.

You: Prove it.

---

[3] These precise statistics are completely made up, but are indicative of what I've observed.

Game on. Let's say you're at the mall, shopping for something you legitimately need.

You: Shoes?

Maybe.

You: Great, shoes!

It doesn't matter. The point is you need something at the mall. You find the item and bring it to the cashier. Here's what typically happens next.

1. The cashier, Ray H., scans your purchase and says, "Ninety-six dollars and ninety-nine cents please."
2. You hand him your credit card.
3. Ray H. swipes your card and hands you a slip to sign.
4. You sign the slip.
5. Ray H. compares the signature on the slip to the one on the back of your credit card.[4]
6. Ray H. returns your credit card to you and says, "Have a nice day."

You: Sounds about right.

Another possibility is you use cash to pay the amount due instead of a credit card.

You: Unlikely.

Perhaps, but since many people do use cash for routine shopping, it's worth highlighting how such a transaction proceeds.

1. The cashier, Angie, scans your purchase and says, "Ninety-six dollars and ninety-nine cents please."
2. You remove a wad of money from your wallet. To ensure you give the cashier the right amount, you count "Twenty, forty, sixty, eighty," <deep breath>[5], "ninety, ninety-five, ninety-six, ninety-seven," and hand over your cash.
3. Even an experienced cashier like Angie recounts the money to ensure her cash register won't be short at the end of her shift:

---

[4] If and only if Ray H. has worked at the store for less than one week.

[5] Turning over more than $80 in cash is where my breathing gets a bit rougher. With credit cards, my number is much higher. You?

"Twenty, forty, sixty, eighty, ninety, ninety-five, ninety-six, ninety-seven." (Hearing Angie count your cash makes it feel as though you're spending your money twice!)

4. Angie puts your money in the cash register and, while handing you a penny, says, "A penny is your change, have a nice day."

From a financial perspective, the two transactions are identical. In both cases, you leave the store with the needed item and you're out $96.99. But when you use cash, you're *literally* lighter in the wallet as you walk away. As a result, you feel poorer when you enter the next store in the mall. Consequently, you just might spend less at the second store or, perhaps, find you don't need anything there after all.

When you spend with cash, it hurts. When you use a credit card, there's no pain.

You: Excuse me? Come to my place when the credit card bill arrives. I'll show you pain.

But you don't *feel* the credit card pain *until* you get the credit card bill. The time lag between when you use the credit card and when you feel the pain is costly.

You: Sounds like an emotional separation again.

Exactly.

You: So now what? What are you going to tell me to do with my credit cards?

Why do you ask? Are you nervous?

You: A little.

Fearful I will tell you to cut up your credit cards?

You: It might not be the first time I've heard or considered it.

You're going to love the name of the next section.

YOU DON'T HAVE TO CUT UP YOUR CREDIT CARDS

You: Really?

Really. You don't have to cut up your credit cards.

You: Okay, this is different.

For most people, cutting up credit cards is an unnecessary and overly dramatic step.[6] Instead, you merely need to recognize something.

You: Recognize what?

And genuinely buy into it.

You: What do I get to buy?

Okay, *buy* was probably not the best word choice. I'll rephrase. You must explicitly acknowledge credit cards cause you to spend more money and to spend more often. You must be convinced credit cards ease your emotional separation from money, making them dangerous even if you pay your entire monthly balance.

You: We started down this road before and I'm still not sold. Reward points have real value. Why should I give up my points?

May I answer your question with one of my own?

You: Sure.

Why do most retailers, from dollar stores to high-end restaurants, accept credit cards?

You: Because it makes it easier for their customers to shop. Besides, why wouldn't stores want to accept credit cards?

Well, for one thing, retailers pay a hefty fee to accept credit cards.

You: They do?

You bet. If a customer pays cash for a $100 sale, the retailer gets $100. But if the same customer hands over a credit card, the retailer might receive only $97. Depending on the retailer and the card used, about $3 of every $100 charge goes to financial services providers, not to the store, hotel, restaurant, etc.

You: So wouldn't the retailer prefer I pay in cash?

Yes.

You: That's the opposite of where I thought this was going. So why do they accept credit cards? Is there a law?

No, no law requires retailers to accept credit cards. Many small merchants still operate on a cash-only basis.

---

[6] If you go over your credit limits and/or do not make your payments, *you* probably do need to take this "tough-love" step. Then again, your credit card company may have already taken care of it for you.

You: So why would anyone accept credit cards?

Retailers know people using credit cards spend more money during each trip, visit more often, and expect their plastic to be accepted. In contemplating a lower amount of anticipated cash receipts versus credit card charges, the merchant rejects a cash-only policy.

For all of those reasons, the shopkeeper, restaurant owner, online ticket broker, and post office willingly pay a fee of about three percent of gross sales to take credit cards. While three percent is a significant expense, accepting credit cards is typically a profitable decision.

You: I get it. Credit cards get people to spend more.

Good. By doing so, you accept the premise credit cards have a cost even if you never carry a balance.

You: Because of the emotional separation.

Yes. You now recognize when you use credit cards, you spend more and you spend more often.

You: I do. Now what?

Your next task is to passionately accept it. It's not too hard and, remember, no scissors are required.

You: How do I "passionately accept it?"

Say it out loud.

You: Say what out loud?

"When I use credit cards, I spend more money and I spend more often."

You: For real?

Yes. You just told me you believed it.

You: But still—out loud?

Yes.

You: This is so weird.

If you're on a plane or a train, or in a café, library, or other public place, you can just mouth the words while looking down. Otherwise, say it out loud:

You: "When I use credit cards, I spend more money and I spend more often." Okay, I did it.

Congratulations. Don't forget it.

DO DEBIT CARDS EMOTIONALLY SEPARATE YOU FROM YOUR MONEY?

I'm often asked if debit cards also emotionally separate you from your money.

You: What do you say?

I tell them, "Yes, debit cards do separate you emotionally."

You: Why?

Debit cards are made of plastic.

You: The material matters?

No, their physical substance is irrelevant. Furthermore, debit cards **are** superior to credit cards since, for the most part, you must have money in your linked checking account to complete a purchase.

You: Why do you say, "for the most part?" You can't borrow with a debit card.

Actually, with most debit cards you can borrow—sometimes without knowing it.

You: What?

Many banks process debit card transactions even when you lack sufficient funds in your checking account. If you don't have true overdraft protection, the bank will assess fees for bounce protection or courtesy overdraft.

You: Some courtesy!

Such fees might be larger than the interest you would have been charged had you used your credit card![7]

You: Disgusting.

Agreed.

You: But let's say I would never exceed my balance using a debit card.

Good.

You: Now what do you think about my using debit cards?

---

[7] While 2010 Congressional legislation made it much harder for banks to charge such fees, they still exist. You are hereby forewarned. Make sure you opt out of any such courtesy overdraft coverage—unless you like the occasional $39 pack of gum.

Debit cards allow you to avoid carrying a credit card, plenty of cash, or <gasp> a checkbook.

You: Carrying a debit card is like walking around with my entire checking account balance.

And that's what concerns me. Cash feels much more finite.

You: What do you mean?

Let's say your goal is to limit your spending to a total of $100 over the next three days. Imagine two different approaches:

1. You leave home with $100 in cash and no plastic.
2. You leave home with only a debit card. This card is linked to a checking account with a $945.78 balance.

Is it possible, despite easy access to nearly $1,000, to track and limit your spending to $100? Of course. But would you? Would you want to?

You: Probably not to the penny, but I might be able to stay close to the $100 goal.

Indeed, you might. But does a debit card keep you more emotionally connected to your money than a credit card? No. You could annoyingly track your spending with each. Furthermore, you do not feel the pain of physical separation from your money when you use either type of plastic. Without the physical loss, the emotional connection is reduced or destroyed, enabling different spending decisions.

You: I'm still not borrowing with a debit card!

Which is why a debit card is superior to a credit card when trying to limit spending. When it comes to retaining an emotional connection to your money, however, neither is anywhere as effective as good old-fashioned greenbacks.

You: Greenbacks?

Yeah, cash. See how separated from it we've become?

LEAVE HOME WITHOUT IT

Instead of taking the scissors to your credit cards, just leave them at home.

You: Isn't that the same thing?

Not quite—leaving your credit cards at home is a much smaller commitment than cutting them up.

You: True.

Before you next run errands, remove your credit cards from your wallet and put them in a safe place. Take only cash with you.

You: How much?

Bring the amount necessary to do your errands. Do not bring an extra twenty or forty bucks just in case.

You: Why not?

You know what happens if you bring the additional money.

You: What happens?

"Just in case" happens. Bring only what you need. When a $59 item on your list is next to a slightly fancier $89 version and you're paying cash, your choice is between surrendering three twenties or five twenties. When you're not simply handing over a piece of plastic for a quick swipe, you feel the immediate pain of parting with more money. Since you want to avoid pain, you make different and better choices using cash.

Furthermore, you won't remember the bells and whistles left behind by passing on the more expensive version. The one you purchased works well for your needs; heck, it was the one on your list in the first place! Stay connected to your money *emotionally* and it will stay connected to you *physically*.

THE MIRAGE

At this point, it's unlikely you doubt the importance of an emotional connection on your ability to save. But just in case, let's talk about the industry best at emotionally separating people from their money.

You: The Internal Revenue Service (IRS)?

No, the IRS takes your money by literally withholding it from your paycheck.

You: I hate that.

Me too, but since you have absolutely no choice in the matter, your emotions don't play a role. How about another guess?

You: Those 900 numbers?

Excuse me?

You: I have a friend who, at the end of his "chats," is definitely both emotionally spent and separated from his money.

Wow—not what I was expecting. I'm shooting for a "G-rated" conversation here, so we're not going to analyze your friend. One last guess.

You: Casinos?

Bingo! Casinos are fantastic at physically separating you from your money. But long before you lose your money by gambling, you lose it emotionally.

WHAT GOES TO VEGAS STAYS IN VEGAS

Visitors to casinos fall into one of the following categories:

➤ Slot machine players

➤ Table-game players (e.g., blackjack, poker)

➤ Players of both types

➤ Observers

Although most of a casino's efforts to emotionally separate you from your money are readily apparent, they're still remarkably effective. Let's say you're going to play a slot machine. To get started, you put twenty dollars in the machine. What's the very first thing that happens?

You: I lose my money.

No, not yet. You will lose it, but you haven't played yet. What happens right after you put in your twenty dollars?

You: I hear noises.

Noises?

You: Like the sound of a bell.

Right, a lot of ding-ding-ding-ding-ding noises. Fortunately, part of your brain knows you haven't won anything and the noise is simply a distraction you should tune out. Unfortunately, another part of your brain is now completely fired up, stimulated, and eager to hear more bells.

You: Kind of like an emotional high.

Yes. Something else happens when you hear the bells.

You: What?

Envision the slot machine. Look right below eye-level. What's happened?

You: I'm not sure.

Your money is gone.

You: But I haven't played yet.

Yet your money is gone. Nowhere on the machine does it say $20. Instead, the slot machine indicates the number of *credits* you have. If you're playing the nickel slots, you have 400 credits. If you chose a dollar machine, you now have 20 credits. No matter the machine, you're emotionally separated from your money *before a single pull of the one-armed bandit*. That matters—

You: Because when I'm emotionally separated from my money it isn't long before I will be physically separated from it.

Well said. Because the slot machine doesn't display the dollar amount of each bet, it's easy to press the "Bet Max" button. Some people put in a twenty-dollar bill hoping it will last them an hour or more. They would never press a hypothetical "Bet $5" button, but they do press the "Bet Max" button. As a result, those 20 dollars might "buy" only seven minutes.

Of course, you might stop gambling before losing all your $20. What button do you press to get your remaining money from the slot machine?

You: The "Cash Out" button.

Correct. Do you get cash out of a slot machine when you press the "Cash Out" button?

You: No, you get a slip of paper.

That's right—you get a piece of paper resembling a receipt.[8] We should call the "Cash Out" button the "Slip Out" button, since you're trying to slip out of the casino with *some* of your money. To convert your little slip into cash, what must you do?

You: Go to a cashier's window.

What's between you and any cashier's window?

You: Many more slot machines.

---

[8] Subtlety implying you actually bought something.

How many?

You: Too many.

So what happens?

You: I might play another one.

That would be my bet.[9] If you make it to a cashier's window, how long is the line?

You: Longer than it should be.

Indeed, even in a relatively empty casino, there's always a line at the cashiers' windows.

You: Why?

The casino alters the number of open windows to ensure a wait. Seeing a line convinces some folks, especially those with relatively small slip balances, to put those last few dollars into nearby machines.

You: Casinos really want all the money, don't they?

Casinos' detailed understanding of how to emotionally separate people from their money makes them incredibly profitable. A casino also applies its magic at table games, where the stakes involved are usually greater.

You: How so?

When you sit down at a blackjack table, the dealer immediately converts your money into chips. Those chips are *like* money, but they are *not* money, making it easier to gamble more aggressively. It's one thing to see your chips disappear—you don't like it. But if you see most of your wallet disappear, you probably stop gambling before the rest of it fades away.

The chip mentality also explains periodic $50 tips to waitresses delivering two bottles of Miller Light®. Would any sober person tip $50 for a couple of beers?

You: I've seen it happen.

I said "sober person."

You: Right. Then, no. But given the chips don't feel like money, I can see someone could tip $50—or lose more than he can afford—in a casino. It's psychology.

No doubt—psychology plays an important role in your financial condition.

---

[9] Pun intended.

You: So leave the credit cards at home and I'm done?

Close. You'll be on your way. Ultimately, your success depends on much more than recognizing and embracing the psychological and financial importance of your emotional connection to money. For instance, you must be honest with yourself about your expenses.

CASE STUDIES

WHY YOU'RE BETTER OFF SAVING $500 THAN EARNING $600

Adapted from a post to the *Beyond Paycheck to Paycheck* blog, June 28, 2010

When speaking on college campuses, I often give students an opportunity to make some money.

You: Seems nice of you.

To get the cash, they must stay after my seminar for a market research study. Since I offer $35 for 30 minutes of their time, nearly the entire audience wants to participate.

You: What do you do then?

I tell them it's a joke.

You: You do?

Yes—I do.

You: That's not nice.

You're right. But it is memorable and I do it to make a point.

You: And what point is that?

How eager most people are to make money.

You: That's not terribly insightful, especially given college students often have very little money.

Perhaps, but contrast this with the same audience's—and just about every other audience's—lack of enthusiasm for saving money.

You: What do you mean?

Well, a college audience ought to be filled with people who would love to save money. Yet most people lament the idea of working to save. I find that both unfortunate and ironic.

You: Ironic?

Yes. If you work hard to save money, you keep 100 percent of what you save. If you work hard to earn money, you keep only about two-thirds of your earnings.

You: Why?

Because of taxes.

You: Right—argh.

So as a society, we should actually be more motivated to save money than to earn it, but my experience says most people are not.

Let me give you a real world experience from my life. Recently, I moved.

You: How did it go?

Not bad, but tiring.

You: You did it all by yourself?

No, the job was too hard and the items too heavy.

You: So you hired movers?

Yes.

You: That can be expensive.

It can be, but it doesn't have to be. When my wife got quotes from moving companies for our anticipated three mile move, each was in the vicinity of $1,000. As such, I started wondering if I could do the move for less without breaking my back—literally and figuratively.

You: And?

I found an answer; hire moving labor but not a moving company. A few web searches later I had a couple of freelance guys show up. They worked their butts off for a fraction of the cost the moving companies quoted.

What did I give up by not hiring a moving company?

You: A name on the truck that didn't say "U Haul" or "Budget?"

Yes, that and a driver.

On the other hand, my additional expenses by doing it "myself" were the $50 cost to rent the truck and the effort of driving the truck. Given I drove a grand total of 16 miles and saved more than $500 in the process, my savings were over $36 a mile. Since I saved—not earned—the money, the $500 won't go on my W-2 and I won't pay taxes on it.

You: Cool.

Think about it this way: **Saving $500 is like earning $750.** The next time you face the possibility of a few more phone calls to save $500, recall how hard it is and how long it takes to earn $750. If you're a high-priced Philadelphia lawyer earning $750 an hour, hire a moving company, but tell me again, why are you reading this book? For the rest of you, enjoy the savings.

BANK FEES AND BILLING ERRORS

Adapted from a post to the *Beyond Paycheck to Paycheck* blog, August 19, 2009

Two recent phone calls saved me money and provided some lessons.

Lesson 1: Michael vs. The Bank Soon to be Formerly Known as the Name Still on Its Sign

First, I called my bricks and mortar bank.

You: Why do you even have a local bank? They are fee central.

You're right; many banks with branches charge a lot of fees. In fact, I went several years without a local bank. Back then, I mailed in the occasional check and took cash out via an ATM. Since my bank levied no ATM charges and reimbursed those assessed by others, I was quite happy.

You: So what changed?

For personal banking, nothing. But starting my own business meant an entirely new world of banking. Most Total Candor® clients pay their invoices by check. Rather than mail checks and wait several days for funds to clear, we opened an account in the neighborhood.

You: So, all was good until . . .

Take a guess.

You: They charged you a fee.

Well done. This was a surprise, since I had compared three local banks' fee schedules when I opened the account years ago. I found I could get a small business checking account with a clever marketing name which, while it assessed no fees, still fully met our needs.

This worked for three years.

[Sinister music plays, growing ever louder.]

Then, one day, out of nowhere, my bank suddenly announced a . . . merger.

[OMG!]

I tried to remain calm but excitement was building. I just knew everything was going to be so much better once my bank eliminated the last five letters from its name!

You: How did you know?

From the numerous correspondences![10]

You: And you believed it?

Of course not! But I did read closely how the fees were going to change. After the merger, I would have a minimum balance requirement or face a sizable monthly fee. Fortunately, the minimum balance was only $100, an amount I always ensure is in the account anyway. So I didn't worry.

You: Foreshadowing an unexpected twist to come . . .

Hey, stop that.

You: Sorry. Misery loves company.

Nonetheless, before the signs even changed outside the branch locations, I discovered a fee in my July statement.

---

[10] "Numerous correspondences" is a shorter and more polite way of saying "endless junk mail disguised as letters, legal disclosure emails which were primarily for marketing purposes and therefore rightly categorized by my computer as spam, flyers with Regis Philbin's picture on it stuffed in the envelope containing my monthly statements, messages in the 'message center' I didn't care to know existed on the bank's web site, and cryptic messages downloaded via my personal finance software." "Numerous correspondences" does not include the blimp that might have flown over Fenway Park displaying video about what a great merger this bank combination was going to be on a night when I was merely trying to see if Daisuke Matsuzaka could get out of the fifth inning on less than 120 pitches.

You: For what?

For "IMAGE CHKS IN STMT."

You: Image checks in statement?

Apparently, yes.

You: What does that mean?

I didn't know either, so I had to ask. Remember when you received your original checks along with your bank statement?

You: Not really.

Along with one's monthly statement, banks formerly sent cleared checks. Presumably to cut costs, most banks stopped including those checks long ago. Today, many banks provide images of cleared checks on monthly statements instead.

You: So how does this relate to your new fee?

Read on for my interpretation of the boardroom play-by-play.

Merger of Equal Brainiacs

At a top secret board meeting in an undisclosed location in a very fancy and expensive New York City restaurant at the corner of 5th Avenue and 61st Street—seated at the elite and highly sought-after "Excess Table"—the collected bank executives needed to make their merger a good idea. After all, the companies had promised synergies to their shareholders!

Like many well-trained executives facing similar dire predicaments of their own making, the team collaboratively brainstormed additional ways to cut costs (i.e., fire even more people). During this process, Archibald Collingsworth, an executive with superior pedigree evidenced solely by his impressive British-sounding name, decided he must have a single piece of paper immediately to most effectively illustrate his point; specifically, that rank and file workers waste too much time focusing on little things which do not matter.

Rather than use the back of any one of the many bogus business receipts held in his wallet, he called a nearby branch of his newfound banking empire. He was instantly put on hold by the receptionist. Never having called a branch before, he was shocked by such "rude behavior," as he called it.

Outraged, he shouted at Julie, the 22 year-old teller/customer service representative/branch manager/receptionist when she returned to the phone.

Archibald: Do you know who I am? You put *ME* on hold? I could fire you and all of your incompetent co-workers right now for such an insensitive act! Bloody hell, is it because so many people are in the branch right now that you must put me on hold?

Julie: No, it's pretty dead in here.

Archibald: Dead?

Julie: Yes.

Archibald: And you put me on hold?

Julie: I was a little upset.

Archibald: Why?

Julie: I was just informed—by email—I've been terminated.

Archibald: What do you mean, terminated?

Julie: Fired, sir. Anyway, I was simply trying to gain my composure before speaking with you. No one else is here to talk to.

Archibald: Why not?

Julie: All my co-workers were fired a few hours ago by some guy named Bristol.

[Archibald nods approvingly across the table to Bristol—the newly named Executive Vice President of Layoffs and Business Card Design—who is on his 5th vodka martini. Bristol tries to nod back but instead knocks over the dijon.]

Archibald: What about the customers?

Julie: I was just going to lock the doors when you called. Only two customers are here now and one of them is sucking on a pacifier.

Archibald: Very well then, Julie. Make sure to really turn the deadbolt on your way out and throw the keys into the sewer.

Julie [obviously in tears]: Yes, sir.

Archibald: Also, and this is very important, I need a single deposit slip for scrap paper. Could you bring one uptown to 5th and—

Julie: But I live downtown, sir, and I was just fired. Am I even going to get paid for—

Archibald: Thanks, sweetie! Tell the maitre d' to bring it to me right away, won't you?

[Click.]

Much to the other executives' surprise, Archibald's conversation with Julie has affected him. To this inner circle who eagerly anticipate his every word, he declares, "You know what? I sense we've maximized our layoffs for now. Let's not fire anyone else until at least Thursday. Indeed, gentlemen, it's now time to create some revenue enhancers."

With that, Graham, an old-timer, decides to take his best shot. He looks at his new golfing buddy and says, "Charles, remember when banks sent customers their cleared checks every month?"

Charles responds, "Sure do, Graham. Wow, that was stupid. And expensive!"

"What if," Charles continues, "we could charge people just to get check *images*? Nobody checks their statements anyway."

"So now something which was once a cost to us becomes a money-maker?" Charles asked.

"Absolutely!" says Graham.

"Graham, you're a genius. Now I know why I merged with you."

A few weeks later I get my IMAGE CHKS IN STMT fee. Thousands of other small businesses do also and most won't look at their statements closely enough to notice.

My response is to call customer service. After the representative verified my identity in a manner so comprehensive a U.S. customs agent would quiver,[11] I informed the representative, "I don't do fees, so can you please tell me what I need to do to ensure I'm never charged for this again?"

She responded all I would have to do is request the previously free check images no longer appear on my statement. I told her to consider it requested. After several minutes of unexplained typing,[12] she asked if there was anything else.

I said yes.

You: What else?

I told her I would like to have the already assessed fee reversed since I wasn't told about it in advance.

You: What happened then?

She disagreed, advising me I was told about the fee. In response, I requested she share with me how I was allegedly informed.

She said the new fee was detailed in some of the paperwork I was sent. Being rather organized, I pulled out the exact paperwork she mentioned and reviewed it with her. Despite dozens of other new fees listed, we could find nothing about a new fee for check images.

She sounded exasperated. She put me on hold again. Now she wasn't the only one exasperated.

She needed to think of something fast.

What she said next was impressive. "There was an insert, completely separate from the paper we were just looking at which had other fees, including a fee for check images.

---

[11] Including but not limited to the last four digits of my social security number, my mother's maiden name, the really mean name my best friend called me when we had a fight in fourth grade after I called him a dork, and the color of my second dog's favorite bowl.
[12] Reminiscent of trying to change a seat assignment at the airport circa 1988.

"Well played," I thought to myself.

I told her I could not prove I did not receive the insert anymore than she could prove I did. In consideration of my relationship with the bank and my belief I wasn't informed in advance, I asked her to remove the fee.

She still wouldn't budge, presumably because she wasn't empowered to do so.[13] I had a decision to make.

You: Time to ask for a supervisor.

Correct, but I decided not to.

You: Why not?

It was only $1—multiplied by three accounts. My primary goal was to ensure the fee didn't recur in the future. I felt I had already invested too much time for $3.

You: Yeah, but still.

Would I really go through all the work of closing accounts and opening them elsewhere over three bucks?

No, I would not.

Will I grow my relationship with my bank as my business grows?

My answer to that question is also no. My bank will simply continue to get the least profitable part of my business. Their actions made my unimportance clear. I'm pretty sure I can mirror those attributes, so I will. Given checking accounts aren't profitable for banks, keeping my accounts open without paying any fees probably does more financial damage to them more than closing them would.

---

[13] Thank you, EVP Bristol.

Lesson 2: Customer Service. On Time.

A few minutes later I called FedEx®.

You: Why?

I noticed an apparent error in my latest bill. A package which ordinarily costs about $5 to ship was billed at over $13.

I told the representative something didn't look right. Before I could even start typing an unrelated email (I expected to be on hold for a while as she developed an answer for why I wasn't right when I actually was.), she told me she would credit my account immediately and apologized four times for their error, an error she obviously had nothing to do with.

That's how to treat people. FedEx made a mistake and caused me to invest some of my finite time to deal with it, yet I came away happier with them than before.

Takeaways:

> ➤ **You have to review your statements.** All of them. Errors will happen and most will not be in your favor.

> ➤ **You won't always get what you deserve** (the bank fee reimbursed, in my case), **but sometimes you'll get more than what you're really asking for** (see page 181 for how I lowered my cable bill and received more services).

> ➤ **No one else will ever care about your money as much as you do.** Your finances are at stake, so you better act like it.

CHAPTER 4

Saving Strategy # 2: Understand and Be Honest About Expenses

"Honesty is such a lonely word. Everyone is so untrue."
—BILLY JOEL

Did you eat lunch today?
You: Yes.

Is lunch something you *want* or something you *need*?
You: I have to eat.

Sure you do. Still, is lunch a want or a need?
You: Food is a need.

Yes, *food* is. But what about *lunch*?
You: Lunch is food!

Where did you have lunch today?
You: Sometimes I bring my lunch to work.

Did you bring your lunch to work today?
You: Today I went out to lunch. Ugh, and I was going to bring my lunch today too.

Feel free to put the book down, bring lunch tomorrow, and read this chapter then.

You: I don't think that will be necessary.

Why not?

You: Because I always say I am going to bring my lunch.

Do you?

You: Don't rub it in.

Since eating is a need and eating out is a want, lunch can be either one. When you choose to spend more of your money by eating out, you do so because you *want* to.

You: So I can't eat lunch out anymore?

Quite the opposite. You can absolutely choose to eat lunch out and still be fiscally responsible. What you can't do is lie about your spending while expecting to become a saver.

NON-DISCRETIONARY AND DISCRETIONARY EXPENSES

In financial jargon, wants are discretionary expenses and needs are non-discretionary expenses. See the adjacent table for examples of both.

Figure 4-1

Examples of Discretionary and Non-Discretionary Expenses

Discretionary Expenses (Wants)	Non-Discretionary Expenses (Needs)
Entertainment	Rent/Mortgage
Dining Out	Utilities
Concerts	Insurance Premiums
Movies	Car Payment
Books	Commuting Expenses
iAnything*	Taxes
*Including but not limited to: Pod, Phone, Pad, Mac, Mic, Pud, Drone, Attack	

You: Discretionary expenses are more fun than non-discretionary expenses.

True. Most non-discretionary expenses, such as taxes and insurance premiums, are annoying requirements of life as an adult. However, other non-discretionary expenses, such as mortgage or rent payments, can bring you happiness.

You: Like when I live in a nice place.

Plus, having no place to live makes it hard to be happy.

You: True enough. So non-discretionary expenses can be either annoying or enjoyable. On the other hand, discretionary expenses are always enjoyable, right?

Actually, some discretionary expenses are not pleasurable.

You: Really?

Yup.

You: What's an example of an unpleasant discretionary expense?

A bad movie.

You: Like Waterworld?

So I'm told. Ultimately, your enjoyment does not distinguish an expense between non-discretionary or discretionary.

You: What's the key difference?

Whether you can affect the expense right now.

You: What does that mean?

If you can do something *today* to significantly change the cost or existence of an expense, the spending is discretionary. If nothing can be done about it now, the cost is non-discretionary.

You: So it's just as it sounds.

Correct—don't you love when that happens? If you can change or avoid an expense, the cost is at your discretion (i.e., the expense is discretionary). If you can't, you no longer have any discretion (i.e., the expense is non-discretionary).

Here are some additional examples of common expenses and their categories.

> ➤ *Housing payments are non-discretionary* because you can't do anything to change your next mortgage or rent payment.

> ➤ *Gasoline expenses are primarily non-discretionary.* Most people spend the bulk of their gas money to commute to work. Not much you can do about it today, is there?

➤ *Gifts and charitable contributions are discretionary.* Since you determine how much to give when you make a gift, you can affect their cost.

DISCRETIONARY AND NON-DISCRETIONARY EXPENSES IN MY LIFE

My discretionary expenses include a family membership at the local children's museum, an occasional dinner out with my wife, a babysitter to watch our young children (so we can actually talk to each other), and a much too rare brewski with the guys I play hoops with. Since I have no obligation to spend until a short while before payment, each cost is discretionary.

Compare those costs with the following expenses which, although similar, are non-discretionary.

Payments to our nanny are non-discretionary expenses. Without our nanny, either my wife or I would be unable to work.[1] Consequently, our nanny's employment with us is a non-discretionary expense.

Although a babysitter does approximately the same things in the evening a nanny does during the day, a babysitter is discretionary—a nanny is not.

You: Even though they do the same job.

Our choice to pay a babysitter is a *want*, since my wife and I don't need to go out to dinner. On the other hand, we do need to go to work. To do so, we *need* a nanny.

You: Give me another example.

As I mentioned, I enjoy playing basketball. Yet, with increasing and disturbing regularity, I land awkwardly on the way down from my remaining two inches of vertical leap. Whether my foot gives out on top of someone else's shoe or just trembles on the remarkably flat and sturdy floor, too often I sprain my ankle, tear my Achilles, or yank my back. When I subsequently visit an orthopedist or podiatrist, the result is a non-discretionary medical expense, even though my clumsiness is related to playing basketball, an activity which is clearly a want.

---

[1] The simple fact you are reading this book is evidence Leslie has been paid.

You: Why don't you just stop playing basketball?

Mom?

You: No.

Within categories you have choices. Take basketball shoes, for example. If you're playing basketball regularly, basic high-tops are required (like a tennis racket is to an avid tennis player.) But top-of-the-line basketball sneakers featuring the autograph and endorsement of someone who can jump over people taller than you aren't necessary.

WHY FINANCIAL HONESTY MATTERS

Being honest about your expenses does not mean frequent ramen noodle lunches and dinner-parties with Spam® as the main course. Like emotionally connecting with you money, understanding and being honest about your expenses allows you to be fiscally responsible *without* being cheap.

Since you can't do anything about non-discretionary expenses in the short-term,[2] you must *understand* and evaluate your discretionary spending to increase your savings rate. When you do, be *honest* with yourself. Remember, discretionary expenses present opportunities—not requirements—for change.

Eliminating all discretionary expenses is both unrealistic and unnecessary. Cutting to the bone is unsustainable over the long-term—you have to live a little. Strict budgets are like crash diets; each might work for a little while, but dramatic overnight lifestyle changes are incredibly difficult to sustain.

So, let's not go there.

You: Agreed.

Focus instead on what is possible by taking one step at a time. If you want to increase your savings rate or simply begin saving, begin by understanding your discretionary expenses. Keep track of your spending for the next week.

---

[2] You can make an enormous impact on your non-discretionary expenses over the long-term, the emphasis of Saving Strategy 3.

You: Just one week?

That's all.

You: Does it have to be next week? I'm super busy.

Yes.

You: Why?

One week from now you can either have this little exercise done and be on your way to saving *or* you could develop another reason why the subsequent seven days are also not good for you to begin the savings process.

You: But I am very busy.

All you have to do is save your receipts.

You: That's it?

Yes. It takes virtually no time to start the process. Save every receipt for every dollar you spend for the next seven days.

You: What about change?

Don't worry about the change.

You: Sweet.

YOU MAKE THE CALL

Since no two people spend alike, the numbers you enter in Figure 4-2 will be unique. Furthermore, different people—even financial experts—could review your reported spending and reasonably disagree on your best savings opportunities.

You: How so?

One expert might recommend you go out to dinner less. Another might suggest you eat out just as often, but spend less each time. Someone else might propose you reduce the frequency of coffee house runs. A fourth person might instead recommend you bring soda cans or bottled water to work and thereby eliminate the vending machine markup.

You: Who's right?

Probably none of them. Only you know what matters most to you. Besides, there is no "right" answer.

You: So how do I go about determining what to change?

Figure 4-2

Track Your Discretionary Spending for a Week

	Sunday	Monday	Tuesday	Wednesday	Thursday	Friday	Saturday	Total
Coffee (regardless of what you say when you order it)								
Vending Machines								
Breakfast out								
Lunch out								
Dinner out								
Drinks out								
Spontaneous clothing purchase								
Entertainment								
iTunes, apps, and any other random digital spending you couldn't have contemplated just a few years ago								
Other Discretionary Spending								

In addition, sometime during your test week, consider how much do you spend monthly on:

Gym memberships
Gifts
Premium cable stations
NetFlix
Charitable contributions
Subscriptions
Other monthly or annual expenses which are truly wants? Allocate a weekly portion on the "other" line.

Review your discretionary spending worksheet and ask yourself these two questions:

    1. Of all my spending last week, what expense was *most* worth it?

    2. Of all my spending last week, what expense was *least* worth it?

What expense do you think you should cut?

You: My answer to question number two.

What's your best opportunity to reduce your discretionary spending?

You: My answer to question number two.

What's your best opportunity to increase your savings rate?

You: My answer to question number two.

You're getting the hang of this.

You: What about the rest of my daily spending?

If you want to increase the amount you save so you can move from income to wealth, you need to cut certain discretionary expenses. But *you* decide which and how many expenses to reduce or eliminate.

You: Do most people have to go through this exercise?

Few people earn enough money to allow unlimited discretionary spending and you're not one of them.

You: How do you know?

People with genuinely unlimited discretionary spending are quite wealthy and don't need books titled *The Savings Solution*. Furthermore, notwithstanding popular images of instant lottery winners, celebrity athletes, and movie stars, many of the nation's millionaires became affluent by consistently spending less than they earned. As such, they don't need tips to save—they've been saving for decades.

You: Fair points.

As you review your discretionary expenses, you'll enjoy identifying opportunities to save.

You: Enjoy? That seems like a reach.

Money in your wallet at a time of the month when there usually isn't: enjoyable. A checking account balance featuring more digits before the decimal point than after it: enjoyable.

You: I'm with you.

Now *you* are in control. When you're living paycheck to paycheck, you're out of control. You're unable to save. By *choosing* what expenses to cut, you're back in control. Eliminating spending for what you value least is far better than cutting highly valued experiences when you suddenly find you cannot afford them.

Despite the enormous benefits from understanding and being honest about discretionary expenses, your non-discretionary expense opportunity is greater still.

You: But you said earlier I couldn't do anything about my non-discretionary expenses.

Over the short-term, that's true. But you're not here to change the short-term alone, are you? Do you want to change your month or change your life?

You: My life.

How?

You: I want to be able to save more.

For those struggling financially, moving from income to wealth requires a life-changing attitude. Spending a few dollars less here or there helps, but not enough to make you an important bank client.

You: Client?

A client is like a customer.

You: I'm already a customer.

I know. I want you to become a client.

Gary: Me too.

Get out of here!

You: So how do I get the real money?

Analyze your non-discretionary expenses, which *you can change over the long-term.*

CASE STUDIES

ANOTHER FANTASTIC UNINTENTIONALLY LOW-COST WEEKEND

Adapted from a post to the *Beyond Paycheck to Paycheck* blog, September 14, 2009

With my wife and youngest daughter away for the weekend, the time was ripe for some serious Daddy-daughter bonding with my four year-old.

From Thursday evening to Sunday night our activities included:

➤ Out to dinner twice

➤ Out to lunch once

➤ Dessert in the North End of Boston

➤ A delicious cold drink on a hot afternoon

➤ Over three hours at two different gyms on bad weather days

➤ A visit to the New England Aquarium in Boston

➤ Several train rides—the girl loves trains!

➤ Her first big-league baseball game at Fenway Park[3]

Does all this sound expensive?

You: Sure does.

Was it?

You: I'm guessing somehow it was not, but how?

You're right. Although a little luck was involved and I'm not including the minimal gas or groceries we used, we spent $55 this weekend.

You: Fifty-five bucks? Impossible.

---

[3] And we heard *Dirty Water,* if you know what I mean.

Nope. The dinners were inexpensive. One of them was a treat to (Old) McDonald's®. Not a staple of our diet, but a good place to go periodically, especially when Mom is out of town and there's a play area. The other dinner was at Chipotle®, which had just mailed me a free burrito coupon. That dinner out was under $4—for my daughter's meal.

You: What about the aquarium?

We're members of the New England Aquarium so the ordinary $30 admission was free.

You: Couldn't I argue you simply prepaid your admission?

You could. But I would counter with the advantages of local memberships. See page 100 for more.

You: How about food while you were in Boston?

Lunch for two at Quincy Market: $11.

Dessert in the distinctly enjoyable Italian neighborhood of the North End: $2.50. Eating a cannoli together on a bench, my four-year-old from one side and I from the other: priceless.[4]

You: Okay, how about the Red Sox tickets?

Free.

You: Free? Who do you know?

It's never a bad idea to meet your dining neighbors, especially at Quincy Market where you're often closer than you'd be in an elevator. Saturday afternoon, my unscheduled dining companions were from Miami. They had come to Boston a day earlier to see the Friday night Red Sox game. Their game had been rained out and rescheduled for Sunday afternoon. Unfortunately for them, their flight back to Florida left a few hours after our lunch together. But, thanks to their generosity, a four-year old went to her first big league baseball game.

---

[4] My daughter now wants to learn how to make "K'noys" in the kitchen with Mom.

You: What about food and drink at the game? You've mentioned how much your daughter eats!

I brought about 3,000 calories for her from home, which was enough for her—barely. Still, I bought a Slurpee® for us to share at 7-11® after the game. For $1.50, I indulged a great little extravagance for a four-year old on a hot day!

You: Parking?

We parked in the suburbs, where parking is $5.50—not the $35 or more they charge for spaces downtown. We rode the T (i.e., the subway) the rest of the way to Boston. My fare was $1.70 each way (little children ride free.) When you're four years old, riding a train is one of the best parts of your day.

*You: You admittedly spent very little during what would seem to be a very enjoyable weekend. But you're into saving, Michael—I'm not. Did **you** enjoy your weekend or were you disappointed at not choosing to do possible but more expensive activities? Or were you scheming ways to spend even less in the future?*

We certainly could have spent more money over the weekend. We could have gone to different places for lunch or dinner. We could have gone to a museum where we weren't members. We could have purchased food at Fenway Park.

We also could have not left the house and cut that $55 right down to zero. But would that be balanced?

I wouldn't trade my weekend with my four year old—and the memories we made along the way—for anything or any amount. Try to achieve such an outstanding weekend soon. It will cost far less than you think and you'll love the feeling.

SAVING TWICE FROM ONE DECISION
Adapted from a post to the *Beyond Paycheck to Paycheck* blog, August 3, 2009

I received an email the other day from Jenny F. of New York City:
"I thought of you yesterday when bragging to my husband how I saved $350/year just by switching my prescription from the drug store to mail order. Not only am I saving money, but it's so much more convenient. Since the prescription arrives at my house, I do not have to make a trip to the drugstore—which really means I'm saving more like $470/year because walking into the drugstore always means spending $10 on stuff I really don't need (e.g., toy car for my daughter, Kit Kat for me, etc). Anyway, I had to tell you about it!"

Jenny's kind note got me thinking. First, I couldn't remember extolling the virtues of acquiring your recurring prescription drugs via mail. It's a great idea. Second, what other saving strategies enable you to save both directly and indirectly?

You: Directly and indirectly? What do you mean?

In other words, a saving strategy where one decision enables you to save in two different ways.

Jenny decided to receive her prescription medicine by mail. Her **direct** savings are the lower co-payment charged to those using this method. Since she no longer visits the drugstore, she avoids any impulsive purchases of candy and toys—her **indirect** savings.

Three additional examples of saving strategies which save money directly and indirectly are:

1. Choosing a home with a small yard and/or a short driveway
Direct savings: Lower home price and property taxes
Indirect savings: Less money spent on landscaping and snow removal

2. Keeping your current cell phone / **PDA** / electronic gadget

Direct savings: No charge for equipment you already own

Indirect savings: No new accessories for the latest gadget plus no new and more expensive monthly plan

3. Taking the family out to dinner

You: What?!

Hold on. Keep reading.

Direct savings: Visiting a less expensive place than if it were just "the two of you," especially if you go to a "kids eat free" place.

Indirect savings: No babysitter!

While eating in is cheaper still, I use the last example to demonstrate saving isn't an all or nothing proposition. Figure out what you really want to do. Then, from time to time, find a way to spend less while still doing it.

CHAPTER 5

. . . .

Saving Strategy # 3:
Lower Your Needs Yesterday

"Yesterday, all my troubles seemed so far away. Now it looks as though they're here to stay. Oh, I believe in yesterday."
—BEATLES, "YESTERDAY"

"When yesterday's gone, yesterday's gone."
—FLEETWOOD MAC, "DON'T STOP"

Of the dozens of spending decisions you make weekly, choices might include:

➤ How many bananas to buy at the grocery store

➤ Whether to purchase flowers for a loved one

➤ Which gas station you choose to fill up at

You: Bananas give me hives all over my—

TMI. Still, not buying bananas is a decision.

Since your spending determines your savings, your daily choices are important. However, only a small percentage of your total spending results from your daily decisions.

You: What? Whose decisions is my total spending based on?

Yours.

*You: But you just said my total spending was **not** based on my decisions.*

Most of your spending is not from your *daily* decisions. Instead, it is largely the result of previous choices—those you made yesterday (or earlier.)

In Chapter 4, we focus on discretionary spending. You complete a table to identify the daily expenses you value most and those which provide an opportunity to save while minimizing lifestyle impact.

LUMP SUMS VS. MONTHLY PAYMENTS

Now we focus on your previous commitments to non-discretionary expenses. Such costs are typically paid monthly.

You: Why is that?

Great question. Most non-discretionary expenses are paid monthly because they are too expensive for the average household to pay in one lump sum.

You: What's a lump sum?

Paying for a whole purchase at once. Few people can afford to buy a house or a car all at once.

You: Can anyone?

Sure.

You: Who? I want names.

I can't give you names, but some people in your neighborhood have probably paid cash for a car. Even you could do so if you wanted to.

You: If it were a clunker, maybe.

Still, you prove my point: at a certain price, you can afford to pay cash for a car. If you purchased such an inexpensive car, you wouldn't have a monthly car payment.

You: But then I'd be driving a piece of $hit. I'm done with that.

I understand; my wife has had more than enough of our ten-year-old Saturn, a car which succeeded a Plymouth Neon, itself driven until it ceased working shortly after its seventh birthday.[1]

---

[1] We finally bought a minivan recently. Until then, we were the rare American family with more kids than cars—and I still drive the Saturn.

Regardless, you *choose* to create a new monthly bill when you buy something you can't afford in a lump sum. As a result, not only do you spend more on the item you purchase, but you also bear an additional cost.

You: What additional cost?

Financing.

You: You mean the interest I must pay?

Exactly. You pay interest to compensate the lender for advancing you the money. Such interest costs are typically significant.

Of the many financed expenses, some examples include:

➤ House
➤ Car
➤ College
➤ Flat screen television
➤ Washer/Dryer
➤ Kitchen appliances
➤ Bed

You: I've bought some of those items.

Most of us have. No problem there. Now, do you see Figure 5-1?

You: Yes, it's right there.

Where?

You: There, on the next page!

Cool.[2] Take some time to complete the table by entering monthly amounts for each non-discretionary expense listed. For any item you don't pay monthly, divide the annual amount by 12. For example, if your real estate taxes are due in two semi-annual installments of $1,800 each, your annual real estate taxes are $3,600. Since $3,600 divided by 12 is $300, list your monthly real estate taxes as $300.

---

[2] I hate when I can't find something in my own book.

Figure 5-1

Monthly Non-Discretionary Expenses

	Average Monthly Spending
Federal Income Tax	
State Income Tax	
Social Security Tax	
Medicare Tax	
Day Care/Nanny	
Housing (Rent or Mortgage)	
Real Estate Taxes	
Homeowner's or Renter's Insurance	
Condo Fees	
Home Repairs/Maintenance	
Home Telephone	
Cable	
Internet	
Water	
Heat	
Electric	
Lawn Care	
Groceries	
Alimony	
Child Support	
Health Insurance	
Disability Insurance	
Life Insurance	
Car Insurance	
Commuting Expenses (Parking, public transportation)	
Gasoline	
Auto Maintenance	
Tolls	
Other	

Compare the numbers listed in Figure 5-1 to the discretionary amounts you determine in Figure 4-2 on page 81. What do you notice?

You: The total of my non-discretionary spending is much larger than my discretionary spending. The list of non-discretionary expenses is also much longer.

Good. It should be, since you ought to be spending more on needs than wants. However, the finding has much broader implications. In order to significantly increase your savings rate, you must examine your larger and less flexible non-discretionary expenses.

You: That sounds difficult.

In some cases, it's impossible.

You: Wow! That's honest.

It's Total Candor®. Yet making such big changes can be *easier* than making small changes.

You: Why?

Two reasons. First, you can achieve a larger financial benefit from making one big decision properly than by making many small decisions perfectly. Second, you face—and must get right—far fewer big decisions than small ones.

By spending money at vending machines, on magazines, for drinks after work, or on runs to the drugstore, people spend far more money on "miscellaneous" than they care to believe. Miscellaneous is yet another reason many people find it hard to save.

You: I'm not going to spend any more on miscellaneous.

Completely unrealistic. You're always going to have random spending. But let's say by paying careful attention to the dozens of unplanned spending decisions, you're able to lower your spending by $180 this month.

You: I could use $180.

It's certainly real money. Now let's say instead of buying a car in April, you buy one in May.

You: So I would hold off replacing my current car for an extra month?

Exactly.

You: I can do that.

Since the car you have your eye on will probably cost well over $180 a month, you would save more by the single decision of delaying your car purchase 30 days than by carefully watching dozens of minor expenses for the same period.

You: What if I really can't wait another month to replace my car?

Why not?

You: I really want a new car and I already negotiated a good deal.

Not good enough.

You: And my current car won't pass inspection without thousands of dollars in repairs.

Much better. If you legitimately can't delay replacing your car, you still have several options to manage this important and large non-discretionary expense. Make sure to read the How to Buy a Car bonus chapter beginning on page 257.

Choosing where to live has similar implications. Once you agree to an apartment lease or home mortgage, you're going to be making monthly payments for a very long time. In the case of a home, expect several *years* of payments before you can reasonably anticipate selling your home without a major financial hit. See the bonus chapter titled When and How to Buy a House, which starts on page 275, for more information.

MAKE A DIFFERENCE TODAY

Periodically, you will have the opportunity to make truly important non-discretionary spending decisions, but these instances are both challenging and rare.

You: How rare?

Just a few times a decade.

You: That's it?

That's as often as you're likely to need a new car or to change residences. Before making such purchases, understand the long-term implications. When you buy a bag of chips and a can of soda from a vending machine, you're probably out about $2.50.[3] While you're clearly overpaying by buying

---

[3] $4.50 in the Bay Area.

on impulse, the total cost is still only $2.50. So your decision, financially speaking, is minor.

But if you err while committing to a new monthly non-discretionary expense like a new car, your decision repeats, monthly, for a long time. Consequently, such a mistake is a big and potentially very expensive one.

Worse, after you sign on the dotted line, little can be done about it.

You: Why not?

The time to lower spending on your needs was yesterday. Now, yesterday is gone.

Before today becomes yesterday, understand the implications of your purchase. You can make a huge difference in your financial life *before* you commit. Think about whether you'll be able to achieve your other financial objectives along with the new monthly commitment.

Most of all, remember: **just because someone will sell you something does *not* mean you can afford it**. Do not assume the car salesman has any meaningful insight to your financial situation.[4] Even if a simple review of your finances would indicate you can't afford the contemplated purchase, don't rely on the bank turning you down. Instead, *you* need to understand what the new monthly payment means to your ability to save and live comfortably *before* you agree to the purchase.

You: I wish I had read this two years ago.

Me too. But if you're already over your head with non-discretionary expenses, look to the future. Consider what you'll do differently the next time you must get a car or move residences. For now, forget the Beatles and go with Fleetwood Mac: "Yesterday's gone, yesterday's gone."

You: What song is that line from?

"Don't Stop" (thinking about tomorrow.)[5]

Better yet, start enjoying free stuff today.

---

[4] He probably doesn't even balance his own checkbook.
[5] How many books about money put songs in your head?

CASE STUDIES

SHOULD YOU REPAIR YOUR CAR OR BUY ANOTHER ONE?

Adapted from a post to the *Beyond Paycheck to Paycheck* blog, June 5, 2009

*H*i Michael,

I own (no car loan) my 2000 Volvo V70 wagon with 140,000 miles, but it needs major work to stay on the road—to the tune of $5,000. Should I pay for the repairs or replace the car? The private party value of the car, once repairs are made, would be $3,000 to $4,000—less than the cost of the repairs.

Here are a few more details about my situation:

➤ My general MO with cars is to buy a newer used car in good condition and drive it into the ground. I don't like to spend money on cars, but I do like reliable and comfortable transportation for my family.

➤ The mechanic who quoted me the repair estimate is fair and has been working on the car since the beginning. We trust him, as much as you can ever trust a mechanic.

➤ Also, the $5,000 estimated for repairs are just the crucial repairs. There are other repairs that aren't critical so we're ignoring those.

➤ My husband and I plan to buy our first house later this year and don't want to spend all of our cash. Even though I would normally tap my savings to buy a good used car outright, this year I am hesitant to do so because we will need the money for our house down payment.

➤ I'm considering financing a car and I'm wondering if I should consider other options, like a new car where there might be some bargains or great incentives.

What do you suggest?

Many thanks!

—Genevive, Maui, Hawaii

Straightforward Answer: Replace your car with either a slightly used or new one and finance it.

More Detailed Explanation:

Aloha. Let's address each of the three decisions you face.

Decision # 1: Replace or fix the car?

As you state, it will cost more to fix the car than it will be worth after the repair is completed. By definition, this means your car currently has a negative value. (This happened to my first car after only seven years and 90,000 miles. You've benefited from 9 years and 140,000 since manufacture so you've done okay.)

It's not a good idea to put money into a worthless asset. You describe your car as needing repairs well beyond routine and expected maintenance. Furthermore, additional identified repairs with corresponding costs are needed in the short-term.

Still, while your car has a negative value to you, it will have a positive value to someone else. Your car would have value as a trade-in, since a dealer would be motivated to sell you another car. (A poor economy will both help and hurt you. The dealer will be excited at the prospect of moving a car, but be less excited about taking your clunker—yet another reason to keep those two negotiations separate, as I discuss in the bonus chapter.)

Net: replace the car and get what you can for it. It's about to become a money pit.

Consideration # 2: Buy a new or slightly used car?

Until recently, this was a no-brainer—choosing a slightly used car was nearly always the savviest financial move. Buying a slightly used car enables you to avoid the painful, instant, and dramatic depreciation suffered by any new car buyer. While a used car may still be your best strategy, it is no longer obviously so. In a down economy, new car prices can fall dramatically. A brief illustration:

My wife and I finally purchased a second car.[6] We fully intended to purchase a slightly used mini-van (insert Dad joke here). But after several weeks researching used vehicles, pricing them, and doing a bit of negotiating with car dealers, the value proposition was notably stronger for a new mini-van.

During a down economy, some manufacturers sell certain model cars at **very** low prices. At the same time, many people keep their cars longer.[7] As a result, it's possible used cars in the specific make and model you're looking for will be limited. The reduced supply and additional demand for used cars during a down market can cause used prices to hold strong while new car prices plummet.

Do your research. Depending on your local market conditions, the car model you desire, and your flexibility in considering other car types, you may be better off buying a new car. Run the numbers, keeping in mind you should expect and plan to keep a new car two years longer than a two-year old used one.

Consideration # 3: Lease, Finance, or Purchase for Cash?

Except in very specific circumstances, I'm against car leasing.[8] Given your intention to drive your next vehicle for a long time and a history of doing so in the past, leasing is not for you. So your real choice is between financing and purchasing with cash. That you are even considering purchasing a car for cash puts you in the great minority. You are only able to contemplate such a step because you either have ample savings, a desire to spend a small amount on your car, or both.

---

[6] Until recently, we shared one sedan. However, with two growing kids and my new out-of-the home office, we ultimately conceded the need for more room and flexibility.

[7] I'm not talking about financially shrewd people who have historically kept their cars until they couldn't run anymore; I'm speaking of the masses who typically replace their cars every three years but now can't afford to do so.

[8] Basically you must be a "car person" and have the financial wherewithal to routinely discard a car after three years. See the bonus chapter.

A huge benefit from paying cash for a car is avoiding interest charges. Furthermore, you won't be in the monthly payment trap. Good outcomes to be sure. But again other factors are at work. Two primary issues influence my recommendation:

First, the economy. If you have the financial strength to be an attractive car buyer (i.e., good credit and a job), you will be eligible for significant financing opportunities not available to less credentialed buyers (or possibly even to you during normal economic times.). It is financially responsible to consider low-cost financing options. During the depths of the last financial crisis, several new cars were available at low or no-interest financing. While I'm not advocating you sign up for an 8 percent car loan interest rate, if you can score a 1.9 percent or 2.9 percent rate, I'd rather see you with the additional cash in your savings account for emergencies or with the ability to increase your retirement savings than buy a car for cash.

Your second consideration is your intended upcoming purchase of a home. If purchasing a car for cash would push you below the 20 percent down-payment required to avoid PMI[9], the cash purchase option should be eliminated. Since you don't seem like a "car person," you should commit to becoming the most attractive home buyer you can be. This means bringing a sizable down payment to closing and arriving in a relatively low cost automobile.

---

[9] PMI is private mortgage insurance. PMI is an insurance you pay for but which benefits the lender—not you—and is required if you borrow more than 80 percent of the value of the home. This is discussed in great detail in the home buying bonus chapter.

FISCALLY RESPONSIBLE, NOT CHEAP—LOCAL SPENDING

Adapted from a post to the *Beyond Paycheck to Paycheck* blog, December 12, 2007

Before I had children, I traveled to Ann Arbor, Michigan several times a year to attend University of Michigan football games (see page 191 for my rationale). Unfortunately, the quantity of my Michigan visits plummeted when I became a father.[10]

Nevertheless, my wife, very young daughter, and I did manage a visit to Michigan in 2006. And, yes, our visit was timed around a certain football game. But this story isn't about football.

You: What's it about?

The zoo.

You: The zoo?

The day after the football game, we caught up with some old friends at the Detroit Zoo.

You: You have friends who live at the zoo?

No, we met at the zoo.

*You: So **you** were living at the zoo when you met?*

No—no one was living at the zoo.

You: Then how did you meet at the zoo?

We didn't meet at the zoo. We met in college.

You: But you said you met at the zoo.

We agreed to meet at the zoo, but the zoo is not where we met—originally.

You: Why didn't you just say so?

I have no idea. My head hurts.

---

[10] I realize some may interpret my use of "unfortunately" in the sentence above as written proof of my immaturity. I disagree. I see it as an explicit recognition of life's tradeoffs. You can still make the "right" decisions yet be somewhat disappointed by what you feel compelled to give up. In conclusion, GO BLUE!

Anyway, we walked with our friends around the zoo with our respective young children in tow. Together, we enjoyed the weather, animals, and conversation. It was a wonderful afternoon. Suddenly, my friend commented, "Michael, you can always tell who the non-members of the zoo are."

"How so?" I asked, quite curiously.

"By their stress level," he replied. "They're trying to see every exhibit before the zoo closes or their kids melt down. Non-members fly all the way from the zebras to the koala bears. They may slow down to see the giraffes along the way, but don't think they have the time to actually stop. Non-members are trying to get their money's worth as quickly as possible."

He's right—I had been there.

You: Because you once lived at the zoo?

No!

You: Just kidding.

While joining a museum or zoo far from home will seldom make financial sense, joining local organizations can have enormous benefits—monetary and otherwise.

An example is my local children's museum. Admission is $6.00 per person. Like most children's museums, they also charge for kids. As such, when my wife and I took our oldest daughter, our total cost was $18. The first time we visited, we probably looked like the crazy zoo people my friend had described. Despite our toddler's satisfaction from playing with shapes in the first room, we quickly moved her from one exhibit to another.[11]

---

[11] Makes you wonder if a child's attention span is really short because her brain isn't fully developed or if other factors are at play.

Furthermore, at $18, it was pricey for only 45 minutes of entertainment before naptime. Consequently, we didn't return to our children's museum for a while after our initial visit. Several months later, my wife informed me she had purchased a family membership at the children's museum.

You: So the person wearing the pants in your family is—

None of your business.[12] Since members can visit the museum at no additional charge, our $60 annual family membership means:

- We **stress less** during our visits. It doesn't matter what our daughter does at the museum or if she's totally disinterested in an exhibit where we had to plead with her to share last time. Sometimes we arrive only an hour before the museum closes. Since we're not trying to get our money's worth out of every visit, each trip is a pleasure.

- We **visit much more frequently.** Instead of being concerned about the admission cost, membership means we go whenever we feel like it. We discovered the museum is a perfect rainy or cold day activity. Plus, it's a great excuse to get out of the house and burn some toddler energy.

- We **increase our tax deductions** and lower the tax we owe, since a children's museum membership is tax deductible. So our true cost to join is less than the $60 we pay.

- We **support an important organization in our community.** Members are the lifeblood of most non-profits.

---

[12] Or the subject of a future book. Stay tuned.

For these reasons, we're members of several similar local organizations. While memberships first appear to be expenses, they actually save us money and allow us to do more. That's a fiscally responsible behavior. On the other hand, deciding never to do things solely because of the cost can make you feel cheap, if not downright unhappy.

I'm convinced my friend at the zoo had it right.

You: But you said you didn't have a friend living at the zoo!

He doesn't live there!

CHAPTER 6

Saving Strategy # 4:
Enjoy Free Stuff

"Sometimes one pays most for the things one gets for nothing."
—ALBERT EINSTEIN

Imagine you're 11 years old. It's Tuesday evening. Because it's summertime, there's no school tomorrow. Immediately upon finishing dinner, you leave the table to play outside. After all, it's still light out and you can hear the other neighborhood children playing nearby.

Sometime later, in the distance, you hear your mother shout your name. So insert your name here:

Your Mother: "<YOUR NAME>!"

You: What?

Your Mother: Come in!

You: Why?

Your Mother: It's 9 o'clock!

You: But Mom!

Your Mother: Come in.

You: Five. More. Minutes. P-LEASE!

I hope you have memories like those. Growing up in New York State, I fondly remember summer nights when the sun didn't set until 9 PM. Recalling how much fun I had playing outside after dinner, I still smile.

You: I remember evenings like those too.

Good. On an evening such as the one just described, how much money did you spend?

You: What?

How much money did you spend playing outside?

You: None.

Exactly. You had no money. You were 11 years old. Only as an adult did you "learn" to equate entertainment with spending money.

You: Why?

Your first real job starts on Monday. Four days later is your first happy hour. Not too far into the evening, you buy your first round.

You: That was a fun night.

Of course it was. So were many of the nights out since then. However, the point of the "Enjoy Free Stuff" strategy is not to eliminate your spending. Instead, the goal is to identify opportunities to reduce certain costs while maintaining or increasing your overall enjoyment of life.

That said, most people need far more than happy hours to be content in their lives.

You: True enough. Even those get old after a while.

Really?

You: Jon . . . from accounting . . . again with the robot impression?

That would get old—it makes sense you would spend on other things. Still, you often purchase restaurant meals, clothes, and entertainment because of a *perceived* need—and a *perceived* corresponding ability—to afford such experiences. Undoubtedly, you can make better spending decisions.

You: How can I learn to make better spending decisions?

Ask a teenager. They probably understand Strategy 4 better than you do.

You: My son/daughter/niece/nephew/brother/sister? Are you crazy?

Yes.

You: You are crazy?

No! I meant to answer, "Yes" to whether a teen typically understands this concept better than an adult.

You: Impossible.

Not so. Ask a typical teenager how her day was.

You: Talk about a can of worms!

Indeed, and her answer is unrelated to the amount of money she spends. A typical teen's life contains plenty of drama but spending money is likely to be a relatively unimportant component. Most teenagers never have enough money for it to meaningfully impact their mood.

You: So what does this mean to me? I'm not 14 and I have no desire to be or act like I'm 14.

You need to enjoy free stuff. Specifically, you need to enjoy *your* free stuff.

You: My free stuff?

Yes.

You: Where is my free stuff?

You have to find it.

You: I don't know where it is. Do you?

No.

You: How is this conversation helpful?

I can help you find your free stuff.

You: Okay, good. Where is my free stuff? For that matter, what is my free stuff?

WHAT IS FREE STUFF?

Enjoyment despite spending little or no money requires some seriously good free stuff.[1] Imagine an hour or an entire day without spending any money.

You: A whole day?

I spend no money several days every month.

You: You must be miserable or cheap. Maybe both?

I beg to differ.

You: I have a hard time buying you can have a good day yet spend absolutely no money.

Funny word choice.

You: Huh?

You said you had a hard time "buying" the concept.

---

[1]   Can you believe that got past the proofreader?

You: You know what I mean.

Yes, I do. Your disbelief is common. Many people initially suspect good free stuff does not exist and, therefore, assume all free stuff must suck.

But free stuff does exist and most of it doesn't suck.

You: I'm still not seeing my free stuff.

Your free stuff is specific to you. For some people, reading a book or a newspaper is good free stuff.

You: Books and newspapers cost money.

Both are free at the library and a newspaper can often be purchased for a dollar or less.[2] Books you already own but haven't yet read are also free—to you.

In addition, your neighborhood has numerous free activities. If you live in a rural community, outdoor pursuits are likely endless and without cost. If you live in an urban area, free or inexpensive museums abound, not to mention ample people-watching opportunities. If you live near the beach, you have an obvious free stuff opportunity.

You: What's that?

Going to the beach!

You: If I live in New Jersey, the beach isn't free.

New Jersey is a strange state. Unless you live in New Jersey, the beach is free. Even if you live in New Jersey, exercising is free.

You: Gyms aren't free.

But running outside is free. Running at a beach is free. Best I can tell, even running at a New Jersey beach is free.[3]

You: I don't like to read or exercise. I don't live near the beach and I'm not an outdoorsy person.

I've met some people like you.

You: What's that supposed to mean?

Nothing. Still, enjoying free stuff goes well beyond "use the library" and "enjoy the outdoors."

You: I'm waiting.

---

[2] Don't nitpick over my "free" which actually costs 75 cents, if your credit card debt is in the thousands.
[3] You need only be faster than one other jogger.

WHAT IS YOUR FREE STUFF?

If you're struggling to identify your free stuff, think young.

You: Excuse me?

When you were young, most days you spent no money.

You: Why not?

You had no money.

You: Right.

Yet you were happy and busy—even after school. Your parents had a word for your activities: hobbies.

HOBBIES

You: How do you know I had hobbies?

Most parents teach their children the importance of hobbies so their kids have something to do. In most families, the amount of money available for children's activities is limited, so low-cost hobbies are formed out of necessity. Still, those childhood pastimes are, quite legitimately, a lot of fun.

You: So I should get into some hobbies?

Yes. Maybe it's time for you to begin cooking again (you have to eat anyway), paint, draw, or scrapbook.

You: Those aren't free.

They might not be totally free, but they're probably a fair amount less expensive than your current entertainment choices. Furthermore, hobbies provide mental health benefits.

You: What mental health benefits?

You're going to enjoy yourself. You might not have been involved with your hobbies in a very long time. Consequently, reengaging might feel like a trip down memory lane. Or, if it's a new activity you've longed to try but haven't found the time to begin, you'll enjoy the genuine thrill of a first time experience. So, not only do you reduce your spending by enjoying free stuff, you also receive bona fide mental health benefits.

FAMILY TIME

Even though my two daughters are still quite young, I have already learned kids are expensive. Even if you buy private label diapers at a warehouse club, you're still going to spend a lot of money on diapers. Formula can be a significant expense even if plenty of breast-feeding is involved.

You: You know about breast-feeding?

I was in the room.

You: It's not the same.

I once worked at Babies "R" Us.

You: You're losing credibility.

This tangent could become uncomfortable.

When you consider diapers, formula, clothing, meals, sports equipment, snacks, school supplies, toys, more snacks, music class, still more snacks and so much more, children are expensive—very expensive. Even the size of your house and cars—and corresponding house and car payments—is influenced by the size of your family.

If you watch every expense carefully, you will still spend a great deal on your children. Even if you periodically or frequently deprive your children, you will still spend significantly on your kids. It's just what comes with deciding to have a family.

Yet, despite children's financial burden, they provide parents with the ultimate free stuff.

You: What free stuff is that?

Themselves.

You: What?

Children don't care about money. Seriously. Of course, you must spend *some* money to keep Children's Services away, but children don't want your money. Yet, if you treat them right, they can give you unlimited happiness—sap intended. Read the sidebars at the end of this chapter for examples of how my children save me money.

Whether it's visiting the playground, hearing my children explain something for the first time, cooking together, singing together, dancing together, building a snowman together, every one of my most precious memories of my two little girls has two common themes. Each experience has been both *priceless* and *costless*.

SPEND TIME, NOT MONEY

When it comes to Saving Strategy 4 and your family, the theme is simple: **Spend time, not money.** You don't need to spend money with your family to have a good time with your family. To a pre-teen, money is irrelevant. Unless you make a specific effort to teach your child about money, he can go a long time without understanding the implications of money. At any age, your child wants you—not your money.

Furthermore, fulfillment as a parent comes not from spending money on your children but from spending time with them. That spending time is *also* a saving strategy is just gravy.

TALK WITH YOUR SPOUSE OR PARTNER—AND SAVE!

Another way to incorporate free stuff into your life is to talk with your spouse/boyfriend/important pet/girlfriend/partner more often.

You: What are you talking about?

When you began your most recent or current relationship, two-way communication (i.e., chemistry) was absolutely critical. Excitedly, you told others how the new person in your life completely "got" you, how you "totally connected," or "simply clicked."

You: I do remember that feeling.

As relationships lengthen from months to years and from years to decades, feelings and priorities change. Add this to your increasing work and possibly child-raising responsibilities; it's understandable why it seems the only way to truly reconnect with your partner is an expensive dinner out.

You: Sounds nice.

It is *nice*, but is probably not *necessary*. Instead of fine dining, try talking as a way to connect.

You: Now?

Now works. So does anytime soon. Instead of running off to do the next errand, working out, or staying late at the office, start a conversation with your beloved. Connect and reconnect. Your results will be priceless and costless.

If your beloved suspects something is going on but can't identify it, tell the truth. Tell him or her, "I'm trying to save money."

When your partner hears your explanation, trust me, you're about to have a very interesting, very entertaining conversation. Is there any better free stuff than that?

You: —

Don't answer that.

You can even have your conversation over a cup of coffee.

You: But I have to make the coffee at home, right?

Nope.

You: Can we go to the coffee shop to have this conversation?

Absolutely.

*You: How is **that** possible?*

Major on the major, minor on the minor. Coffee is minor.

CASE STUDIES

HOW A SWING SET KEEPS YOU BALANCED

Adapted from a post to the *Beyond Paycheck to Paycheck* blog, June 8, 2007

When our nanny occasionally leaves before my wife gets home, I take a break from writing to watch my daughter. When this happens, I play with my two-year old for 10 or 20 minutes until my wife returns.

Not yesterday.

The weather was nice and my wife needed to prepare for a book club she was hosting. (No, they're not reading *Beyond Paycheck to Paycheck*, but it isn't for my lack of trying.) With the extra time, I honored my daughter's request to go to the playground, a short walk away. All was blissful as she ran from one thing to another— the climb-on toys, the slides, and a little counter we pretend is a lemonade stand—before she raced to the swings.

"On Daddy. On Daddy," she said as I placed her on my lap and began to swing back and forth, just as we had done many times before. Yet this instance would prove to be dramatically different— she began to sing "Row, row, row your boat."[4]

Her melody grew louder and I soon joined her. In response, she raised her voice and I, sensing no one nearby, raised mine. Soon we were both shouting, "Merrily, merrily, merrily, merrily, yife is buttadeem!" repeatedly—loud enough for people in Maine to hear us.

You should have seen her face! Her smile went from ear to ear. (I bet mine was nearly as big.) The song made my whole week.

What does this have to do with money? Plenty! Yesterday's memorable moment cost nothing. Zero dollars, zero cents. Heck, by walking, we didn't even use gas. The playground was a good reminder of just how cheap some of life's biggest thrills are.

Furthermore, our visit highlighted a key benefit of the small hole in our child care: an opportunity to keep in balance. I'll eagerly take advantage the next time such an opportunity presents itself. Will you?

---

[4] The words aren't clear from a two year-old but, since the tune is unforgettable, you ultimately figure out what she is singing.

SCORING BIG LABOR DAY DEALS—WITHOUT SHOPPING

Adapted from a post to the *Beyond Paycheck to Paycheck* blog, September 11, 2009

I had one heck of a Labor Day holiday weekend.

You: What did you do?

Since the weekend represents the unofficial end of summer—

You: Why is that?

First, school starts immediately afterward. Second, it's already getting cool here in New Hampshire.

You: Seriously?

Seriously. On a bike ride early yesterday morning I thought, "I'd be more comfortable with gloves on."

Still, the weather was gorgeous over the weekend and we were thrilled to stay around town.

Friday Night

Last Friday night I took my daughter for a walk after dinner and wound up across the street in the neighbor's yard for a nice chat. After my wife got the girls to bed while I mowed the lawn, we just chilled in the house—connecting.

Total Friday Night Spending: $0

Saturday

My wife got up wicked early Saturday morning.

You: Wicked?

Wicked is a New Englander's way of saying "very." Anyway, she got up with the sun to go running. I fed the kids until she got back.[5] Then, I left to play "basketball" from 7:30 until about 9.

---

[5] It's not that my wife went on a short run; it's that my kids can eat for an hour or more straight.

You: Why is basketball in quotes?

Basketball is a game played by basketball players. "Basketball" is the game I play. After hoops, I met my wife and girls at the playground near the farmer's market they visited while I played basketball.

You: You mean "basketball."

Point taken. Anyway, the playground was beaming with activity and we ran into several of our friends.

We returned home for lunch. Soon after, my brother arrived from Connecticut. When my youngest daughter woke up from her nap, we went to the beach. There's almost nothing better than watching little kids play at the beach. Bonus: with my brother there, I was able to abdicate child-care responsibilities for about 10 minutes and go for a swim in the ocean.

You: Why only ten minutes?

It's New Hampshire; the water's cold!

You: Oh, right. The ocean's wicked cold there.

Excellent use of "wicked!"

On the way home from the beach, we picked up some pizza from a local place we really like. After wolfing down the pizza and getting the girls to bed, we all caught up. A good time by all.

Recap of Saturday and Saturday night activities: Run (wife), basketball (me), playground, visit from family, beach, pizza dinner.

Total Saturday/Saturday Night Spending: $28 (pizza)

Sunday

After breakfast on Sunday, we walked downtown. Well, my brother, my wife, and I walked. The baby was in her stroller and the 4-year old was on her bicycle. On the way, my brother noticed the tires on the bicycle seemed flat. A quick squeeze proved it—almost no air in either tire. So we rerouted to a gas station to get air (my pump broke a while ago). I was slightly outraged to learn both nearby gas stations charged $0.75 for air.

You: There was a charge for air?

Yes.

You: And you paid for it?

Yes.

You: How can you possibly give saving advice if you're paying for air?

Um.

You: Stuck?

Kind of. I know it sounds ridiculous, but what was I supposed to do?

You: You couldn't blow air into these tires, I suppose?

No.

You: Okay, you're off the hook for now, but if this becomes a habit, we're going to have to talk.

Fair enough. Anyway, after our "air purchase" we went to a park down by the river—

You: Isn't that something Chris Farley said?

Yes.

You: Cool.

Anyway, we hung out, did some people-watching, and walked back home for lunch.

While the baby napped, we sat in the backyard, enjoying the fresh air and pleasant company. After my brother left and the baby awoke, we went back downtown to a restaurant where we could eat outside by the water.

You: Sounds nice.

It is. I love eating outside. Our short summer means limited opportunities to take advantage. We had a great meal. Then we went home, got the kids off to bed and relaxed—just my wife and me.

Recap of Sunday and Sunday Night Activities: Walk downtown, enjoy riverside park, hang out with family, enjoy outside air (not to mention the swings), delicious dinner by the water

Total Sunday/Sunday Night Spending: $7

You: How does all of that cost only $7? You went out to dinner!

Besides dinner (and air), nothing else cost money. As to dinner, I had some frequent dining points.

You: What the heck are those?

Many of the independent restaurants in my town joined forces a few years ago and created a loyalty program. I've accumulated sufficient points and decided to cash some in. (By the way, the $7 was a rather generous tip, demonstrating the restaurant wasn't too expensive anyway.)

Monday

Monday was more of the same. We went on a hike we'd never done before with the girls. Then we came home for lunch and the baby's nap. Late afternoon was spent teaching my four year old how to shoot hoops (on a 5' basket) and how to hit a ball with a bat. She's not bad at either! My wife made a great dinner and we talked about how much fun the weekend was.

Recap of Monday and Monday Night Activities: Hike, teach my daughter two new sports, hang out with my wife, delicious home-cooked meal

Total cost for Monday: $0.

Weekend Summary

It was never our objective to spend so little money this weekend. When people wonder how others can have a good time without spending a lot of money, I wonder how they came to believe doing so is difficult.

Can you copy any of these ideas? Add your own?

MONEY DOESN'T FALL FROM TREES, BUT LEAVES DO

Adapted from a post to the *Beyond Paycheck to Paycheck* blog, November 7, 2007

We had stunningly beautiful autumn weather in New Hampshire yesterday. To take advantage, my wife, daughter, and I took a long walk together.

For years before we started a family, my wife and I took countless walks together. Admittedly simple, walking has always been something we really enjoyed. With the increased time pressure a child brings, our walks are much more sacred. Far fewer occur and, when they do, there are three of us—never two. But, as a proud father, I'd never trade my new life for the one I had before.

As we walked across town, we ran into friends similarly out for a morning stroll with their children. We formed a "stroller parade" for a few blocks before we each went our ways. (We had already promised our daughter a visit to the playground and, while adults experience plenty of spontaneity with a young child, it's the child's whims—not the grown up's—which are followed. A mid-course change in plans was not advisable.)

Which was just as well. We completed our walk to the playground. Up and down on the see-saw we went. I was on one side, my daughter on the other, with my wife "spotting" her. A true blast. The little one loved the thrill of the slides as well. But the morning took on an entirely new meaning when we discovered an enormous pile of leaves up the hill from the park.

Anyone growing up in an area where the leaves fall annually has memories of lying down and jumping in the piles. Born and raised in New York State, I was fortunate; every year I had such an experience. But my wife is from New Mexico; if she had jumped into a pile of cactus needles, she might *still* be uncomfortable.

Alas, in New Hampshire there are few cacti, so the three of us played vigorously, tackling one another and throwing leaves all around. It was suddenly easy to recall how autumn felt as a child.

Yet it was a totally different experience as a parent. "Truly special," my wife and I agreed as we walked home. And my daughter has talked about "pouncing in the yeaves" every day since.

Was it a great morning? Sure, but it was much more. If nothing else good happens until December, I've already had a great month. Last Sunday's experience at the park is something which will be with me forever: my daughter's first time playing in the leaves. We made a memory together.

Any guesses how much money I spent Sunday? Can you create merely one day like that later this month?

TAKING ADVANTAGE OF THE RULES TO SAVE A FEW BUCKS: AIRLINE EDITION

Adapted from a post to the *Beyond Paycheck to Paycheck* blog, September 10, 2009

My youngest daughter sure earned her wings this summer.
You: What do you mean?
In the last month, she's flown to Florida and Arizona.
You: How old is she?
One and a half.
You: Isn't it crazy expensive to fly your daughter around the country?
Flying alone with a baby 18 months old is crazy. Is it expensive? Not at all. Actually, it's free.
You: Does your wife work for an airline?
Nope.
You: Is your little girl cashing in your frequent flyer miles?
No.
You: So what gives?
Airlines allow lap children to fly for free.
You: What's a lap child?
Like it sounds, a lap child is a child that flies on the lap of an adult.

You: Rather obvious now.

No worries. As long as the child is less than two years old, air-lines—at least the major ones—don't require a separate ticket for your child.

You: Sounds like a deal.

It's a huge deal. But it's not for everyone.

You: You said that already. The child has to be less than two years old.

Yes, but furthermore, the parent(s) have to be willing to keep their child on their lap for the duration of the flight—not to mention taxi, take-off, landing, and waiting for a gate to become available because someone in a Omaha control tower had to use the restroom.

For us, taking advantage of the lap child policy is a no-brainer. But I know some parents who won't do the lap child thing and instead choose to pay for an extra ticket. To each their own.

Visiting My Family

When I realized I had a frequent flyer ticket about to expire last month, I used the ticket to visit my folks in Florida. For no extra charge, I brought the baby and, just like that, the 1½ year old thrilled her grandparents and great-grandparents with a rousing rendition of "Bwok-ee!"

You: What's "Bwok-ee?"

Broccoli.

You: Cute.

Yes, but if you're one of the grandparents or great-grandparents related to the baby making the aforementioned sound, "Bwok-ee" isn't just cute, it's better than *Phantom of the Opera*.

Visiting My Wife's Family

When Southwest Airlines posted a $99 maximum fare sale to travel anywhere in the U.S. several weeks ago, we purchased a ticket for my wife to visit her relatives in Arizona—a trip she had contemplated for a while. Guess who's riding on her lap all the way to Phoenix and back? You bet—my squishy 1½ year old.

Visiting Nobody's Family

We like to get away once each winter.

You: Away?

Away from the very cold temperatures characteristic of a northern New England winter. We usually try to get away around winter's halfway point (February). But not this year.

You: Why not?

Our youngest child turns two in mid-January. By moving our trip up several weeks, we need only three tickets rather than four. That's a 25 percent savings on air travel.

Just by understanding the rules—and using them to our advantage—we're saving big money on air travel this year. Furthermore, our youngest is visiting (and being hugged and kissed by) relatives throughout the country. Meanwhile, our oldest daughter, now four and a quarter years—

You: And a quarter?

Yes, and if you forget that part she *will remind you.* Anyway, my oldest had a wonderful weekend with her mother when I went to Florida with the baby. This weekend, father and older daughter will have some incredible bonding experiences around New Hampshire. What's not to like?

How can you take advantage of the rules to save money and enjoy yourself? Saving is not merely about spending less; it's just as important to get the most from the money you do spend.

With children, your memories are priceless—just like the MasterCard commercial. Unlike MasterCard, the best memories are also costless.

CHAPTER 7

· · · · · · · · · · · · · ·

Saving Strategy # 5:
Major on the Major, Minor on the Minor

"Worry often gives a small thing a big shadow."
—SWEDISH PROVERB

As a highly motivated fifth grade student, my wife[1] Laura periodically stressed over her spelling tests. Fortunately, Laura's mother calmed her by reminding Laura to keep things in perspective, saying, "It's just a spelling test, Laura. Major on the major, minor on the minor."

You: I haven't heard that expression before.

I never heard anyone else say it either, but it's the perfect mantra for this saving strategy.[2]

You: What does it mean?

Major on the major, minor on the minor means don't sweat the small stuff. If you have to stress over something, make sure it's about something important.

---

[1] We were not married at the time. She was in the fifth grade. I was in the seventh. She was in New Mexico. I was in New York. Yes, I plan, but not *that* much.

[2] Furthermore, it's a nice way to honor her memory.

IT'S JUST COFFEE

Warning: I am about to contradict numerous financial experts.

You: Why?

When it comes to helping people save, the popular financial advice boils down to just one tip. Yet the more I read other financial experts' books, newspapers, magazines, and web sites, the less I am convinced of their conclusion. Ultimately, they want you to believe the world's financial problems would be solved immediately if only we could eliminate one thing: coffee shops.

You: Oh yes—I've heard that plea before.

Indeed, the "solution" is everywhere. But the claim is nonsense.

You: You think so?

YOUR PROBLEM ISN'T STARBUCKS™

You: You've got my attention.

If you visit Starbucks five times a day or spend $100 or more weekly at any coffee shop, you *do* have problems. But your money issue is the least of my worries.[3] Of course, most people don't visit or spend at Starbucks to such an extent. What many financial talking heads miss is nobody—including the most coffee-addicted person you know—can find ten grand a year by pinching pennies at Starbucks. **You will not fundamentally change your financial life negotiating with or avoiding a barista.**

You: I like you.

Thanks. Just remember: coffee is a minor expense and you should minor on the minor.

You: Meaning?

Put only minor emphasis on minor expenses. How about another example?

You: Okay.

IT'S JUST SALT

You're walking down the aisle at your—

---

[3] You have an addiction, my friend.

You: Really? This is exciting. My wedding!

No. You're walking down the aisle at your neighborhood supermarket.

You: Well there's a buzz kill.

No doubt. Instead of your friends and family on either side, you have soups on your left and pastas on your right.

You: Oh.

You're shopping from your grocery list, reducing impulse purchases.

You: What's an impulse purchase?

An impulse purchase is something you buy without any forethought. For example, you were just walking around, doing your thing and—boom!—the *Speed 2* DVD is in your cart. When you shop from a list, you are far less likely to buy things you don't need.

You: Got it. So I'm in the supermarket—

Yes, and you're pushing your cart. As you get to the end of the aisle, you see salt on the shelf. Upon seeing the salt, you suddenly recall running out of salt last week. You think to yourself, "I should get some salt."

You: Impulse purchase, don't do it!

False.

You: False?

False.

You: Why?

Think about the risk.

You: What risk?

Think about what's at stake.

You: The purchase of salt.

Yes—and it's salt you need. You simply forgot to put it on your list.

You: Fair enough.

Good. Now, if instead of simply buying the salt, you pick it up, note it costs 59 cents, and think, "I wonder if this ever goes on sale" or "Might this be cheaper at Wal-Mart™?"

You: Sounds very responsible.

It sounds crazy.

You: Crazy?

Crazy!

You: But what if I could spend less on the salt?

STOP THE MADNESS!!

You: Strong words!

We're talking about salt. Your total purchase—and the total amount at risk—is less than a dollar. If you're a heavy salt user, you make a salt purchase every few years. Over the course of your entire life, you will spend less than six dollars on salt.

You: I never bothered to calculate my lifetime salt expense.

Nor should you. Salt is a minor expense. You should absolutely never think twice about buying salt.[4] Salt doesn't matter.

You: What about—

Even if you have a five cents off salt coupon at home, do not stress over the wrong thing. Step back from the shelf and purchase the salt. Move on with your life. Don't think about the salt purchase again.

You: Major on the major, minor on the minor.

Exactly.

WHAT IS A MAJOR EXPENSE?

You: So what is an example of a major expense?

A house is a major expense.

You: I assumed anything in the six figures was major. I understand coffee and salt aren't major. But there's a big difference between a $5 latte and a $250,000 (or more) house.

True.

You: What about the stuff in between?

Well, a major expense is a different dollar amount for everyone.

You: Why?

The calculation of a major expense depends on your income, age, and net worth.

You: So now what?

I'll give you a definition you can use.

You: A definition I can use?

---

[4] From a financial perspective. Your primary care physician might have a different opinion. In the meantime, put down the chips.

Yes, so you can determine when a potential purchase is a major expense for you.

You: I'm ready.

Regardless of your income, age, net worth, or anything else, **a major expense is anything you can't afford to pay for in its entirety when you buy it**.

In other words, a major expense means you're signing up for monthly payments and finance charges.

You: Finance charges?

When you finance a purchase, you will pay back not only the amount of the purchase but also interest—every month.

You: Like with a car?

Yes. You also pay finance charges anytime you use a credit card for a purchase and don't pay the entire outstanding balance when you receive the bill.

In addition to a car, another obviously major financial decision is choosing a place to live.

You: Like when I buy a house.

Yes, but also if you sign an apartment lease.

You: Why? A lease isn't nearly as expensive as buying a home.

True, but when you sign an apartment lease, you agree to make a series of monthly payments.

Major expenses are major because they:

➤ affect the amount you spend this month and many future months

➤ determine if and how much you are able to save during every future month during which you will need to make a payment

➤ require the use of thousands, tens of thousands, or hundreds of thousands of your precious dollars over the months and years you commit to make those payments

You: I've got it. Major expenses are a big deal.

Absolutely. Not only because of the large amount of money at stake, but also because major expenses become non-discretionary for a long period of time.

You: Right. What else?

Consider two additional points when evaluating major expenses. First, just because a purchase is a *major* expense doesn't make it a *bad* expense. Most non-urban folks need a car to commute to work, so a car is not a bad expense. Obviously, everyone needs a place to live. So neither cars nor housing are bad expenses. But they're clearly major decisions.

Second, while the definition of a major expense won't change over time, the dollar value will. In other words, what constitutes a major expense changes over the course of your life.

Major expenses are quite different than a cappuccino, huh?

You: Even with salt.

You put salt in your coffee?

You: No.

Phew. To successfully major on the major, step back, think about, and carefully evaluate the implications of the purchase decision *before* you actually sign anything.[5] Be sure you can *and want* to live within the new monthly cash-flow constraints your major purchase will require.

HOW TO MAJOR IN MAJORING

We discuss lowering your needs yesterday in Chapter 5. When you make a major purchase commitment, you pledge to make a series of monthly payments. If the monthly payment amount proves too high, this obligation alone can create financial havoc on your life.

You: How so?

First, the overwhelming monthly payment restricts your ability to spend money on other things you might now prefer. Second, the monthly burden dramatically reduces the amount you can save. In extreme but not unusual circumstances, such an obligation makes it *impossible* to save. In such a case, you struggle to make ends meet despite carefully limiting your daily spending.

You: How do I avoid such a fate?

For one thing, don't be house poor.

---

[5] If you don't have to sign anything, it's probably not a major expense. Unfortunately, if you've ever tried to purchase a car part at an auto dealership, you've learned the opposite isn't true.

You: What does that mean?

House poor means owning a home but being unable to afford anything else.

You: Like those people in the big house who live without any furniture?

Probably.

You: Or curtains?

Do you live in southern California?

You: No.

Then, yes, those without curtains probably can't afford curtains—they're house poor.

Because of the large amounts involved, getting major purchases right is critical. Yet such big decisions are also hard to get right because you face them infrequently. As a result, learning from experience is difficult.

On the other hand, you need to get such decisions correct *only a few times in your entire life* to live comfortably. Review the bonus chapters about car and home buying at the end of the book for a detailed discussion of life's most important major purchase decisions.

MORE MAJOR EXPENSES

Major expenses include more than cars and homes. What other spending decisions do you think are major?

You: I'm not really sure.

Some televisions are major expenses.

You: TVs are major expenses?

Maybe.

You: How do I know if the TV I'm considering is a major expense?

Would you finance the new TV?

You: I'm not sure yet.

If the only way for you to buy the TV is to sign up for a series of monthly payments, then for you that TV is a major expense.

You: But my buddy just got one and I think he makes about what I make.

Perhaps your buddy makes more than you do. Maybe his spouse makes more than your spouse. Maybe he doesn't have the same expenses in his life as you do (e.g., kids or parents to support, tuition, real estate taxes, student loans, DQ™ and White Castle™ runs, etc.). Of course, your friend could also be deep in debt.

You: I suppose I don't know how he was able to afford the TV.

Or *if* he could afford it.

You: Fair point.

The only thing you know is he *has* the TV, not how financially easy—or difficult—it was for him to buy it. Let's give him the benefit of the doubt.

You: He's a nice guy.

That has nothing to do with it.

You: Still.

Let's say he can afford the TV and you, absent financing, can't afford it.

You: That sounds right, but it doesn't feel right.

Life's not fair.

You: Excuse me?

In this case, life isn't fair means two people with identical incomes contemplating the same purchase can face different definitions of affordability.

You: So let me get this straight. If I can't afford the TV without financing it, you're telling me not to buy it and using "Life isn't fair" as a justification?

Not necessarily.

You: Then what are you telling me?

Anything you must finance is a major expense. But major expenses aren't automatically bad expenses to avoid. Periodically, you can and should make major purchases. However, those decisions require careful consideration.

You: So, the TV?

Classifying the new TV as a major expense no more means you shouldn't get it than your alter ego's financial recklessness means he should. Instead, first consider the implications of the potential purchase. You might determine once you get the TV you will have absolutely no money to spend on any other entertainment for the next six months.

Armed with that information, you *could* decide to wait until next year to buy the new TV.[6] In the meantime, you could save some money for the TV, possibly reducing the need to finance it. So delaying the purchase is a possibility.

You: One which leaves me without the TV I want.

Yes. Another possibility is to say, "I don't care. I'm comfortable without any spending money for six months. I really want this TV. With this TV in my home, my friends will visit all the time; I won't need any spending money."

You: Is choosing that path irresponsible?

No, not if it's the truth. If you believe and can withstand the sacrifice a major purchase requires, it's irresponsible for you NOT to buy something you truly desire. But if you're lying, the only person who will be burned is you.

You: Example?

Sitting on the couch, looking at your new 95" TV, unable to pay for basic cable: not priceless.

TAKE MAJOR EXPENSES SERIOUSLY AND YOU'LL HAVE LESS OF THEM

If you take a deliberate approach to major expenses, your major expense threshold will increase.

You: What?

While the definition of a major expense does not change, its dollar value adjusts. Furthermore, if you are careful about your next car or housing decision, your required monthly payments will be lower.

You: Your theory being I can do better than the last time.

Exactly. In addition, being thoughtful about major expenses—majoring on the major—helps you twice.

You: Twice?

Since you spend less every month, you save more—the first reason and primary focus of the chapter so far. But another important benefit of majoring on the major is your future purchase decisions are less likely to be major.

---

[6] When the cost will probably have plummeted.

You: What do you mean?

When you keep your monthly payments affordable, you are able to save more.

You: Because I have the same income but a lower monthly bill.

Precisely. As a result of increased savings, you're less likely to need financing for future purchases—you have money in the bank! When a big expense does not require monthly payments, it's not a major expense for you. As you know, the same purchase could still be a major expense for a peer earning the same salary you do.

You: Life isn't fair, buddy.

A phrase easier to say than to hear, no?

You: Did I sound too eager?

Not at all, my friend. Anyone can do what you're about to do. Anyone can choose to strategically and intentionally lower their non-discretionary expenses to free up future cash-flow. When you do, you save more.

You: Awesome.

This approach also gives you flexibility.

You: Flexibility?

Saving gives you options. Just ask Sandra.

You: Who?

Sandra, from page 10.

You: Oh yes.

COFFEE, SALT, PIZZA: IT'S ALL THE SAME

Major on the major, minor on the minor. Focus on things that matter. If you prefer the pizza from House of Pizza over the pizza Lots of Pizza makes, but House of Pizza charges an extra two bucks a pie, get the pizza you like! You won't be able to retire earlier by eating lousy pizza your whole life. Those people who retire comfortably don't get there by eating cardboard pizza or, for that matter, skipping lattes.

Much bigger issues, such as majoring on the major, are at play. In addition, don't forget to spend time with people you like.

You: What's that got to do with saving money?

Plenty.

CASE STUDY

TEN ANNOYING WAYS TO LOSE A LITTLE MONEY
Adapted from a post to the *Beyond Paycheck to Paycheck* blog, July 6, 2009

I'm a big fan of major on the major, minor on the minor. Too many people spend too much time trying to save money in small ways while missing truly big opportunities. As a result, they continue to struggle.

Still, even I have spent and lost small amounts of money I'm not happy about. In each case, my previous choices caused me to lose or spend money in the following annoying ways.

1. **Expired parking meters:** Frustrating no matter the situation, but enough to drive a man insane when caused by someone who keeps on talking despite having nothing to say when the meeting was clearly over. Cost: $10 (New Hampshire) to $45 (Los Angeles).

2. **Change in between the seats of the car:** I can see the coins. I can't get them. I've tried. More than once. Cost: Unknown, but estimated between 55 cents and $2.14.

3. **Blackjack:** Do the laws of probability not apply to me? I know how to play, but I've just lost seven straight hands and am now approaching my psychological dollar limit. But I'm so due. Maybe just two more hands? Cost: Highly variable and occasionally zero. But usually a bit more.

4. **Sales tax:** I have lived in sales-tax-free New Hampshire long enough that a $1.08 bill for something priced $0.99 feels like a total con job. Cost: Minimal, because I just don't buy many big ticket items away from New Hampshire.

5. **Bank fees:** While I've paid an incredibly small total (i.e., less than ten bucks) in bank fees during my lifetime, they are so annoying I remember them forever (See page 67). Bank fees are sooooo optional. Don't pay them. Choose

your banks and accounts wisely and say goodbye to bank fees forever. Cost: $7.00.

6. **Library fines:** While library fines obviously don't qualify as a big mistake, you only pay them if you're forgetful, lazy, careless, or all of the above. I try not to have any of those attributes, so a library fine is more of a personal insult than one of monetary significance. Cost: About 10 cents, but it stings.

7. **Grocery items on sale at the shelf but not at the cash register.** Whether because the computer wasn't updated for the sale, a sign was misplaced, or I accidentally picked up the 150-sheet size ultra light white version of discount brand X toilet paper instead of the 150-sheet size ultra light off-white version of discount brand X toilet paper, the price comes up at $0.50 cents more per unit at the cash register. I've bought three because of the sale. Next comes the most annoying choice of my day. Do I say something or swallow the $1.50? I bet you know the answer. Now, I am annoying! Cost: $0.00.

8. **Free refills which weren't:** I remember once being charged an extra $1.99 because the free refills promotion had ended but I didn't get the memo. Cost: $1.99.

9. **Ridiculous taxes on rental cars, hotel rooms, and airfare.** Not a whole lot you can do about those highly annoying fees. In case you're curious why rental car fees and hotel room taxes are so high, it's because the out-of-staters who pay those taxes can't vote in the state where the taxes are assessed. Bummer. My only workaround: rent a car away from the airport, like in the center of the city. You can save some serious dough, especially on long-term rentals. Cost: Over $100 a year.

10. **Lab fees:** How much could an x-ray of a busted ankle cost? It took less than 3 minutes once I met the tech. Survey says:

north of $100, even with decent insurance. Thanks, now my ankle and my wallet hurt.

Bonus annoying way to lose a little bit of money:

11. **Refused coupons:** My wife goes through the Sunday newspaper inserts periodically and grabs coupons for items we regularly buy. I tend to do the warehouse club shopping in my family. Recently, I presented the cashier a coupon for 50 cents off eggs which my wife cut out of the paper just hours earlier. Yet, said coupon is summarily, thoroughly, and publicly rejected because my wife, in her haste, has accidentally snipped off the month's portion of the expiration date.

How does the jury find?

"Guilty! We can't accept a coupon without the expiration date, you not so clever thief!"

That it is a manufacturer's coupon—so the retailer doesn't actually pay for the coupon—is irrelevant. That my bill is north of $150 and the coupon is $0.50 is not of the least consideration.

The coupon czar, an authority figure so designated by her prominent nametag imprinted "Joan S." says "Absolutely not." Highlighting her decision-making as one of the most annoying people in New Hampshire is of small comfort.

CHAPTER 8

Saving Strategy # 6:
Enjoy Being With People You Like

"Friendship is like money, easier made than kept."
—SAMUEL BUTLER

You're 16 or 17 years old.
> *You: No I'm not.*

Pretend.

You: Oh.

After seemingly forever, you finally received your driver's license last week. Now, it's 4:30 PM on a Friday. You have access to a car—freedom at last.

The phone rings.

You: Hello?

Your best friend: Hi.

You: Hi! What's up?

Your best friend: Not much. Just got off the phone with Jordan. A bunch of us are going out. Want to come?

Do you remember your response?

You: I'd say "Where are you going?"

Wrong!

You: What?

Think about it for a minute. The question is not what you'd ask your friend/spouse/life partner/significant other today. Instead, the question is what you would have said to your friend when you were 16 or 17.

You: It was different?

Very different.

You: I give up.

The line you uttered next was:

You: Who's going?

Your best friend: Lots of people—Trish, Trisha, Pete, Chappy, Bill, Kelly, Craig, the other Craig, Matt, Beeker, Sumit, and Pat are all definitely in.

You: Pat's going?[1]

Your best friend: Yeah.

You: I'm not sure yet—I was talking to Dave and Wendy earlier, so I might be with those guys tonight.

Your best friend: Oh yeah—Riley is also hanging with us.

You: Riley Jones?[2]

Your best friend: Yes, Riley Jones.

You: $#^$@ Dave and Wendy. I'm with you guys.

"WHO?"—NOT "WHERE?" OR "WHAT?"

As a teenager, the place you spent your free time was relatively unimportant. Where could you go when you were 17 anyway? If your high school social opportunities were anything like mine, your options were pretty limited:

- the movies (most expensive)
- the bowling alley (most competitive)
- a friend's house (most comical)
- your own house (most terrifying)
- the beach (most seasonal)
- the diner (most French fries)
- the parking lot *outside* the pizza joint (most pathetic, since we weren't actually inside the pizza joint)

---

[1] Pat is really, really annoying.
[2] Riley is really, really hot.

Fortunately, your entertainment venue opportunities gradually improve as you age. Unfortunately, you might ultimately have this conversation:

Your significant other: Don't make plans for Saturday night. We're going out.

You: Cool. Where?

Your significant other: That new bistro place that just opened on Market Street. It's called Uptown Molly's or something like that.

You: Downtown Polly's?

Your significant other: Yes. That's it.

You: I've heard good things about that place.

Your significant other: Me too.

Only upon arriving at the restaurant do you learn another couple is joining you and your significant other.

You: That sounds ridiculous. Why wouldn't I know who I was meeting for dinner?

Because you don't really care.[3]

You: I do care.

Sure, you might care a little bit. But the first question most adults ask when making their plans is "Where?"[4]

You: Why does "Where?" vs. "Who?" matter?

While the "Where?" establishes how much an evening costs, the "Who?" determines how much fun you have! When you prioritize "Where?" over "Who?," you pay more for what is less important.

Think about the last time you went out with a friend or co-worker spontaneously.

You: Last Thursday I grabbed a couple of appetizers with Chuck from accounting.

Really?

---

[3] Or you live in a family like mine and your spouse was about to tell you about the other couple, but you wound up interrupted by your children so many times you simply stopped trying to finish your conversation.

[4] While many things have changed since you were a teenager, today's adolescents still ask "Who?" first. Go ahead; listen in on a teenage conversation. I dare you.

You: No, you got me. I went out with Casey from sales. How did you know?

Accountants and spontaneity don't go together.

You: So I have observed.

Me too.[5] Did you have a good time eating apps with Casey?

You: Yes, it was a good time.

Good. How much did you spend hanging out with Casey?

You: Not too much—maybe $10 or $15. It was a pretty inexpensive evening considering how much fun we had.

Although the evening was fairly low-cost, your enjoyment was top-notch. Casey (the "Who?") mattered much more than the location (the "Where?") or your selection of appetizers over entrees (the "What?"). "Who?" always matters most.

Have you ever gone out to eat at an expensive restaurant?

You: Sure. Nothing wrong with that, is there?

Probably not.

You: Hmmm.

Can you recall feeling disappointed after one of those dinners?

You: Most of the time, they were great. But sure, a couple of times were disappointing.

Why?

You: Once, we sat next to a couple who brought their crying newborn—I could barely hear my date talk. Another time our waitperson was beyond a little snooty. But, as I said, most of the fancy dinners I've had were great.

So most of your expensive dinners were positive experiences, but not every one?

You: That's what I'm saying.

Makes sense. Thinking back on all of your dinner dates, what was the most important factor in making an otherwise forgettable evening a truly memorable one?

You: My date.

---

[5] Of all the places I worked, only at accounting firms were happy hours scheduled more than three weeks in advance—with a menu.

Exactly, it was "Who?" you were with. Even if the "Where" and the "What?" are amazing, only the "Who?" can make an experience magical. If you can afford an expensive restaurant meal and value the experience, enjoy. But don't spend money you don't have in a failed attempt to have an experience you desire but cannot obtain.

MODERATION AND LIFESTYLE CREEP

You: What does "lifestyle creep" mean?

Many people fall victim to the belief certain restaurants, vacations, and cars—once more than satisfactory on their former salaries—are no longer adequate given their higher incomes today.

You: Well, it is nice to move up in life.

I hear you. I spend more on certain things now too. For example, I eat less Ramen™ noodles and I drink more Tropicana™ orange juice.[6] But any spending increase should be less than your income increase.

You: Huh?

I've seen people start new jobs upon graduating college and immediately spend as a successful thirty-something might reasonably afford. Still, the entry-level salary doesn't provide the ability to live like a mid-level executive. That the new graduate is confident he'll one day reach a higher income level is irrelevant.

Any time you receive a pay raise, you have a fantastic opportunity to improve your life in two ways:

1. You can increase your saving without cutting back on your spending.

2. You can increase your spending without cutting back on your saving.

Don't blow it by focusing on the second one alone! Instead, move up in moderation. Let's say you get a raise.

You: Sounds good.

---

[6] In Chapter 10, I explain exactly how the author of a savings book eagerly drinks a premium brand of orange juice most mornings.

You'll probably want to increase your standard of living as a reward for earning your raise.

You: Amen, brother.

What, specifically, does increasing your standard of living mean to you?

You: A new couch.

If you can afford one based on your understanding of majoring on the major, go for it.

You: Some new clothes.

Seems reasonable.

You: A better car, a new house, a more extravagant vacation, more shoes, eating out more often and at nicer places, the new handheld electronic gizmo of the month, another computer, better seats at the theatre . . .

Take a breath.

You: That was fun.

And, as you surely realize, completely unrealistic.

You: Why?

Did I say your income doubled or did I say you got a raise?

You: You said I got a raise. How much?

Three or four percent.

You: But that's what I usually get.

Could you afford all those lifestyle changes on a three or four percent increase?

You: Of course not.

Even with a 10 or 15 percent raise, you couldn't afford the enormous lifestyle creep you just described. Nonetheless, it is still appropriate to increase your standard of living as your income increases.

Saving is not about endlessly depriving yourself; it's about making choices in favor of what truly matters to you. When you can afford it, improve your life in the one or two areas you've identified as highly important. Don't attempt to change your entire lifestyle at once. You'll never be able to afford that.

You: Ever?

Probably not. But if you honor the Total Candor saving strategies, you might eventually be able to afford much of what's on your current dream list.

You: What about the dream lists I might make in the future?

Achieving those dreams is far less likely.

You: Why? What do you know about my future dream list?

It will be very different from today's dream list.

You: How so?

Products and experiences you currently aspire for become merely acceptable once you can easily afford them. Instead, you will desire what is just out of your reach.

You: But that's how I feel right now.

That's how we all feel right now. It's how we've always felt and how we will always feel.

You: How annoying!

Totally.

You: Why is it this way?

Striving for what is just out of reach is human nature. You are, I am fairly certain, a human.

You: That's some endorsement.

Facts are facts. Understand the following.

➤ You can't have everything you want right now.

➤ You will always want more than you have.

➤ By implementing the saving strategies, you can achieve most of what you deem critical fairly quickly.

➤ Through fiscal discipline, everything reasonably on your current dreams list is achievable over the long-term.

➤ Unless you change the lens through which you view personal finance, self-reliance, and financial independence, you will never feel completely satisfied since your constantly upgraded dreams will stay just out of reach.

You: Isn't that depressing?

I don't think so. I think it's rather uplifting.

You: Uplifting? How is that uplifting?

Recognizing you might not be able to achieve *future* dreams isn't much of a sacrifice. By definition, we're talking about only forgoing things you're not even currently contemplating. On the other hand, over the long term, you can achieve much of what you strive for today.

You: Sounds better.

One of the most important steps to achieving your dreams is to complete Figure 8-1.

Figure 8-1 is a blank personalized dream worksheet. By completing the form, it becomes *your* personalized dream worksheet. (For one of many possible takes, review Figure 8-2, which shows a completed worksheet.) Keep in mind there are no right or wrong answers.[7]

Once committed in writing, dreams become legitimate goals—and you're on your way. Still, you'll need to overcome several challenges. Like the obstacles we discuss in previous chapters, you're prepared to conquer them. Your next strategy is to triumph over recurring minor expenses.

---

[7] You can download the form from on my web site at www.totalcandor.com/dreams.php and complete it on your computer. This will be particularly helpful if, like me, you can't read your own handwriting five minutes after you scribble something down.

Figure 8-1

Envision Your Dreams

My Name: _____   Date Created: _____

Revision Dates: _____

These are my dreams. I will strive to realize these goals over the time frames
indicated. They are my true priorities, financial and otherwise, and I am willing to
make sacrifices in order to achieve my true aspirations:

Immediate Goals – within one year	
Financial Goals	Non-Financial Goals

Short-Term Goals – one to five years	
Financial Goals	Non-Financial Goals

Mid-Term Goals – five to ten years	
Financial Goals	Non-Financial Goals

Long-Term Goals – more than ten years	
Financial Goals	Non-Financial Goals

Figure 8-2

Envision Your Dreams

My Name: _____   Date Created: _____

Revision Dates: _____

These are my dreams. I will strive to realize these goals over the time frames indicated. They are my true priorities, financial and otherwise, and I am willing to make sacrifices in order to achieve my true aspirations:

Immediate Goals – within one year

Financial Goals	Non-Financial Goals
Pay off all high-interest debt	Make good impression on employer
Establish a great savings profile & emergency fund	Eat healthier
Contribute to 401(k) plan – up to employer match	Spend more time networking socially than socially networking

Short-Term Goals – one to five years

Financial Goals	Non-Financial Goals
Consumer debt free	Get promoted/Go to graduate school
Increase 401(k) contributions rate to 10%/Fund Roth IRA	Spend more time with family
Establish outside savings	Take a hobby to the next level

Mid-Term Goals – five to ten years

Financial Goals	Non-Financial Goals
Debt-Free (besides mortgage)	Buy next home (or first)
Salary of $X	Really nice vacation
Experienced Investor	Get a pet

Long-Term Goals – more than ten years

Financial Goals	Non-Financial Goals
Net Worth of $X	Buy vacation home
Financial Independence	Teach others how to be financially successful on any income
Pay for child's education	Bliss

CASE STUDY

WHEN YOU SPEND LESS, YOU GET MORE VALUE OUT OF LIFE

Adapted from a post to the *Beyond Paycheck to Paycheck* blog, December 24, 2008

We received over a foot of snow last Sunday. This dumping was on top of another foot we received less than 24 hours earlier. Needless to say, Sunday was a day the entire family, save for my numerous shoveling excursions, remained inside. It could have been a boring day.

It wasn't.

At the end of the day, my wife and I agreed we would probably remember our evening's primary activity for a very long time.

You: What did you guys do?

We made a memory.

You: How?

We made dinner together. The whole family.

You: Isn't your youngest kid an infant?

Technically, yes. So we made her supervisor and she monitored the situation from her high chair. But my wife, older daughter, and I made dinner, assembly line fashion, with calming but festive music in the background.

You: iPod sound system?

No, the boombox I got in 1991. See? The precise music player is meaningless. So was the fact the dinner's ingredients cost less than $20 and fed us all for **two** nights—plenty of yummy leftovers! The memory was from the genuine closeness of enjoyable *family time*, not *family money*.

It was the second time something like that happened in a week.

You: Something like what?

I received far more value than I expected.

You: What was the other time?

Last week, my wife and I went out to lunch.

You: Uh-huh.

We met in the middle of the day and had a meal together.

You: I didn't need a definition of "lunch."

I didn't mean to offend. Meeting someone for lunch is routine for many people. However, since my wife and I both run small businesses, we often don't feel we have the time for lunch out of the office. But, last Thursday, we decided to make the time.

You: Okay, so you had lunch together. Why is this a big deal?

Can you handle the truth?

You: Jack?

No, it's still me, Michael.

You: Darn! I still want the truth, though.

Good. While my wife and I have not gone out to lunch often because of time pressure, we also don't do lunch because eating out is an easily avoidable expense. To that end, we nearly always bring our lunches from home.

Still, we had such a nice time last week that we agreed to meet for lunch more often.

You: Increasing your spending.

Certainly, but not by nearly as much as the value we received from a $10 lunch.

You: That's really cheap for two people.

True. We had a coupon, so it won't be as inexpensive next time. But again, it wasn't the cost we focused on. It was each other. *When you focus on spending time, not money, you get a lot more value for your dollar.*

Extra bonus: you live in balance.

What could you do and receive top value? Why aren't you doing it already?

CHAPTER 9

. . . .

Saving Strategy # 7:
Don't Blow Off the Recurring Minor

"Chains of habit are too light to be felt until they are too heavy to be broken."
—WARREN BUFFET

Cable Company: Thank you for calling Tronvision Cable. This is Meredith R. How may I help you today?

You: Hello Meredith. I'm moving, so I need to change the address where I receive service.

Cable Company: Congratulations on your upcoming move! I'll connect you to the billing department.

You: Billing?

Cable Company: Yes.

You: Okay.

[Heinous music plays for 30 seconds followed by a booming male voice touting new technology and bundles offered by TronVision followed by—]

Cable Company: Thank you for calling Tronvision Cable. You've reached the billing department. This is Jon. How may I help you?

You: Hello Jon. I'm moving so I need to change the address where I receive service.

Cable Company: Well, this is the billing department.

You: Yes, I know.

Cable Company: We don't process moves in the billing department.

You: I didn't think so.

Cable Company: Do you have a billing question?

You: No, I'm just moving.

Cable Company: So how can I assist you?

You: It doesn't sound like you can, Jon.

Cable Company: Before I transfer you to our move team, is there anything else I can help you with today?

You: There's a move team?

Cable Company: Yes. All they do is process moves. They will be happy to assist you.

You: Is that a new division not all TronVision employees would have heard about yet?

Cable Company: No, the move team has been around longer than I've been at TronVision.

You: How long have you been with TronVision, Jon?

Cable Company: Oh, a while now. Let's see . . . about six weeks.

You: Thanks.

Cable Company: Is there anything else I can help you with today?

You: No thanks, Jon. Just the transfer.

Cable Company: I'll transfer you now to the . . . um . . .

You: The move team.

Cable Company: Right. Transferring.

[Dead silence for about 10 seconds followed by a fainter version of what you heard before—heinous music playing for 30 seconds followed by a booming male voice touting new technology and bundles offered by TronVision followed by more music and the booming voice again. The process repeats itself for seven minutes.]

Cable Company (thick accent): I apologize for any brief delay you may have experienced and thank you for calling Tronvision Cable. You've reached technical support. This is Soresh. How can I help you?

You: Can you process a move?

Cable Company: What do you mean by "move?" I do not know anything about "moves." What seems to be the problem with your service and can I have your customer account number information please?

[Click. You hang up. Thirty minutes later, you call again.]

Cable Company: Thank you for calling Tronvision Cable. This is Phil. How can I help you?

You: Hi Phil, I'm moving.

Cable Company: I'll transfer you to our move team.

[One second pause.]

Cable Company: Hello, I understand you are moving.

You: Yes. Wow, that was fast.

Cable Company: Yes, Phil told me you were moving.

You: Yes, but still.

Cable Company: At TronVision, we seek to exceed your expectations every time you call—you are a valuable TronVision customer. My name is Warren and I will guide you through our streamlined move process.

You: Because you're on the move team.

Cable Company: Yes, I am. When would you like your move to take effect?

You: Next Thursday.

Cable Company: I can arrange for your service to stop at your current address next Thursday. I will also start service at your new address next Thursday. Is that what you would like me to do?

You: Sounds perfect.

Cable Company: While I am processing this change, may I also tell you about our current move specials?

You: Sure, I guess.

Cable Company: I see you have our extended basic cable plan right now. Is that correct?

You: I believe so.

Cable Company: You currently have our extended basic cable plan. I can offer you the same plan at the same rate in your new home. In addition, you qualify for a free three-month trial of our TronVision cable-plus program. With this program, you receive six premium stations including

ABO, Lotsomax, Gotime, and DSPN-5, DSPN-6, and DSPN-Obsession. Ordinarily, TronVision cable-plus costs an additional $29.99 a month, but is totally free for the first three months if you order it with your move.

You: It's totally free for three months?

Cable Company: Yes, it is. If, after the third month, you are enjoying the cable-plus program, you don't have to do anything. Your service will continue and the $29.99—that's less than a dollar a day—will be added to your subsequent bill. Shall I include TronVision cable plus in your plan at no extra charge?

You: Sounds like a no-brainer.

Cable Company: It is. No one turns this down; it's our best offer.

IS IT WORTH IT—TO YOU?

Why would you say yes to the TronVision cable plus offer?

You: Because I get something for nothing.

Why do you think the cable company makes the offer?

You: I have wondered about that. I guess because some people try such packages and decide to keep them.

Yes, that's one reason. Also, some customers won't remember agreeing to the additional service, let alone recall the need to cancel the service at the end of the trial period. Regardless, the consumer has just agreed to an additional $30 a month ($360 per year) for supplemental programming.

You: Are you saying it's not worth it?

For who?

You: For me.

I don't know.

You: How about for you?

Definitely not.

You: Why are you uncertain it's worth it for me, but convinced it's not worth for you?

I know my TV-viewing habits; I don't know anything about yours. I currently watch so little TV I periodically contemplate cutting cable entirely. I certainly don't need any stations beyond those I pay for now.

You: So why don't you cut out cable?

Because I need cable to watch the Red Sox games.

You: There's radio.

A newspaper tells you the scores the next day too. Although I hate how expensive cable is, I obviously think it's worth it.

You: Why do you say so?

I value watching the Red Sox on TV more than the cost of the monthly cable bill. If I didn't, I would have already canceled the service, but I haven't and don't plan to do so.

Only you can determine if you value specific expenses, like regular and premium cable packages, more than their costs. *You* must decide if the sacrifice is worth it.

You: The sacrifice?

Yes, in terms of forgoing your other spending and saving opportunities. If an expense is worth it to you, go for it. If not, pass. It really is that simple.

FREE TRIALS

Do not accept free trials with the intention of canceling service before payments are due.

You: As with TronVision cable plus?

Exactly.

You: Why not?

Because you won't cancel.

You: I think I usually do.

If so, you're an exception. Many people are so busy they struggle to complete their everyday responsibilities. Few find it easy to remember let alone create the time required to place an optional phone call to the cable company.

You: Especially since there was a good movie on one of those premium stations last night.

Exactly. Free trials allow for easier lifestyle creep. No one likes giving up something they enjoy. Free trials are a psychological maneuver companies use to successfully increase consumer spending.

You: What do you mean?

As you correctly stated, the TronVision cable plus free trial initially provides you with something for nothing. Three months later, your choice is quite different. At that time, you can either increase the amount you pay for *the same thing* ($29.99 monthly vs. no charge) or you can cancel *your* cable plus service. At that time, your options are either giving up money or giving up services.

You: Neither option is particularly attractive.

No, they're not. Either your spending goes up with no benefit to your lifestyle or your lifestyle goes down without any benefit to your ability to save. Yet most people do not view their choices in such a way three months later.

You: How do they look at it?

They don't.

You: What?

Ninety days later, few people contemplate their enjoyment of TronVision's cable plus programming versus its cost. Many will forget about the three-month deadline entirely. Still others will determine they like the service, paying an increased amount they can no longer recall.

You: Won't people eventually remember the package isn't free?

One benefit to the cable company of a longer trial period is it's harder for the consumer to remember to cancel. (Things are harder to remember the longer the period of time in which you need to remember them.) Furthermore, many people pay their cable bills automatically by credit card or by a recurring debit from their checking account. Combine automatic bill payment with e-statements and many folks never witness their cable bill being paid or observe the details of their service.

Out of sight, out of mind, out of wallet.

MINOR VS. RECURRING MINOR

You: But in Chapter 7 I learn to minor on the minor. Since I don't need to finance thirty dollars, cable plus is just a minor expense. If I legitimately focus on the major expenses, can't I avoid sweating the small financial stuff?

It's true—thirty bucks is definitely a minor expense and not nearly as important as buying a home.

You: So that's it?

No, of course not. Big differences exist between minor expenses and *recurring* minor expenses. While you can minor on the minor, you can't blow off the recurring minor.

You: Recurring minor?

Recurring minor expenses occur repeatedly. The additional $29.99 cable charge isn't a one-time event. You're agreeing to be billed $29.99 repeatedly until you stop the service. The package costs $360 a year, $3,600 over a decade, unless you take action.

Recurring minor expenses are very different from a truly minor expense such as coffee at a café.

You: Why? I have a friend who buys coffee every day. Isn't that a recurring minor expense?

Many other financial experts would say yes.

You: But?

I do not.

You: Why not?

Every time you buy a coffee—

*You: **My friend** buys the coffee.*

Right. Every time your friend buys a coffee, she makes a proactive decision—right then—to incur the expense. She has a daily opportunity to decide the purchase is not worth it.

You: So my friend can still order her coffee even if she goes to the café almost every single day?

If your friend wakes up most mornings longing for *that* coffee, she may conclude it's worth $5 a day ($1,300 a year) to do so. But if she enjoys ordinary coffee just as much or is only stopping at the coffee shop to delay getting to work for nine minutes, hitting the snooze button is a much less expensive option.

You: So it's up to me?

It's up to *your friend*.

You: Right. That's what I meant.

Your friend's truly minor decision is based on what she values at the time she incurs the cost.

Perhaps she might not be in the mood for coffee on a given morning. Maybe she runs late and doesn't have time to stop. Either way, she makes the decision to spend or the decision not to spend every day. She must do something to spend her money.

On the other hand, a recurring minor expense works differently; you must take action *not* to spend on a monthly package you previously agreed to accept. Since procrastination and inertia are the human paths of least resistance, when a one-time decision is automated, it is likely to continue for a very long time.

You've probably already signed up for numerous other recurring minor expenses, some of which are automatically taking your money right now.

You: Ugh. What are they?

AUTOMATIC MONTHLY EXPENSES

Common examples of recurring minor expenses include:

➤ Cell phone
➤ Netflix™
➤ Gym membership
➤ Bank fees
➤ Insurance premiums (e.g., auto, homeowner's/renter's, health, life, disability)
➤ Internet access

Each of the recurring expenses above results from your previous commitment to a certain dollar amount. Absent a move on your part, you pay those amounts, or possibly more, for the rest of your life.

You: Possibly more?

When your gym or health insurer raises its rates, they notify you of the effective date and the new amount. Since your payment is made automatically, you are not required to take action. Even if you don't open the letter notifying you of the rate change, you simply and conveniently pay the higher rate.

You: For the rest of my life?

Have you ever received a call from your cell phone company informing you they are going to stop charging you a monthly fee?

You: Of course not.

Even if you join a new gym and cease using your old gym, you pay for the original gym until you cancel your membership.

As I said, since human nature is a combination of procrastination and inertia, we proceed with the status quo. Why else do people still root for the Chicago Cubs?

You: Pardon?

Wrigley Field often sells out yet the Cubs haven't won the World Series since 1908. If cheering for the Cubs isn't an example of doing something simply because you've done it before, I don't know what is.

You: As opposed to doing something because it makes sense, right?

Aha! A south-sider!

You: What?

Inside baseball joke. Here's another example. As of early 2010, AOL collected more than $85,000,000 in *monthly* subscription revenue.

You: Why? What do you get paying for AOL that you can't get for free?

I don't know. I looked and I couldn't figure it out. I know AOL's sub-scriber revenue continues to plummet. People cancel every month. Still, more than four million AOL subscribers pay $85,000,000 every month for something the rest of the world has figured out is available for free.

You: That's some seriously expensive procrastination.

Indeed, we're talking many years worth of procrastination. Remember, each recurring minor expense provides you an opportunity to minimize your cost while maximizing the value you receive. Understanding your genuine preferences and being honest about what you truly value are critical. As the AOL example proves, some expenses just go on and on and on and on and . . . Consequently, you simply can't blow off recurring minor expenses.

Let's talk about some common recurring minor expenses and what you can do to minimize or eliminate the excess of their cost over the value you receive.

You: Sounds good to me.

CELL PHONES

When you shop for a new cell phone plan, you make several choices. Your first choice is to terminate your current plan.

You: Is that a bad thing?

It depends. Is the new plan you're considering more expensive than the one you would cancel?

You: I'm not sure yet.

It's rare people change cell phone plans and save money. Is your current phone still working?

You: Yes.

Then why shop for a new cell phone plan now?

You: I really want a new phone.

I hear you. That's how it is for most people, since phones come out with new bells and whistles all the time. Consequently, a two-year old phone can seem like an antique.[1]

Still, how important is a new phone? Is it worth more than the monthly plan rate increase multiplied by the 12 or 24-month minimum contract?

You: I'd have to think about it.

That's all you should consider. Only you can determine if you'll receive value exceeding your additional cost.

When shopping for a cell phone plan, the number of included anytime minutes is another critical decision. Finally, you must also choose between an all-inclusive plan and one where you pay per use for other services, such as text messaging and web access.

Choose plans which make the most sense for your needs, not necessarily the plans labeled "best value" by nearby promotional materials or those confidently suggested by sales representatives.

It can be much cheaper to select all-inclusive text messaging for an extra $5 per month rather than to pay 25 cents for each text message sent

---

[1] Of course, if you own an iPhone, today's new release by Apple™ has permanently embarrassed what you bought last Thursday.

or received. But if you anticipate sending or receiving only five messages per month, it's obviously cheaper to pay 25 cents per use.[2]

The same logic goes for minutes. Pay for what you use—not for what you might use if minutes didn't cost anything. Also, don't pay for 1,000 minutes because you have no idea what you use now. Before switching plans, take 10 minutes to research what you currently use.

You: That sounds annoying.

It is annoying. But not as annoying as later realizing you're paying an extra $20 every month for minutes you'll never use. Don't give away $240 a year because you don't want to complete an annoying 10-minute project. Unless you currently earn $1,440 per hour or more, you made the wrong decision by blowing off analyzing this recurring minor expense.

You: $1,440 per hour?

Someone who earns $1,440 per hour earns $240 in 10 minutes. So theoretically, such an individual could ignore this annoying project and come out even.

You: But almost no one makes that much money, right?

No.[3] So do the math and save.

Finally, if you have very good cell phone service inside your home, consider purchasing a higher minutes-per-month plan and disconnecting your landline telephone service completely for extra monthly savings.

NETFLIX®

A leading online movie rental service, Netflix is a want, not a need.

You: It doesn't feel that way.

Still, you know it's a want.

You: I guess.

Are you on the right Netflix plan?

---

[2] If you're under 30, you don't have to think about this very long; you've probably sent and received 20 texts since the beginning of this chapter. If you're asking yourself, "Is a text the same as an email?" you should pay per text.

[3] Almost no one. A quick calculation reveals that LA Laker Kobe Bryant makes about $50,000 in only ten minutes. Of course, that doesn't include the time he has to put in during the playoffs. But it doesn't include the $16,000,000 he earns in endorsements either.

You: Netflix has multiple plans?

Yes. My personal experience with Netflix demonstrates the importance of being realistic when considering entertainment-oriented recurring minor expenses.

My wife, Laura, signed up for Netflix in November 2007. The plan she chose provided for a DVD we selected to be mailed to us. When we were done watching the movie, we would mail the DVD back to Netflix and another DVD would be sent to our home. Although there was no limit to the number of movies we could watch and the monthly cost for the plan was about nine dollars, I was hesitant. Still, I went along.

You: Why?

Why was I hesitant or why did I go along?

You: Both.

I was hesitant because, given our harried lifestyle, I wasn't sure we'd watch more than one movie per month. Given a nearby Blockbuster® rented DVDs for $5, Netflix seemed comparatively more expensive.

You: Why did you go along then?

In the interest of marital harmony.

You: That's it?

Laura was also eight months pregnant. You do not doubt the decisions of your beloved when they are going through incredible, soon to be followed by intense, discomfort.

You: You're a smart guy, Rubin.

Actually, she was pregnant with our second child; I like to think I'm a quick learner.

You: So then what?

We had another girl.

You: Congratulations, but that's not what I meant. What happened with Netflix?

When the first movie arrived, we watched it almost immediately. We mailed it back to Netflix. Sure enough, a few days later, a second movie arrived.

Total cost for the second movie: $27.

You: Twenty-seven dollars for one movie rental?

Yup.

You: Netflix isn't that expensive.

Netflix isn't expensive if you regularly watch and return the movies it sends you. But the second movie we received from Netflix stayed on top of our DVD player for three months.

You: Three months? What happened?

Allyson happened.

You: Who's Allyson?

My youngest daughter. She was born after we watched the first movie but before we watched the second movie. Since Allyson was due in the middle of winter and my wife was to go on maternity leave, Laura thought she would have plenty of time on her hands. She expected to need movies to keep her sane during the long periods of time when she would have little interaction with those able to do more than drink milk and fill diapers.[4]

Still, I was not surprised there proved to be even less time for Laura to watch movies after Allyson's birth. If both our two year old (Hannah) and our newborn were asleep at the same time,[5] I knew what my wife would do, no matter the time of day.

You: Go to sleep herself.

Absolutely.

You: Given the Netflix situation played out as you expected, did you tell your wife, "I told you so"?

Heck, no.

You: Smart man.

Second kid—learning curve.

After Laura agreed $27 was a ridiculous amount to pay for a movie rental, she canceled Netflix. But a year later she signed us up for a less expensive Netflix plan where we were limited to just two movies per month. Now that Allyson's out of the newborn stage, relaxing twice a month sometimes happens.[6]

---

[4] That my Ph.D. wife had resorted to several consecutive weeklong *Dawson's Creek* marathons while home with our oldest daughter further strengthened her "I *need* Netflix" argument.

[5] Parents of young children have a name for this phenomenon: a %$^# miracle.

[6] But usually not for two hours in a row.

Whenever you're presented a service plan choice, always choose one that matches your needs, not your aspirations. Monitor your use every few months. Pay for only what you can truly enjoy—it usually takes only a few minutes to change or cancel your service. Don't be shy; it's *your* life and *your* money.

GYM MEMBERSHIPS

Gyms charge a variety of fees including initiation fees, monthly dues, and daily use fees for non-members. Many gyms also have other services you can choose to add on to your base membership monthly dues.

You: Such as?

Towel service or tanning, for example.

You: Do you use the tanning option?

We've obviously never met in person.

You: So you're either very tan or very not.

I live in New Hampshire and have the pigment to prove it.

You: Gotcha. Do you belong to a gym or are you going to argue a gym is an extravagance?

I do belong to a gym. Although I have always exercised consistently, I have not always belonged to a gym.

You: So what's the right decision for me?

Just like with Netflix, joining a gym should be based on 1) what you value and 2) your expected usage.

Don't join a gym because it has the newest equipment if you tend to work out only by attending aerobics classes. Similarly, a robust class schedule is irrelevant if you only enjoy working out in the weight room. If the monthly fee to join the gym you are considering is $49, a daily user pass for non-members costs $10, and you expect to visit three times a month due to your travel schedule, don't join! Pay $10 each time.

You: But don't you think I'll go to the gym more often if I join?

What do you think?

You: I don't know.

Me neither.

You: But the guy at the gym said I would.

I'm sure. Figure out what works for you and choose a corresponding gym. Only you know your lifestyle.

INITIATION FEES

Although I can't prove it, I've concluded initiation fees primarily exist so gyms can promote a discount on something other than the monthly membership rate.[7]

Unless you live in a particularly underserved area, you have multiple gyms to choose from. Every gym in your neighborhood is a competitor to a gym you consider joining. Use that fact to your advantage by asking about promotions and specials. Mention competitor's offers and advertisements.

In addition, ask about discounts for monthly automatic payments or for pre-paying for a quarter or a year.[8] If you typically work out with a friend, or if you and your roommate/spouse/significant other just moved to the area, ask about two-for-one specials. Gym owners love to increase their membership bases as much as their revenue bases, since every member is another potential referral source.

But if you don't ask, you don't get.

BANK FEES

Bank fees suck.

You: Language, Michael?

No, seriously, they suck. The suck because, of the billions of dollars of bank fees charged by financial institutions, the amount which helps individual savers is zero. Bank fees also suck because they literally suck *your* money away from you.

You: What if I pay bank fees or don't know if I pay bank fees?

Stop.

You: Stop?

Yes.

---

[7] An exception is very high-end gyms. Is it more important you belong to a high-end gym or that you are healthy—physically *and* financially?

[8] If you can afford it, prepaying can save you significantly—another benefit to keeping your costs down elsewhere so you have savings set aside.

Figure 9-1

A Brief History of Bank Fees You Should NOT Pay-EVER

Bank Fee	What You Did (or Did NOT do) to Cause the Fee	How High the Fee Could Be	How to Avoid the Fee
Overdraft Fee	You withdraw more money from your account than you have in the account	From $20 to hundreds of dollars each time	• Don't spend money you don't have. • Stay aware of your account balance. • Use your check register. • Link your savings account to your checking account to avoid overdrafts.
Paper Statement Fee	You receive paper instead of electronic statements or request a copy of an old check	Several dollars per month or per request	• Request electronic statements. • Determine if you really need an old check before requesting it.
Courtesy Overdraft Fee	You withdraw or spend more money than you have in the account and the bank, as a courtesy, allows the transaction to occur anyway	$20 to $40 per time, plus $5 or $10 a day until you pay it back. Many times, a single transaction causes hundreds of dollars in fees.	• See overdraft fees above. • Since the bank can't perform a courtesy overdraft without your consent, revoke your standing authorization by contacting customer service.
POS (Point-of-Sale) Fee	You use your debit card as a debit card (by entering a pin code) at a cash register	10 cents to $1.50 per time	• Find out if you'll be charged extra for using your debit card (increasingly rare) and, if so, just sign for the transaction.
ATM Fee (out of network)	You make an ATM withdrawal at a machine that is not your bank's	$6 or more ($3 or more by your bank, plus $3 or more by the owner of the ATM)	• Only use your bank's ATM. • The next time you have to buy something, ask for cash back using your debit card • Plan ahead and bring cash.

Money Order/Cashier Check Fees	You purchase a money order or a cashiers' check	$10 or higher	• Do you really need one? • If so, can it be avoided with proper planning next time? • Get one at the post office or a retailer, where it is likely to be less expensive.
Monthly Maintenance Fee	You have the wrong bank account for your needs.	$50 or more each month!	• Ask your bank what you can do to avoid monthly fees. • As required, maintain minimum balance, establish direct deposit, or forgo interest to eliminate the maintenance fee. • If you can't find the no-maintenance fee account for you at your bank, you're at the wrong bank.
Check Fee	You requested those rectanglular pieces of paper that say "Pay to the Order of" on them.	$25–$35 for a single box of checks	• Stop using checks and start using online banking. • Purchase checks online for less; search "cheap checks," for example. • Get an account with free checks and use them only use if no other payment option is available. One hundred checks ought to last you many years that way . . .
Minimum Balance Fee	Your balance goes below some arbitrary minimum set by the bank.	$12 or much more	• Choose an account without such a fee. • Be sure you never go below the minimum. • Set up alerts if you are getting close to the minimum, though that requires you have money elsewhere to immediately transfer as well as have time to deal with such clerical concerns at the drop of a hat. You don't-or your balance wouldn't be so low in the first place.

You: How?

First, review your most recent bank statement.

You: Um—

It doesn't matter how long it's been since the last time you looked at your bank statement—you're not at Confession. As you review your bank statement, look for line items such as:

➤ Maintenance/Account fee

➤ Overdraft fee

➤ Paper statement fee

➤ Courtesy overdraft fee

➤ POS fee

➤ ATM fee

➤ ATM surcharge

➤ Money order/Cashier check fee

Also, be on the lookout for two of my favorite and most descriptive charges:

➤ Fee

➤ Bank Fee

Banks have every right to charge you fees they disclose in advance. You also have rights, including the right to structure your financial affairs in such a way as to avoid bank fees entirely. You can even cease using banks that charge fees.

You: Seriously?

Absolutely. I don't pay any bank fees at all. Follow my logic:

➤ I hate things that suck.

➤ I avoid things that suck.

➤ Bank fees suck.

➤ Therefore, I hate and avoid bank fees.

You: You gotta love the transitive property.

Indeed, the transitive property is my favorite of all mathematical properties. The only rational conclusion? Don't pay bank fees.

You: But how do you avoid them?

At most banks, certain accounts are available with no fees for the "right" person. Get the right account by being the "right" person—ask how.

Furthermore, certain institutions, including credit unions and online-only banks, charge very few bank fees to any of their customers.

Since it's impossible to get any value or any enjoyment from a bank fee, paying one is simply fiscally irresponsible. Commit to cutting them out. Entirely. Forever.

Note the summary of common bank fees on pages 164 and 165, why they are charged, and how to avoid them.

Frustrated with all the fees? Consider a credit union, a local (not national) bank, an Internet-only bank, or a bank affiliated with a brokerage, each of which are less likely to nickel and dime you.

INSURANCE PREMIUMS

In *Beyond Paycheck to Paycheck*, I discuss insurance policies such as auto, homeowner's, renter's, health, life, disability, accidental death and dismemberment (AD&D), and dental in great detail. Instead of repeating the information here, let's discuss your biggest saving opportunity related to insurance.

You: What is it?

A periodic review of your policies.

You: Ugh. Why?

To ensure each policy still makes sense for you. Keep the following two rules in mind when making any insurance decision.

1.   Never risk a lot for a little.
2.   Do not insure what you can easily afford to lose.

You: How do those rules work in practice?

One example is a higher deductible.

You: What does that even mean?

A deductible is the amount you pay in the event of a claim.

You: I'm still kind of hoping for English.

Let's say you get into a car accident.

You: Now that sentence I understood. I didn't like it, but I understood it.

If the damage to your vehicle is $5,000 and you have a $100 deductible, you will owe $100 and the insurance company will pay $4,900.

You: So the deductible is the amount I pay in the event of a claim.

Well-said.

You: Thank you.

You're welcome. However, a very low (i.e., $100) deductible will cost you more in insurance premiums (i.e., the amount you pay for coverage) than a higher deductible.

You: Why?

Two main reasons. First, since your deductible is so low, the insurance company will need to write a bigger check every time you make a claim.

You: Makes sense.

Second, the insurance company is likely to have to deal with you more often. That's expensive.

You: Why will they have to deal with me more often?

Because you can make a claim for a $350 accident, whereas someone with a $500 deductible wouldn't bother to call.

You: Why not?

Why make a claim for a $350 accident if you'd have to pay for the whole accident anyway (since a $500 deductible exceeds $350 of damages)?

You: You wouldn't.

Exactly. Consider higher deductibles, especially for auto insurance policies. Establish an emergency fund so you can easily tolerate the increased expense you would need to pay in the event of a car accident. Fortunately, the lower premium charged by a higher deductible plan makes it easier to establish an emergency fund in the first place.

You: That's helpful.

Thanks.

*You: Not you—the discount from a higher deductible **helps** make my emergency fund grow.*

Right. It does.

You: Are there other opportunities to save on insurance?

Plenty.

You: Preach on, brother!

Amen.

You: You're supposed to say that at the end.

Oh.

You: Please continue.

I'm on it. Another way to save on insurance premiums is to take advantage of a group discount.

You: What kind of group discount?

Check any you might qualify for including professional associations, alumni associations, or AAA.

When you obtain quotes or review your insurance policies, ask your agent about any opportunities to save. Common discounts for auto insurance include being a safe driver or having a short commute. Owning an older and/or less expensive car also means lower insurance costs.[9]

Another great way to save on insurance is to keep all of your policies with the same insurance company. Many insurers provide additional discounts to those with multiple (e.g., auto and homeowner's) policies. Take advantage and save.

No one is impressed by a costly insurance policy. Keep your costs as low as possible for appropriate coverage. By investing 60 minutes a year, you can save a good deal of money with absolutely no impact to the quality of your life.

You: Seriously, where's the sacrifice?

The sixty minutes.

You: I can do that.

Good. Do it today.

---

[9] Yet another reason why new cars cost far more than the typical consumer expects.

INTERNET ACCESS

You: I need access to the web.

I know. Just make sure you're not overpaying for it. Whether you have dial-up,[10] high-speed through DSL, cable, satellite or a new technology that came out while *The Savings Solution* was at the printer, you're likely paying a monthly fee.[11] These rates fluctuate frequently. Incentives are offered to new customers and to those who purchase more than one service from the provider (e.g., phone service and/or cable TV service in addition to Internet access). When you start service, get the best deal. Then, when that deal expires—

You: Expires?

When the introductory three, six, or twelve month period is over, you'll be automatically charged a new rate. That rate will be higher.

You: How do you know it will be higher?

You wouldn't have accepted a special introductory rate unless it was lower than the normal rate, right?

You: Of course not.

Therefore, the regular rate will be higher than the introductory offer.

You: So now what?

Do you have any ISP brand loyalty?

You: Huh? What does that mean?

Do you care whether you access the web via a DSL connection, a cable connection, or another way? As long as you're getting high-speed Internet access do you really care how?

You: Heck, I'm not sure what I have now. I just know it works. My significant other took care of it when I moved in.

---

[10] There's nothing particularly useful to see down here, but like dial-up, you're delayed . . . waiting. Soon you'll be able to return to the main text and continue with what you were doing. It shouldn't be much longer now, but it could be. Sometimes it depends on the time of day. Other times, your slower speed is just random. But when you're ready to move up to high-speed, just stop reading this footnote. Okay, now the rest of the page is fully loaded.

[11] Unless your neighbor's wireless router's name is "Linksys," in which case there's a great chance no password is required to get free Internet access. But—technically—this is stealing. No matter how effective or tempting, stealing is endorsed neither by the 7th saving strategy nor the 8th commandment of any widely practiced religion.

Look in the newspaper, your mailbox, and online to see the current deals. Then it's time for a phone call to your provider to see what you can do to keep your rate from increasing dramatically upon the expiration of your introductory offer.

You: Sounds annoying.

It is annoying.

You: Being annoyed seems like a theme with Saving Strategy 7.

Reducing your recurring minor expense by spending a bit of time once or twice a year is annoying, especially when you're thinking about it. But when you free up cash-flow as a result of those brief calls and can therefore afford to a) save more, b) spend more on other things you truly enjoy, or c) both, you feel—

You: Satisfied.

Not annoyed, that's for sure.

You: Seriously, I just did it.

Congratulations. Getting the same products and services for less while eliminating spending on things you don't genuinely value are easy fiscally responsible actions you must take. By doing so, your ability to save increases without any corresponding decline to your lifestyle.

ANNUAL FEE CREDIT CARDS

Don't pay an annual fee for a credit card.

You: But if I don't pay an annual fee and I pay the entire new balance monthly—

You're using a credit card perfectly.

You: Won't they close my account or reduce my limit or something? I've heard those guys can be pretty greedy and if they're not making any money on me—

You're wrong.

You: They're not greedy?

No comment.

You: Then what am I wrong about?

They're making money on you.

You: How?

Every time you swipe your card, the merchant is charged a fee, sometimes multiple fees. A two to three dollar fee is fairly standard for a $100 transaction.

You: Wow.

Do not pay an annual fee to use a credit card.

You: What about rewards programs?

I've paid annual fees to gain access to reward programs at times.

You: Now?

Be honest about what you get for what you pay. Revisit your decision every year. If you think you'll earn rewards worth more than the annual fee, a rewards card could be a good idea.

You: Why wouldn't it definitely be a good idea?

First, you're guessing how many points you'll earn. You could easily overestimate your point generating activity. Second, after signing up for the rewards credit card you may subconsciously begin to use the card more often to get maximum advantage of your reward benefit.

You: C'mon!

I can be pretty frugal and even I've heard little voices rationalizing, "Yes, Michael, it's an extra $50 but it really isn't $50 because if I spend the $50, I'm closer to X, Y, or Z in my rewards program." Fortunately, I realized I was being dumb and dumped most of my rewards credit cards.

The last reason you shouldn't pay an annual fee for a reward credit card is you can get one for free.

You: Excuse me?

Some credit card's reward programs do not charge annual fees.

You: Really?

Yes, including cards which give you hotel points and those which give you cash back.

You: A cash-back credit card is a reward card?

It's the ultimate reward card. Using a cash-back card is like receiving a discount on everything you purchase. If you're going to use a credit card, a no-annual fee credit card with a cash-back reward is hard to beat.[12]

Here's some easy math: Add up all the annual fees of the credit cards in your wallet. If the total is greater than zero, you should seriously examine it. Eliminating annual fees represents yet another easy opportunity to easily increase your savings without affecting your lifestyle.

RECURRING MONTHLY EXPENSES FROM DAILY DECISIONS

Expenses like gym memberships, insurance premiums, and credit card annual fees are caused by infrequent and rarely revisited decisions. However, other recurring minor expenses result from decisions you make every day. Unfortunately, most people effectively put such daily decisions on autopilot too.

You: Why?

Many people live a familiar routine whereby their decision to spend—which *should* be made at the time of the actual purchase—becomes so automatic it is ultimately made without any conscious thought. Examples include:

➤ Dry cleaning
➤ ATM fees
➤ Coffee shop visits
➤ Vending machines
➤ Lunch at work
➤ Manicures/pedicures
➤ Massages
➤ Happy hour (or some other regular dining or drinking arrangement)

---

[12] This sentence starts with, "If you're going to use a credit card." But remember Saving Strategy 1: since no credit card can help you stay emotionally connected to your money, the best option is still to use cash. But if you're going to use a credit card, pay as little as possible for the privilege.

DRY CLEANING

If you do not work in an environment requiring you to wear high-end clothes, dry cleaning is not a need. It's a want.

You: But my clothes say "Dry-Clean Only."

In that case, dry cleaning is a need for your clothes—not you.

*You: But they're **my** clothes.*

Clothes which are a lot more expensive than you may have initially realized. Lesson number one: be sure to consider the cost of dry cleaning when buying clothes. Other ways to save on dry cleaning include wearing your dry-clean clothes less often and wearing them more times between dry-cleaning. Last, clean your silk and linen in your home.

You: I don't have dry-cleaning equipment at my place.

Use the gentle cycle on the washing machine and hang dry.

You: Do you do that?

No.

You: A-ha!

A-ha nothing. My wife does it for me[13]—I'm not even allowed near the washing machine anymore.

Look at how much you spend on dry cleaning monthly. Ask yourself if it's worth it. It won't be. Severely cut your dry cleaning expenses. Take the money you spend at the cleaners and put it in the bank or spend it on something you actually enjoy, like new clothes that don't say "Dry Clean Only" on them.

ATM FEES

ATM fees are another wasteful everyday expense giving you nothing in return. Paying three bucks, five bucks, or more to withdraw $50 or $100 from your bank account is absurd.

You: Five bucks?

ATM owners frequently charge $2 to $3 to non-customers. It's also common for banks to charge a similar fee to customers who use a non-bank owned ATM.

---

[13] Reason # 4,358(b), subsection iii, I am a VERY lucky guy.

You: So there might be two fees for the same ATM withdrawal?

Yes.

You: Oh, that's ugly.

Very ugly. Don't do this.

You: So it's worth it to avoid those ATM fees?

Yes, it is worth the effort to:

➤ cross the street to **use your bank's ATM.**

➤ **change banks** if you or your job moves so the once convenient ATM is no longer so convenient.

➤ **plan out your week** and the amount of cash you need so you don't need to hit the ATM on Monday, Tuesday and Thursday.[14]

➤ **ask for cash back** at a retailer when making a debit card transaction so you can effectively receive a fee-free ATM withdrawal.

➤ **ask your bank about how you can receive widespread access to ATMs without paying fees.**

You: Now why would they offer me that?

Because you're a very important customer.

You: I am?

If you keep following the saving strategies, you will be soon enough.

COFFEE SHOPS

You: Whoa! You give a free pass on lattes elsewhere in this book. What gives?

Calm down—you might still be able to have your latte and drink it too.

You: MIGHT? Where are you going with the coffee shop category?

Make sure your coffee shop spending matters. Make sure it *really* matters. If it does, you retain free will to enjoy your beverage. But do not go to the coffee shop only out of habit.

You: I don't.

Good. Skip the café for a day. What happens? Do you really miss it? If not, it's a good indication your regular visits are a habit, not something

---

[14] Unless you can use an ATM that won't charge you any fees. Still, why are you going to the ATM three times a week?

you value highly. If you miss your coffee experience, then pick up your regular latte tomorrow.

You: Doesn't sound too hard.

For just two weeks—

You: Two weeks?

Yes, for the next two weeks visit the coffee shop half as much as you do now. See how you feel. If you're just as happy as when you went more frequently, enjoy the savings (and the coffee you're still drinking), but if you're miserable, go back to your former comfortable ways. No real harm will be done and you'll have saved a small amount in the process.

You: But why go through this process if I already know the answer?

You could be wrong. This exercise verifies whether you truly value the coffee shop experience or if you just visit out of habit. Your goal is to remove all expensive low-value autopilot-spending habits so you can focus and spend on what truly matters to you. It doesn't matter which category the latte winds up in. As long as you are truthful to yourself, you win with either outcome.

VENDING MACHINES

With just a little planning, you can completely eliminate the money you spend at vending machines.

You: But I get hungry!

Me too—trust me. I've been known to eat lunch before 11 AM.

You: Solid eating habits, I see.

I could do better at times. But rather than focus on caloric consumption, this personal finance 101 lesson is short and sweet.

You: Like the bag of cookies behind A4?

Quite possibly. Stop buying the small snack packs from vending machines. Instead, buy a family pack of snacks at your grocery or discount store and put a bunch of them in your work desk or locker. Purchase and store drinks the same way.

You: Won't the soda get warm?

Good point. Use the refrigerator. If none is available, drink water—it's healthier anyway.

See what just happened? Now you can eat the same snacks, enjoy the same lifestyle, and spend less money, enabling you to save more for your future.

LUNCH AT WORK

Spending money by eating out at work is a daily expense that really adds up. You could save a small fortune by bringing lunch from home.

You: Should I?

Maybe. If you have credit card debt, you should brown bag your lunch every day.

You: Every day?

Every day except when there is a free lunch.

You: There's no such thing as a free lunch.

True, so you should brown bag it. Bringing a lunch from home is an easy, quick, and significant win.

You: What about people who pay their credit card bills monthly but aren't exactly rich?

Eating lunch out is a question of value. When I worked in a corporate environment I occasionally struggled with this question. At my first job in Detroit, we were prohibited from eating at our desks and no break room was available. Since Michigan weather prohibits eating outside most of the year, we had to eat at local food establishments.[15] But every job I've had since then has allowed me to choose between bringing my own lunch or—as 99 percent of my co-workers did—going out to lunch.

Although regularly going out to lunch costs real money, not going out to lunch means missing one of the most important and enjoyable parts of any workday.

You: Tofu?

No, not for me anyway. I'm referring to socializing with others and enjoying the opportunity to get to know your co-workers in a more relaxed setting.

Contemplating the costs and benefits of eating out led me to different conclusions at different points in my career.

---

[15] I say "food establishments" because "restaurants" seems *way* too generous a description for the places I chose to frequent.

You: About those costs—

Here's why buying lunch everyday can be expensive:

Figure 9-2

Annual Savings By Reducing Your Lunch Spending

Daily Cost of Eating Lunch Out	Brown Bag Cost Estimate	Potential Daily Savings	Eat Out 4 Days	Eat Out 3 Days	Eat Out 2 Days	Eat Out 1 Day	Eat Out No Days
$ 5.00	$ 3.00	$ 2.00	$ 96.00	$ 192.00	$ 288.00	$ 384.00	$ 480.00
$ 7.50	$ 3.00	$ 4.50	$ 216.00	$ 432.00	$ 648.00	$ 864.00	$ 1,080.00
$ 10.00	$ 3.00	$ 7.00	$ 336.00	$ 672.00	$ 1,008.00	$ 1,344.00	$ 1,680.00
$ 12.50	$ 3.00	$ 9.50	$ 456.00	$ 912.00	$ 1,368.00	$ 1,824.00	$ 2,280.00

Assumes 48 weeks a year, due to holidays and vacations. Your savings will be greater if you keep your brown bag cost below $3 by bringing your drink from home and periodically using leftovers.

STAY HUNGRY, MY FRIENDS

As a young professional on a typical entry-level salary, it hit me one day that the Number Five Value Meal at McDonald's™ cost the same no matter your income. There was no means testing at Burger King™ either. My boss's boss—a great guy who periodically joined us for lunch—paid the same amount for the combo meal as I did. Given his higher salary, the $4.99 lunch was an incredibly easy expense for him to digest.[16]

How many people do you know who, upon a promotion or significant raise, change the places they visit for lunch? Many don't even go out with the same folks anymore. Dumb. Eating at the same places means avoiding lifestyle creep. Bonus: you retain a good reputation with the workforce you need to be effective and succeed with at your new role.

---

[16] The large fries were another matter entirely.

At my second job, where I was permitted to eat lunch in the office, I chose to do so periodically. But not every day. If a good group of people was going to lunch, I'd keep my brown bag lunch in the refrigerator for the next day.

What I hated to do and consequently tried to avoid was to purchase lunch outside of work only to bring it back to the office to eat alone. To me, doing so was a big waste of money since I wasn't benefiting from the social aspect of an out-of-the-office lunch, just paying the cost for one.

There's no right answer when it comes to eating lunch out—unless, as I said before, you're paying credit card interest. Can you convince a friend to bring his/her lunch a couple days a week? If so, the two of you can eat together outside or in the break room. You'd get the double benefit of affordable lunch spending and socialization.

Regardless, do what works for you. Spend on what you value. But there's no shame in bringing your lunch to work.[17] Similarly, eating lunch out from time to time is totally acceptable.

RECURRING MINOR EXPENSES REALLY MATTERS

When you pay attention to your recurring minor expenses, you free up cash-flow. By generating additional cash-flow, you obtain the ability to spend with comfort on items you value highly. Before long, desires which once seemed consistently just out of reach or totally unreasonable become attainable. To achieve this new lifestyle requires only your commitment to focus on what really matters. You know such an approach makes sense for your life; why not for your money too?

---

[17] Ironically, my first employer—the one who prohibited us from eating at our desks— ultimately filed for bankruptcy. Disclosure: the bankruptcy had little to do with an audit of employee lunches. Its audit of a rather large energy trading company in Houston was the real culprit.

CASE STUDIES

CAN A TELEMARKETER SAVE YOU MONEY?

Adapted from a post to the *Beyond Paycheck to Paycheck* blog, February 28, 2008

My cell phone rang in the middle of a busy workday yesterday. Although I didn't recognize the number, I answered the call. After a long pause indicative of an approaching telemarketer, our conversation ensued:

Other Party: Hello, Michael?

Michael: Yes. Who is this please?

Spr&#t: This is Spr&#t. We are calling to make sure you are getting the most value from your wireless plan. We periodically review our customers' plans and offer them opportunities to save.

Michael: I'm in the business of saving—you have my attention.

Spr&#t: We are pleased to offer you the opportunity to increase your minutes to 700 minutes per month for only—

Michael: Didn't you say you reviewed my account?

Spr&#t: Ummm. . .

Michael: Is it in front of you now?

Spr&#t: Yes, Mr. Rubin. I see—

Michael: I used like 50 minutes last month and my wife perhaps another 100. Why would we increase our minutes to 700 and pay more? Said another way, how would I save money with a bigger plan?

Spr&#t: You are correct Mr. Rubin. You would not benefit from a higher minutes per month plan. However, we could offer you a third phone for just—

Michael: Our oldest child is just now getting to the point where she doesn't try to eat our home phone. We might be interested in getting her a cell phone, but your latest models are so small they present a choking hazard. So, I don't think so.

Spr&#t: We also could also add to your account—

Michael: It seems like all your ways to "save money" would actually increase my monthly bill. It doesn't seem like I am going to save in the way I had hoped when we started our conversation.

Spr&#t: No, Mr. Rubin, probably not.

Michael: Hey, you have a great day!

Spr&#t: *You too, sir. Thank you for choosing Sp#$ percentt.*

# # #

I hope my call didn't use two of my "anytime minutes." We only have another 500 left on the lowest family plan offered. Too bad pay-as-you-go wireless companies don't market as aggressively to me. Then again, if you can save me money, eventually *I'll find you.*

HOW I LOWERED MY CABLE BILL

Adapted from a post to the *Beyond Paycheck to Paycheck* blog, August 12, 2009

I waited too long to negotiate my cable bill. You shouldn't.

Although I usually follow my own advice, I'm far from perfect. It's one reason why financial advisors should periodically review their affairs with another competent planner.

You: Do you?

Yes, I consult a trusted advisor for big financial decisions. However, I handle minor issues myself. Doing so requires a commitment to tackle them. Today, I'll share my experience dealing with my cable company.

You: Why?

Four main reasons:

1. To demonstrate you can save money and/or get more value from a small amount of time and effort.

2. To show you customer service is inconsistent and how one seemingly useless call can be followed by another which has you shaking your head asking, "Why?"

3. To illustrate there are as many answers to your service and billing questions as there are potential representatives who could answer your call.

4. To experience what I advise and maximize my saving opportunities instead of relying on my memory of how things once worked.

Rubin's vs. the Cable Company

When we moved to New Hampshire, we opted for the cable company's "triple play" package which provided cable TV, phone, and high-speed Internet access for $99 a month for 12 months. It was the best deal for the services we wanted. All was good.

We began to pay full-rate when the deal expired a year later. The new monthly bill was $162. Consequently, calling and haggling another deal with the cable company went on my to-do list.

It stayed there. Way too much time went by before I did anything about it.

You: Why?

I'm human. I didn't really want to deal with the cable company and I was legitimately busy.

You: Those are just excuses.

No argument.

You: So what finally happened?

My wife volunteered to call the cable company.[18]

You: How'd she do?

Not bad.

You: How so?

Simply making the call put her ahead of my pathetic performance to date. Furthermore, she received a lower rate just by dialing. Before she even asked for a price concession, the representative

---

[18] Like one might "volunteer" for jury duty.

told her, "Based on your account history, you're due for another package discount." Just like that, the representative offered my wife a $50 monthly discount, a savings of about 30 percent.

You: Sounds pretty good to me. Did she take it?

She couldn't.

You: Don't tell me you're a guy who doesn't empower his wife.

Nothing could be further from the truth; my wife needs no empowering from me.[19]

You: So why didn't she take the cable deal?

The cable company told her she could not make changes to our account because I had originally set it up.

You: That's stupid.

I agree.

You: So did you call the cable company yourself and take the deal?

I called but I didn't just take the deal.

You: Why not?

Male pride.

You: Really?

No.[20] I wanted to save even more money.

Instead of taking the deal, I thanked the representative for her offer, but said I really needed to get back under $100 a month for all three services.

You: How did the representative react?

She told me she had offered us the very best rate available unless we upgraded our cable package.

You: That doesn't make any sense.

I agree. Furthermore, I didn't want to upgrade my TV package. But the representative made it very clear: if we were willing to upgrade our cable package, I could get the number (i.e., a monthly

---

[19] On the other hand, I need permission—preferably in writing—to buy milk which isn't organic.
[20] Maybe a little.

bill under $100) I wanted to reach. I allowed her to explain the counter-intuitive opportunity further and it soon became clear what the cable company was thinking.

You: And that was?

They would lower my monthly bill because they anticipated I'd pay an additional amount for "On Demand" or "Pay Per View" programming which would be instantly available as part of the upgrade. I knew we wouldn't be tempted so I went for that deal—we barely have enough time to watch "The Office."[21]

Although not necessarily by design, we clearly bargained very well. A classic negotiation strategy is to have two individuals on one side, one which can make decisions but isn't very accessible and the other who does most of the talking. My wife took the latter role. By later entering the process, I started at the price the cable company had already agreed to and negotiated down from there. As a result of our two phone calls, our bills are about 45 percent less than they were previously and we'll receive a slightly better package.

You: Until that deal runs out.

True. Next time I won't wait so long to call.

If you're still waiting to make your call, end the procrastination. Make your best deal today.

Operators are standing by.

FISCALLY RESPONSIBLE GYM MEMBERSHIPS

Adapted from a post to the *Beyond Paycheck to Paycheck* blog, December 14, 2007

You: Are you about to argue gym memberships aren't necessary because you can run and exercise outside?

No. I live in New Hampshire. Yesterday it was 15 degrees outside.

---

[21] Fact.

You: That's cold.

Wicked cold.

You: Right.

Such frosty days make for some tough outside running weather. Still, regardless of their state of residence, a gym membership is a complete waste of money for some people. People who should not spend any money on gym memberships include:

➤ Those who say, "If I join a gym, I'll go more often because I'm paying for it." Wrong. If that's his primary reason to join a gym, he still won't work out frequently. Following this strategy, he's now not only out-of-shape but he's poorer. Why spend money proving he's wrong?

➤ Those with free gyms available at work.

You: That's not much of a list.

True. Since keeping fit helps a person maintain good health today and might also reduce his long-term medical expenses, many people could benefit from a gym membership.

You: So you're giving me the green light to join a gym?

If you'll use it and don't already have a free one at work, absolutely.

You: Cool.

Still, keep a few things in mind. First, visit a few gyms before joining one. Most gyms offer complimentary trial periods ranging from one visit to one month so you can determine which gym is the right gym for you. Take advantage of such offers at two or three different locations.[22]

---

[22] Remember Saving Strategy #4: Enjoy Free Stuff? I'm not advocating you rotate through all the gyms in a 50-mile radius to avoid paying gym membership fees for two years, but why not delay the beginning of your monthly dues while you figure out the best gym for you?

Evaluate how each gym matches your needs and wants. If you never swim, the Olympic Size pool doesn't matter. If you love exercise classes like Spin,[23] make sure classes are available at times you can attend.

In many cases, the local Y presents a viable low-cost option. Before you rule it—or any inexpensive gym—out based on reputation, be sure to visit. You might be pleasantly surprised.[24]

Once you determine the **right** gym for you, you can join comfortably, knowing you've chosen wisely. But don't just join.

You: What? Are you paying attention? Did your editor skip this section?

Relax.

You: Dude, you just contradicted yourself in consecutive sentences and the book's already been printed. I should be calming you down!

It's going to be okay.

You: First, you tell me to comfortably join the gym. Then, in the very next sentence, you tell me not to join. What's going on here?

I want you to join the gym that meets your needs. But before you actually join, you'll need to pretend you're at a car dealership.

You: What?

A car dealership. A place where you would go to buy a car.

You: I know what a car dealership is. But why am I pretending I'm at a car dealership when I'm actually at a gym?

What must you do at car dealership to get a decent price for a car?

You: Haggle?

Yup.

You: Really? At my gym?

Nope, it's not your gym **yet**. It will be your gym after you get the best price. To do so, find out what membership specials they're running or have recently offered.

---

[23] With the good-looking instructor.
[24] Or have a really funny story to tell.

You: Anything else I should consider as a fiscally responsible gym member?

My wife and I once joined the same gym and pre-paid for an entire year. By doing so, our savings compared to the monthly rate were tremendous. Even better, the gym offered us the same deal the next year. We took it and saved a chunk of change.

Your health insurance may reimburse part of your gym dues.

You: My health insurance company never told me anything about any fitness center reimbursement.

Neither did mine. So I called them. You should too.

You: Did you get any money back?

Yes.

You: Was it worth it?

Now I get about $200 back every year.

You: That answers my question.

When you add 1) the partial reimbursement from my health insurer, 2) the savings from joining with another person, and 3) the savings from prepaying, our effective gym rate is significantly less than their "sticker price."

Get the same gym at a far lower cost.

You: Good call.

No doubt. A fiscally responsible gym member has a healthy wallet to go along with that body.

CHAPTER 10

. . . .

Saving Strategy # 8:
Spend With Comfort on
What You Value Most

"If you don't have good dreams, you've got nightmares."
—"Boogie" Sheftell, played by Mickey Rourke, in *Diner*

THE IMPORTANCE OF FOLLOWING YOUR DREAMS

Y*ou: I follow your "Don't be cheap, be fiscally responsible" theme. I'm glad you're not all over me with antics like, "Stay out of coffee shops or you'll be poor for life!" I'm even with you on not blowing off recurring minor expenses.*

So far, so good.

You: I still have an issue.

No problem. What's the issue?

You: My dreams.

What about your dreams?

You: I took the time to list my dreams in Chapter 8.

Good, that's an important exercise.

You: Yet I don't see how I'll achieve my financial dreams. Your advice allows me to save and to understand the importance of saving. But I need any changes I make in my life to enable my dreams, not merely allow me *to save. The lure of my long-term dreams makes my short-term sacrifices possible. I'm reading **The Savings Solution** to achieve my dreams. Sorry if I'm going on, but do you know what I mean?*

Do I ever?! I live in the real world too. I also want things I don't have. But, I'll confess: I could buy many of my dreams right now.

You: You could?

Sure. But I haven't.

You: Why not?

Just because I can buy them doesn't mean I can afford them.

BUY ONLY WHAT YOU CAN AFFORD

You: Why the distinction? Is it because you'd be spending more than you make?

If buying something means I won't be able to meet my savings goals, I deem it unaffordable.[1] Although I could purchase many of the items on my personal dreams sheet by withdrawing money from savings, I choose not to.

You: But you have achieved some of your dreams, right?

Indeed—those I could afford.

You: Have you achieved any dreams I could relate to? Your dreams don't solely consist of ideas like "Save 15 percent of my gross pay," right?

I spend money.

You: What financial dreams do you regularly achieve? What do you spend big money on?

Items and experiences I value highly.

*You: What **are** those items and experiences? I want examples! What's your vice? You said you are human, so you must have a vice!*

"Human," huh? I've been called worse. Okay, I went to a big public university in the Midwest.

You: Ohio State?

Dagger through my heart. No. I attended, the University of Michigan.

---

[1] While that's what affordability means to me, it's a decent definition for anyone.

FOOTBALL IS A BIG DEAL—OR NOT

You: Your tuition must have been due years ago. I'm taking about your current spending. Besides, education isn't a vice.[2]

Hang in there. Long after I graduated, I continued to attend several football games a year at the Big House.

You: The Big House?

That's the nickname for the University of Michigan Football Stadium.

You: You probably paid no more than $75 a ticket. Such an expense makes sense since you're a sports fan. But it's hardly a big expense, Michael. I mean, seventy-five bucks a couple of times a year isn't exactly a vice.

Let me go on. While I paid about $75 per ticket, each game ultimately cost me about $500.

You: Whoa—that's a lot of hot dogs! How could you possibly spend so much money at a football game?

It wasn't at the concession stand, where I'd spend perhaps $3 on a hot chocolate at the colder games. Usually, I didn't even spend that for fear of missing a play or two while away from my seat.

You: Then how does a game cost you $500, if a ticket is only $75?

When the game is in Michigan and you live in New Jersey, a typical weekend including air-fare, game tickets, and meals can easily cost $500.[3]

You: You flew to Michigan for football games?

Yes, several.

*You: To be clear, you traveled to Michigan to **watch** the game, not to **play** in the game, right?*

I'm 6'1" and nearly two-dimensional.

You: Excuse me?

I'm thin.

You: So?

It's a major understatement to say I don't have a football player's physique.

---

[2] Just ask Pink Floyd.

[3] It would have cost far more if not for great friends who let me stay with them. Thank you Erin and Mitch, Carl and Catherine—Go Blue!

You: Gotcha. So you'd travel by plane to Michigan from New Jersey to watch football games?

Yes. As I've moved, I've traveled to Michigan games from Boston, Chicago, New Jersey, and New Hampshire.

You: So you're rich, crazy, or both.

I'm definitely not rich and I'm married to a psychologist.

You: Point being?

If I were crazy, I would have been diagnosed long ago.

You: But you have to admit it's hypocritical to provide saving advice when you admit to spending $500 to fly to watch a football game—

That was nearly always televised at my home.

You: Oh, this is nuts.

To you, yes. But not to me. And it isn't crazy to the many other thousands of spectators who come to Michigan games from great distances. On the other hand, I imagine if I offered *to pay you* $500 plus expenses to attend a Michigan football game, you'd probably decline.

You: I've got better and more important things to do with my free time.

As expected. However, I highly value the experience of a Michigan football game, including:

> the mile-long walk among throngs of people to the stadium,
> the players taking their warm-ups as the crowd fills in and the excitement builds,
> the marching band's initial playing of "The Victors," with over 110,000 fans singing along, and
> the team running on to the field and jumping up to touch the "Go Blue!" banner.

I cherish every moment.

You: So I can tell.

I hope so—everything I've just described occurs before the game begins.

You: Wow. I see you're really into the experience, so it must be worth it to you. Still, it's something I would never do.

I know. You have your own Michigan football game.

You: No, I don't.

WHAT REALLY MATTERS TO YOU?

Look at your dream sheet again. Think broadly. If you don't like Michigan football, your analogous experience could be going to the Horseshoe in Columbus or the Swamp in Gainesville. If it isn't football, it might be a trip to Fenway Park in Boston or the Staples Center in Los Angeles.

You: What if I'm not into sports?

It could be seeing the New York City Ballet in a performance of "The Nutcracker" at Lincoln Center or listening to the National Symphony Orchestra play at The Kennedy Center in Washington, DC. Perhaps you're not into theatre, sports, or traveling. Instead, your aspiration could be new high-end shoes, jewelry, or a day at the spa.

Still not you? Maybe you hope to start an art collection or splurge on a new technology gadget that plays music, surfs the web, text messages, takes pictures, rotates your tires, and, if you know just how to use it, makes phone calls.

If you're alive, you want something.

You: But I can't afford what I really want.

Maybe not.

You: So I'd rather not admit I want it in the first place.

Why not?

You: If I admit I want something, I'll probably get it—even if I can't afford it.

A common problem!

You: And a rather depressing one.

Whether you live paycheck-to-paycheck or save, you never obtain what you really want, right?

You: If I admitted what I wanted it in the first place, you would be right.

Fair enough. More importantly, you're still not confident the path you are on will allow you to achieve your dreams in the future.

You: Now you get it.

Okay. Good. This is simple. Your problem is caused by your failure to prioritize.

YOU'LL ONLY GET WHAT YOU REALLY WANT IF YOU ACT AS THOUGH YOU REALLY WANT IT

*You: My failure to prioritize? You should see my to-do lists! You should see what is on my plate—both at home and at work. I **only** prioritize.*

Perhaps you are doing a great job prioritizing your *time*. But both time and *money* are finite resources. In the same way you can't make the day 25 hours long, you can't simply add money to your checking account without taking it from somewhere else.

You and I live in the real world; a world which is filled with real constraints. As a result, prioritization is critically important. What would happen if you prioritized everything on your to-do list as most important?

You: That's not possible.

I know it's not possible, but what would happen if you tried to run your life like that?

You: It would be a disaster. Since things that really needed to get done would not be, chaos would reign. It would be as though I wasn't prioritizing at all, so the results would be poor. I'd be unhappy at home and probably a disappointment at work.

Prioritizing everything as very important is as impractical as it is defeating. Prioritizing everything as highly important is equivalent to not prioritizing at all.

You: We're on the same page.

Now, let's return to spending. How do you prioritize your spending?

You: I don't understand the question.

Likely because no one previously asked how you prioritize your spending.

You: Regardless, I still don't get the question.

PRIORITIES, PRIORITIES, PRIORITIES

Prioritization is a different way to look at the familiar issue of not having enough money for everything you want. Today, you're probably not prioritizing your spending.

You: I certainly don't think about it that way.

Few people do. As a result, you are left with the same chaos and stress you previously described in the hypothetical scenario where you did not prioritize your time.

As a result, key financial choices are made based on how much money is in the bank when the decision has to be made.

You: Not the best way to make a decision.

Of course not. For most people, paycheck-to-paycheck living goes something like this:

Payday: Easy day for spending. Pay off a couple of nearly overdue bills, go out to lunch, and grab a gift for yourself or someone else.
Corresponding Money Attitude: A cross between relaxed and relieved.

Four days prior to the next payday: Before leaving for the restaurant, verify you have enough money in your checking account. Yup, you can go out tonight as long as it isn't too expensive.
Corresponding Money Attitude: Aware.

Two days before payday: Before leaving the house, check the account balances online. You have enough money to pay for gas on the way to work and one other thing you need to get done. Bill that came in the mail last week will have to wait until next payday. Ugh, and rent (or mortgage) payment is due next week also.
Corresponding Money Attitude: Frustrated.

Day before payday: Look online at bank web site. Balance still positive. "Phew." Will pay that other thing tomorrow. May have to pack lunch or conveniently ask friend to pick up lunch today with, "I'll get you tomorrow" comment.
Corresponding Money Attitude: Stressed out.

Whether the above feels familiar to you personally, it's a very common cycle in society today. As I state in Chapter 1, studies put between half and two-thirds of all Americans living paycheck-to-paycheck.

You: Why does it play out that way?

Although many people struggle to save, most will do anything to avoid our bank balances dipping below zero. We don't want to bounce checks. We do want to pay our bills. Taken together, when we see our checking account balance at $8.38, we find a way to dramatically lower our spending.[4]

MATERIAL BENEFITS OF SPENDING LESS

With Saving Strategy 9, we talk about ways you can trick yourself into spending less of your paycheck. Here we emphasize the material benefits of spending less.

You: The material benefits of spending less? Sounds like an oxymoron.

Like jumbo shrimp?

You: Or poor trust-fund-baby.

Well-said. In fact, the material benefits of spending less are real. Most importantly, doing so allows you to spend with comfort on items or services you value most highly. By obtaining the discipline to prioritize your spending, you're able to save. When you review what genuinely matters, you find things to cut. Not only things you don't need, but also items you routinely overpay for.

You: Like the examples in Chapter 9.

Yes—don't blow off the recurring minor.

You: Right.

By prioritizing your spending, you will be able to spend more on expensive things.

You: This is so not like other personal finance books.

I know! Wait until we get to the section about not budgeting.

You: Surely, you jest.

Yes, but not about budgeting and don't call me Shirley.[5]

---

[4] During college, I once withdrew five dollars from an ATM. At the time, only one ATM on campus allowed you to withdraw money in $5 increments. I doubt it's even possible today.

[5] Kareem Abdul Jabbar has had significant financial problems in his life. If you don't get the relevance of this fact, you've obviously never heard of Ted Striker nor laughed out loud at airport parking announcements.

YOU CAN SPEND ON EXPENSIVE THINGS JUST BECAUSE YOU WANT TO

Although I'm not rich, my trips to Michigan for football games are affordable. I can take such periodic weekend trips to the Midwest or splurge on Red Sox tickets because I make those expenses high priorities in my life.

You: Why?

Because I value them highly. If I didn't, I wouldn't have the money for the expense. Furthermore, while I wouldn't be able to afford it, I wouldn't care.

You: Like me. I have no desire to go to Michigan.

But you do have aspirations on hold because they seem unrealistic based on your financial situation today.

*You: They're **not** realistic.*

Fine, not today. But what about a year from now or two years from now? Start taking the actions outlined throughout this book, *focusing on what really matters* while referencing your dreams. In fairly short order, you will be thrilled to discover what's not only possible but also relatively easy to achieve. Furthermore, the things you dream about today will turn out to be even better than you imagine.

You: Now how do you know that?

Let's say going to a very exclusive restaurant is something you crave. When you're out at such a dinner and know you can afford it, the food tastes better.

Perhaps attending a big-time sporting event is something you dream about. When you're at the Super Bowl with great seats and you know you can afford it, the field looks better and beer tastes better.

When you can afford to live your dream, it will be better—no matter what the dream is.

You: Why?

Because all you're thinking about is the dream.

You: What else would I be thinking about?

How you're going to afford it.

You: But if I've prioritized it beforehand, I know I can afford it.

Exactly.

You: Making the experience much more enjoyable.

Now you understand the bona fide material upside of spending less.

You: Doing so allows me to spend with comfort on items I value highly.

Yes, even if such goals seem like far-off dreams today. Here's your super-simple plan:

1. Go ahead and dream.
2. Prioritize your spending.
3. Live your dreams.

One of the best ways to speed up this important process is to hide your money.

You: Hide my money? Like in a Swiss bank account?

Not quite. You can hide your money right here in this country.

You: Who am I hiding it from?

Yourself.

You: Why am I hiding it?

You won't spend what you don't see.

You: True. How do I hide it?

Glad you asked.

CASE STUDIES

FIVE WAYS TO BE (OR NOT TO BE) FISCALLY RESPONSIBLE

Adapted from a post to the *Beyond Paycheck to Paycheck* blog, August 27, 2008

Successful sustainable saving requires fiscal responsibility while avoiding a cheap lifestyle. Your time on Earth is too short to constantly deprive yourself. Instead, live in balance.

Since examples are helpful, here's a list of ten ways I am fiscally responsible and not cheap. But the list comes with a twist—it's actually two lists of five. First are five ways I am fiscally responsible and perhaps, to others, cheap. Second are five ways I am not cheap and to others, perhaps, completely reckless with my spending.

You be the judge. To me, it's all about balance.

Top Five Ways I Am Fiscally Responsible

1. We reuse sandwich bags.

At both my home and office, we recycle virtually everything possible. To that end, we reuse certain items, like sandwich bags, most people discard after a single use. While environmental friendliness motivates our behavior, we spend less on items like sandwich bags, freezer bags, and paper than we would if we simply trashed them.

2. We have just one car.

By a ratio of two to one, my wife and I have more kids than cars. While a one-car family won't work for everyone, it's viable for many people who think otherwise.

Must I rent a car on occasion? Indeed. Does the rare rental car expense approach the cost of owning a second car? Not even close. With no payment, no insurance, no maintenance, and no gas on a second car, we come out way ahead. Bonus: we drive less.

3. Our car has been around a while.

The car we own is a seven year-old Saturn. Since our first car was seven years old before it died, we've had only two cars in 14 years.

Leasing gets you a new car every three to four years for a lower monthly payment than buying the same car. But if you purchase a car and keep it beyond the length of the car loan, you own a car but have no car payments.

Congratulations! You've entered the Promised Land of Savings. You can easily save more every month until you purchase a new car. It is no wonder those who reach the Promised Land of Savings once do so repeatedly.

No difference exists between your lifestyle during the last month of the car loan and the first month without the payment, yet you can easily save the $389.50—or whatever it was you were paying for the last few years—for a long time to come.

4. We genuinely enjoy cheap thrills.

Many weekend days we spend virtually no money. Last Saturday, we went to the public pool—a huge thrill for my young daughters—and brought a picnic lunch with us. Cost: $2.00 total plus a small amount for groceries.

On Sunday evening, we went to the beach and took a zillion pictures of the girls. It was at sunset and the photography and emotions were spectacular. Total cost: $0.00, although we'll spend a few dollars printing pictures later.

Spending time with friends, at their homes or ours, is another free or minimal cost activity which usually winds up being among the highlights of any weekend.

5. We drink store-brand soda.

When it comes to soda (or, as my Midwestern friends say, "pop"), we don't care if it's a Pepsi® product, a Coke® product, or a generic one. We refuse to pay more than $0.99 for a 2-liter bottle of soda. So when store brand ginger ale is 77 cents and they want $1.33 for 7-Up®, the ginger ale goes in our cart. We wouldn't call store-brand soda a thrill and it doesn't make a big dent in the grocery bill, but when you're buying 45-cent strawberries (see page 19), you've got to do something to save at the supermarket.

Now, the flip slide.

Five Ways I'm Not Cheap

1. I pay for experiences other people avoid.

Before I had children, I routinely paid airfare to Detroit, plus the expense of a rental car, *just* to see a 3.5-hour long University of Michigan football game live. Since I moved from Ann Arbor in 1996, I've done this upwards of five times a season. The cost varies for each weekend, but averages around $500 per trip. My expenses would be much higher if not for the generous hospitality of friends who live nearby.

Since the weekend is an absolute thrill for me, the money I spend is totally worth it. However, spending hundreds of dollar to visit Ann Arbor for a day or two would be extremely wasteful for most other people. (e.g. Penn State fans).

2. I don't camp.

Instead of staying at a hotel, you can save a lot of money on vacation by camping. But that's a non-starter for me. I've authentically camped only once in my life, with a bunch of business school students in Utah during a week of non-stop ~~fun and sun~~ pain and rain. I came home and announced to my fiancé the trip was the most fun I never wanted to experience again.

It certainly costs more to stay in a hotel, but doing so dramatically increases the value and the effectiveness of my "re-charge," making the additional expense worth it. But I know others who find greater revitalization from sleeping under the stars. Those people should continue to do what they're doing, but I'm happy to see them on the hiking trails the next day.

3. I drink Tropicana® orange juice.

Yup, that's what the guy who wrote *The Savings Solution* drinks nearly every morning. "Liquid gold" a friend of mine once called it! I realize my OJ choice flies in the face of the 77-cent soda decision, but it works for me. I don't drink coffee—I'm allergic to caffeine— and **Tropicana orange juice** is my in-the-home splurge (But, if I'm at a restaurant for breakfast, I'll have water please.).

4. Up north, outerwear really matters, especially in the winter.

Although my monthly spending on clothing approaches zero, I own one pair of Timberland® boots, one L.L. Bean® raincoat, and one phenomenal winter coat. None were cheap. I purchased the boots before the aforementioned trek to Utah in 1998, the raincoat in 2001, and the winter coat back in 1996. The boots still make hiking—the ultimate cheap thrill—more comfortable while the raincoat has saved me during many a brisk rainy Saturday afternoon in Ann Arbor.

When I went to Filene's® in Boston to buy a winter coat, I told the clerk I walked to work. I also informed her I wasn't into style.[6] Instead, I simply wanted the warmest coat available. She showed me a coat. I put it on. Within seconds, I began to sweat.

It cost what it cost. It still keeps me toasty twelve years later and has been worth every penny, especially when you consider the many cold winters it helped me through.

---

[6] My girlfriend begrudgingly verified this fact.

5. A diamond really is forever.

As a mineral, diamonds are worthless. Yet there I was, handing over a sum of money exceeding the value of my car, for a single diamond.

Although buying an engagement ring for my girlfriend wasn't purely a financial decision, I avoiding being talked up by the jeweler. I also didn't buy the ring at an expensive retail store with a patented color box. Instead, I bought the stone in Boston's diamond district, where prices are relatively competitive.

I had two thoughts in mind as I spent a large sum to purchase an incredibly small object.[7] First, I was only going to purchase an engagement ring once. Second, my girlfriend would wear whatever I bought every day.

Every single day.

For the rest of her life.

So I splurged. Call me crazy. But I still smile when I see it on her finger. It was—and still is—totally worth it.

TEN WAYS TO SAVE MONEY WHILE RUINING YOUR LIFE

Adapted from a post to the *Beyond Paycheck to Paycheck* blog, July 22, 2009

If you're already saving (i.e., living *Beyond Paycheck to Paycheck*), making any of the following decisions is absurd.[8] However, if you are living paycheck to paycheck, your financial predicament might compel you to make some of the otherwise poor choices below. As such, this list highlights a few ways you sell yourself short by not saving. (Nothing the rest of this book can't help with, of course.)

Ten Ways to Save Money While Ruining Your Life
Or, said another way,
Ten Ways to Be Cheap Yet Financially Irresponsible.

---

[7] If you include not vomiting from once-in-a-lifetime nervousness, I had three thoughts.

[8] Yes, I've been absurd from time to time. I am not proud of it.

1. Comparison-shopping cold medicine

If you, your significant other, or your kid is sick and needs medicine, go to the store and buy some medicine. Period. That's it. You don't first go to the drug store, then the grocery store, and then visit drugstore.com to see who has the best price. You buy the freaking medicine. If you want to save money on OTC medicine, comparison-shop only within the first store you visit.

2. Regularly avoiding nights out with friends

You: Why spend money I don't want to on a place I didn't choose?

Because you only live once. If you like the people who you would be going out with or need a change of scenery, go out. You don't have to order something expensive nor must you agree to evenly split the bill if half the group orders fillet and the other half—your half—asks for soda water with a slice of lemon. You don't have to spend a lot to have a good time, but you do have to leave your house to retain your sanity.

3. Using a dial-up Internet connection

I just called your home to explain why high-speed is much more convenient, but your line was busy.

4. Not replacing old shoes or sneakers

Because I buy new sneakers so infrequently, I just re-learned how great new sneakers feel. But it wasn't good for my feet (nor would it be for yours) to wear shoes to the point I didn't recall what an arch felt like.

5. Driving an Unsafe Car

During the last 16 years, I've owned a total of two cars. Obviously, I'm not a "car person," so I benefit from the no-car-payment strategy. But such a plan isn't for the flashy. Few young ladies were impressed with my red Plymouth Neon back in the day, and no one awes the Saturn sedan I cruise through town in now.

However, if I ever felt my car wasn't safe and couldn't be reasonably repaired, I would get rid of it immediately. I can't imagine putting my safety behind my desire to avoid a car payment. You shouldn't consider it either.

6. Not giving to the important causes in your life

We all have soft spots for certain missions. Find the special causes which speak to you and give generously to them. Give time and give money. You will get far more back than you put in, often in ways you don't understand. Withholding charity costs you far more than the check you could write to help others.

7. Not updating sporting equipment

Thanks to multiple sprains and torn ligaments, my weak ankles require I wear braces whenever I play "basketball." I'm smart enough to take the extra ten minutes every time I play to put on the braces. But I'm still an idiot because my ankle braces are more than four years old and were, therefore, not effective in preventing another ankle sprain a few weeks ago. You might not need new gear every season, but you do have to replace your equipment periodically. Don't be so cheap it costs you.

8. Delaying a visit to the doctor to save the co-pay

Even if you have a high co-payment like I do, it's not a good idea to delay seeing the doctor if you are sick or have sprained your ankle again. It might cost you more in the long-term, since your illness might become more serious and costly.

9. Not bringing water on a hike even if you have to buy it

I don't like purchasing bottled water. (You know what Evian® spelled backwards is, right?) Nonetheless, I drink a lot of water. When I'm home, this is easily accomplished without buying a bottle.

But since I don't like filling a thermos at a public restroom, you'll probably see me with bottled water when I'm traveling.

It wasn't always so. Years ago, my girlfriend and I would often go on lengthy hikes and invariably forget to bring water. Without a container and not wanting to spend money on bottled water, we went without. But water is important on a warm summer day on a very long hike, even in Michigan. Don't be dumb—buy the water.

10. Skipping a vacation

If you can't afford a vacation, don't go on *that* vacation. Go on a vacation you *can* afford. If you can't afford any vacation-related expense, then take time off and spend time locally. If you have paid vacation time, you can afford a vacation. Find one. Life is too short.

SAVING MONEY WHILE YOU'RE SPENDING IT

Adapted from a post to the *Beyond Paycheck to Paycheck* blog, December 24, 2007

My wife and I are expecting our second child next month. I would have preferred a December due date to take advantage of an increased child tax credit and additional personal tax exemption, but you just can't plan everything.

Before child number two arrives, my wife and I really wanted to get a night away—just the two of us. Since we haven't slept more than 15 feet from our first child since she was born and baby number two's impending arrival means now is likely to be our only chance for a night away for years more, we are ready. So we scheduled a little R & R in Boston for a Saturday night in mid-November.

Unfortunately, our daughter got sick the night before, so we postponed. You just can't plan everything.

We rescheduled the quick getaway for a month later.

Unfortunately, our daughter got sick the night before, so we postponed. You just can't plan everything.

Our daughter is remarkably healthy, mind you. Furthermore, we didn't cancel our plans over some little cold. On the contrary, she had the fun stuff which keeps parents awake all night. Persevering, we rescheduled for this past Saturday night.

Fortunately, no one got sick and we had a great time.

You: What does this have to do with saving money?

Plenty. In going away for the weekend, we enjoyed—and spent—far more than we would during an ordinary weekend. Still, we never threw the baby out with the bathwater.

You: Interesting idiom to use.

Saving Strategy 8, Spend With Comfort on What You Value Most, not only motivated us to take our mini-vacation in the first place, but also guided our entire weekend. Specifically, it led to a nice meal in Boston's North End.[9] It also meant dessert afterwards.

But there's also a flip side to the strategy.

You: Which is?

Do **not** spend highly on things you do not value.

You: Such as?

Parking. Generally speaking, I hate paying for parking. But I *particularly* dislike overpaying for parking. The hotel where we stayed charges $35 to self-park your car for a single night. During the workweek, when all the neighboring lots are full and street parking is non-existent, you probably wouldn't have much of a choice but to park at the hotel's expensive lot. But I figured nearby lots would cost much less on a Saturday night with the business travelers gone. Still, before I drove into a neighboring lot, I decided to invest five minutes—

You: Invest? Five minutes?

---

[9] If you've never been to this neighborhood in the Hub, you've missed some seriously ridiculous wicked good Italian food.

You can invest more than money. In fact, time is one of your most valuable assets (Remember the miracle of compounding interest in Chapter 2?). Although I decided to invest five minutes to pursue street parking, I found a spot less than three blocks from the hotel in just two minutes. I paid $1.50 at the meter for time before the spot became free for the weekend.

Rather than pay $35 to park overnight, we paid $1.50. While I drive an old Saturn, street parking might not work for someone with a newer and more expensive car. If so, add another way to the list of how nice cars cost far more than their purchase price.

Developing ways to reduce spending without cheapening one's life is the biggest obstacle people face when they haven't started saving, preventing many from moving *Beyond Paycheck to Paycheck*. They simply can't imagine reducing their spending without becoming cheap and miserable. Splurging for a big city getaway while simultaneously minimizing money spent on parking is a simple example of finding a way to save while still thoroughly enjoying yourself.

Yet, saving while spending won't work every time. Had it been pouring rain when I arrived in Boston, I might not have liked the idea of carrying luggage three blocks in a downpour—but then I would have valued the parking much higher. On a decent-weather day like last Saturday in Boston, I'd much prefer to use my $33.50 elsewhere, like on a Red Sox ticket.

You: The Red Sox? In December?

You just can't plan everything.

CHAPTER II
. . . .
Saving Strategy # 9:
You Won't Spend What You Don't See

"Most people should learn to tell their dollars where to
go instead of asking them where they went."
—ROGER W. BABSON

WHERE DOES MOTIVATION COME FROM?

For more than twenty years, top-notch University of Michigan student-athletes received motivational and inspirational lessons from legendary head football coach Bo Schembechler. At the other end of the athletic spectrum, my lanky build and safety-first parents led me to volleyball. With all due respect to my coaches Tom, Pam, and Duane, there was only one Bo.

Consequently, my greatest collegiate influence was Professor Griffin. As I discuss in Chapter 2, Professor Griffin first told me about the miracle of compounding interest, imparting more financial wisdom on me in a single hour than any person before or since. As a direct result of his single lecture, I immediately began saving aggressively upon entering the workforce.

It was easy to do.

You: Why was it so easy? Most people have a hard time saving on their first job's income.

I was a perfect candidate to save aggressively.

You: You had Professor Griffin's lesson.

Yes, but there was more to it than that.

You: What else?

My parents paid for the lion's share of my college expenses.

You: That's huge.

Indeed, I was extremely fortunate for my parent's capable generosity.

You: What else?

The third key element of my savings foundation was surviving college with limited spending money. Other than groceries, I lived on a $100 monthly stipend from the bank of Mom and Dad. (Although I received another $100 for groceries, the first $100 had to pay for copies at the library, my share of utilities at the home I shared with five other "men," all forms of entertainment, (e.g., cover charges, meals outside of my house including the all-too-rare date, and movies), Taco Bell® at 2 AM, and so on. Without a car, I didn't have to worry about a car payment, gas, or insurance, however.

You: I know plenty of people who had it worse.

Me too. But I learned to get by with fairly little. There was absolutely no money for splurging. Consequently, when I received an offer to become an entry-level personal financial planner at a public accounting firm in Detroit, it was as though I had struck gold.

You: The pay was that good?

Not really. The salary was ordinary for a college graduate's first "real" job. However, the compensation was a lot more than the $200 a month plus rent ($319) I had lived on during college. When I moved out of the "house" I shared with five other overgrown guys averaging 6'2", I didn't move to an upscale apartment. I moved to a marginally[1] nicer place with a roommate in a nearby town. As a result, my share of the rent increased by 50 cents a month.

---

[1] At the new place, the refrigerator did *NOT* leak an as-yet-undetermined liquid. Also, if you were to hypothetically place a ball down in the middle of the living room floor, it would *NOT* roll quickly to a corner. Ahh, college housing.

You: That's it?

Yes. My rent for my first year out of college was only fifty cents more than what my parents had paid for my rent during my last year of college. I also purchased a car.

You: What kind?

A Plymouth Neon. The negotiated purchase price was $12,800. Although my Neon did have a 10-disc CD changer, it was a pretty cheap ride. Since I had minimized the two biggest expenses a new graduate incurs[2] (i.e., housing and car payments) I didn't need to spend significantly more than I spent senior year. Yet now I had a real job.

You: Still, it's not like you were making $100,000 a year right out of college, right?

Far from it. I made less than a third of that amount. But it was still a giant raise. In fact, it represented the biggest percentage pay increase I ever received.

You: Makes sense, since you were starting from practically zero.

Right. Armed with small monthly recurring expenses, low standard of living expectations given my entry-level salary, and Professor Griffin's lesson about the miracle of compounding interest, I made a very easy, very aggressive decision.

You: What was that?

I decided to participate in my 401(k) at the maximum allowed percentage.

You: You mean up to the amount your company matched?

No. Unfortunately, my first job didn't offer an employer-matching contribution.

You: Bummer. So what percentage did you contribute?

I started at 19 percent.

You: Nineteen percent of your gross pay?

Yes.

You: That's a lot of retirement saving.

Yes it was.

You: Why 19 percent?

---

[2] Two glaring exceptions are people who move to a city like New York that doesn't require a car and/or those with significant student loans.

That was the most allowed by my plan.

You: My plan doesn't even allow me to contribute that much.

Neither did mine!

You: Then how did you contribute 19 percent?

When I handed the 401(k) enrollment form to my Human Resources representative requesting the maximum contribution the form permitted (14 percent), she remarked to me I was saving a lot. In response, I explained how my tax professor had convinced me of the importance of saving early in my career. Furthermore, I told her I was committed to saving the maximum. At that point, she let me in on a little secret.

*You: A secret? With your HR representative? Sounds juicy! What **was** the secret?*

Sorry—too much build-up. Alas, although the 401(k) enrollment form indicated a maximum 14 percent contribution rate, some people, it turned out, could contribute more.

You: Some people?

Yes.

You: That doesn't seem fair.

I agree with you, but I didn't make the rules.

You: So what was the deal?

People on the low-end of the pay scale at my employer were permitted to contribute up to 19 percent of their gross pay to the 401(k) plan. Those who made bigger bucks were limited to the 14 percent listed on the form (and sometimes even less).[3]

You: Weird.

I thought so too. Nonetheless, after learning of the true limit, I had the following conversation with my HR representative:

Michael: I would like to contribute the *real maximum* of 19 percent.

HR Rep: Sure. Would you like to make the 19 percent contribution effective with your first paycheck?

Michael: Why not?

---

[3] These varying limits were partially due to *discrimination testing* required by the Internal Revenue Service (IRS), meant to ensure meaningful benefits of 401(k) plans go to typical employees, not solely to the higher earners.

HR Rep: It is administratively impossible for us to process your 401(k) contribution request in time for your first pay period. However, we could process your contribution for your second or third pay period and arrange to take enough out of that paycheck to make up for the one or two paychecks we miss.

Michael: Sounds good.

HR Rep: You realize you might wind up with one paycheck which would be less than half of your normal pay?

Michael: No problem. The only way I'll have to deal with a one-time 50 percent or more 401(k) contribution rate is if I receive two outsized paychecks beforehand.

HR Rep: True, but—

Michael: Those one or two big paychecks will leave me with plenty of money. I'll easily be able to get through the period when I receive an unusually small net pay due to the one-time catch-up 401(k) plan contribution.

HR Rep: You're sure?

Michael: I am. I have no money now so this won't be too big of a test.

As a result of this conversation, I contributed 57 percent of my third paycheck to my 401(k) plan. From the next paycheck until I left that job two years later, I contributed 19 percent of my gross pay twice a month, every month.

You: Was it difficult?

No. Since I started saving right away, it was easy. If I had waited a year to begin contributing to my 401(k), I'm sure it would have been much more difficult.

You: Why? If you waited a year before saving in the 401(k), you would have received much bigger paychecks, built up a safety net, and spent a bit more.

While you might be right, it's unlikely. Certainly, it's not what happens for most people who don't contribute to their 401(k) plans.

You: Why not?

Because we become accustomed to living on our full net pay. We spend what we see. As a result, we anticipate the pain of even a 5 percent 401(k) plan contribution. But if we never receive the 5 percent in the first place, it's easy to continue to live without it.

That's what I did when I first started. I simply lived on *what was left*. And that amount, by my standards, was plenty. Quite honestly, it was more than enough.

You: Even to pay for all those trips back to Michigan games?

One perk of working in Detroit was living in Michigan, so the cost of attending Michigan football games was meager compared to what it cost when I subsequently lived elsewhere.

You: Is that why you took a job in Detroit?

Contrary to the opinion of some family members and dear friends, no, proximity to Ann Arbor was not the reason I took a job in Detroit.

During my first year as a real-world employee, I realized I didn't care for the town I moved to after graduation.[4] When my lease ended, I moved to a nicer place in Ann Arbor.

You: Lifestyle creep.

Yes it was, but just a mild case. In fact, when I contemplated my next apartment, *I didn't consider what I could afford* based on my gross income.

You: You just winged it?

No, I viewed the affordability of my next apartment solely from the standpoint of my *net* income.

You: Your net income being your gross income less your income taxes.

And *also subtracting my 401(k) contributions.* I based affordability on my current monthly cash-flow—including saving. I never considered what I could afford if I ceased contributing to my 401(k).

You: Why not?

Since it was money I never saw, it was as though it wasn't mine. Those retirement funds consisted of money I didn't consider to be mine.

Said another way, it was my *future* money, not my *today* money. As a result, 19 percent of my gross pay wasn't available for me to see. More importantly, it wasn't available for me to spend. My starting point for all spending decisions was *after* saving 19 percent of my gross pay.

---

[4] In retrospect, that the name of the town started with "Yps" should have been a clue.

My approach undoubtedly kept my spending decisions more practical. Still with a roommate, my share of the rent increased by a mere $41 when I moved back to Ann Arbor. The small increase solidified my ability to save aggressively, especially since my raise earlier in the year was $208 per month.

THE SECOND REAL WORLD, OR WHEN IT'S NO LONGER FUN LIVING WITH SOMEONE YOU'RE NOT SLEEPING WITH

As my income increased in future years, saving became easier still. While my expenses have increased significantly—

You: Why have your expenses increased so dramatically?

I'm now married with two children. I could go on about the appetite of my two girls, but trust me; together they eat more groceries than I did in college. I now live in a home with three bedrooms. My roommate is my wife, not some random guy who also wants to live in the same neighborhood I do. While my wife brings in money today—after a million years in school—the kids don't chip in.

You: Don't you think they should learn financial responsibility? You don't want them freeloading.

My kids are very young.

You: Oh.

My wife and I have been married more than eleven years. Despite our expenses increasing during that time, we've always saved a healthy percentage of our incomes. We've done so by consistently making spending decisions assuming a certain level of saving. For example, we've *never* lived on what our net paychecks would have been if we ceased retirement plan contributions.

You: You've got to admit, Michael, few people live that way.

Actually, many folks do.

*You: What? Most people do **not** save a big percentage of their incomes.*

Correct. However, many people *do* make spending decisions which don't reflect their net income. Instead of spending *less* than they make (as I do and as you will), many people spend *more* than they make. As a result, they struggle from paycheck to paycheck.

YOU CAN SPEND—JUST NOT MORE THAN YOU HAVE

Don't follow the masses by spending just a little bit more than you make. That herd mentality is the recipe for disaster which might have you struggling today.

Turn over a new leaf. Spend a bit less than you make. From this point forward, imagine you make less than you do. Spend that reduced amount. Save the difference.

You: Impossible.

No, it's not. Sustainable saving is achievable with the right approach and attitude.

You: You're not going to deliver one of these hokey self-help speeches!

Definitely not. Now is *not* the time to roll out the yoga mats. The only attitude shift necessary is your approach to saving. Most people permit their savings rate to be the consequence of their earlier choices.

You: Meaning?

For them, saving is about what they have left at the end of the month. Said another way, the amount they save is the result of the spending decisions made previously.

You: Makes sense.

It makes sense, but it doesn't work. Instead, you've first got to think about saving. By doing so, your spending decisions will be based on what you can truly afford—*after saving*. As a result, *you* choose the amount you wish to save, rather than saving only what is left at the end of the month.

When you view saving as a must-do item and prioritize it accordingly, you spend less. When it seems like there isn't anything in your checking account (because there isn't—the money is in another account you don't follow daily), you spend less.

HOW TO SPEND LESS THAN YOU EARN

To spend less than you earn, first follow the previous eight simple saving strategies. Doing so allows you to creatively and enjoyably spend less without cramping your lifestyle.

You: Then what?

The key to successfully implementing Saving Strategy 9 is automation.

You: Automation?

You won't find an easier way to save than by automating your savings.

You: I'm still not sure what you're talking about.

In Chapter 9, we discuss the importance of monitoring recurring expenses.

You: Such expenses add up.

That's right. Even relatively minor expenses, like cell phone and cable bills, become financially meaningful after many months and years of payments. Such bills are dangerous because you make the spending decision only once yet are billed every month forever. To make the bills stop, you must take action.

You: Like cancel service.

Right.

You: Geez, it's like getting off a drug.

A fairly dramatic analogy, but such subscription services are indisputably hard habits to break.

You: Why are you bringing this up again?

To remind you of the power of automation. In Saving Strategy 7, automation works against you. In Saving Strategy 9, you learn how to put automation to work for you. Instead of placing expenses on auto-pilot, put savings on auto-pilot. Set up your financial life so, absent any additional effort on your part, you automatically save. If you forget to save, you still save. Make your financial life so you must consciously "turn off saving" to spend every dollar.

You: How do I arrange for automatic savings?

MORE THAN THE 401(K)

A 401(k) plan is the best place to start. However, automatic savings are about more than your 401(k) plan.

You: Good, I don't have a 401(k) plan.

Unfortunately, you are not alone. While some people might have a 403(b) or a 457 plan which work similarly to a 401(k) plan, others have no workplace retirement plans. But anyone can arrange an Automatic Investment Program (AIP) through an Individual Retirement Account (IRA).

AUTOMATIC INVESTMENT PROGRAMS

You: But aren't you supposed to contribute several thousand dollars to an IRA?

You can do so, yes.

*You: I don't have several thousand dollars hanging around. I'm reading **The Savings Solution** for crying out loud!*

I know. You don't have to contribute several thousand dollars to an IRA all at once. You can sign up for the AIP offered by most IRA custodians.

You: But what if I can't afford the minimum investment required?

You're wrong.

You: Excuse me?

At Vanguard™, for example, the lowest required automatic savings amount is one dollar. The least frequent contribution period is annually.

You: A dollar a year?

Right. An amount you admit you could afford, correct?

You: Yeah, I could sign up for $1/year right now with no problems.

Of course, a buck every year is below the savings level I hope you'll achieve, but its mere possibility is evidence large sums of money are not required to save for the future. Although greater dollar amounts were once necessary to begin an IRA, they are no longer required. No matter how little you have already put aside, you can begin saving for the future today.

IT'S NOT "PAY YOURSELF FIRST," IT'S "PAY YOUR FUTURE SELF FIRST"

The "Pay yourself first" doctrine is well-known in the financial planning community.

You: What does "Pay yourself first" mean?

Before you pay your bills, before you spend money on anything from required groceries to discretionary concert tickets, pay yourself first by saving something.

You: And your thoughts? Do I have to do this too?

When you automate saving as discussed, you're already paying yourself first. It's as though the first bill of the month is you.

You: Me?

Yes, you.

You: I'm a bill?

Yes, although instead of paying yourself first, you're paying your Future Self first.

You: My Future Self?

From "The Office" episode "Branch Closing"

Jim Halpert: I don't have a ton of contact with the Scranton branch, *but* before I left, I took a box of Dwight's stationary. So, from time to time, I send Dwight faxes. From himself. From the future.

Jim Halpert: [Reading fax] Dwight, at 8 AM today, someone poisons the coffee. Do **not** drink the coffee. More instructions will follow. Cordially, Future Dwight.

[After Dwight reads the fax, he observes Stan walk out of the kitchen with his coffee. Dwight runs to Stan and knocks the cup from Stan's hand while screaming "NO!"]

Even more likely: you'll thank *me* later for my advice to pay your Future Self.

You: What are you talking about?

In some ways, the bill you pay to your Future Self is like any other bill. You should pay the bill when it's due—don't skip it. After all, it will cost you in the long run if you miss a payment.

On the other hand, don't treat the bill like any other bill. Because, unlike a utility or credit card bill, when you pay your Future Self, the money doesn't leave You.

You: It doesn't?

It leaves Current You's checking account, but it's still Your money.

You: My Future Self's money.

Right. And your Future Self is part of You. Current You pays Future Self.

You: This is weird.

Look at the Figures 11-1 and 11-2 which show the Universe of Money and how it exists for those living paycheck to paycheck.

Figure 11-1
The Universe of Money

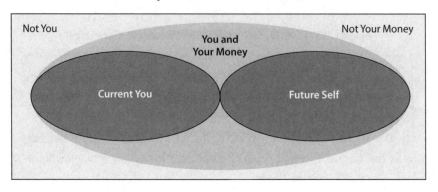

Figure 11-2
Your Universe of Money, If You're Living Paycheck to Paycheck

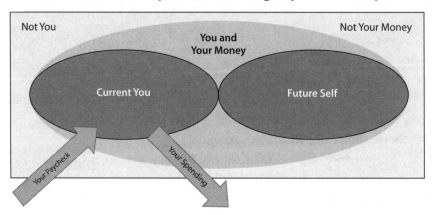

Your Future Self bill should be the rare payment you enjoy making. It's also the only bill that doesn't lower your net worth.[5]

You: A bill which doesn't lower my net worth?

---

[5] In fact, your Future Self bill can increase your net worth.

SAVING IS ABOUT MORE THAN RETIREMENT PLANNING

The benefits of automatic savings go well beyond retirement plan saving. For example, establishing an emergency fund is a main concern.

You: What should my priorities be?

See Chapter 7 of *Beyond Paycheck to Paycheck*. No matter the reason you're saving, you'll be more successful once you automate the process.

Let's say you're eager to begin Saving Strategy 9. As a result, you go to your payroll department and request 10 percent of your pay to be deposited in your savings account with the rest of your paycheck to go to your checking account. This major step forward is represented in Figure 11-3.

Figure 11-3

Your Universe of Money, If You're Saving for Retirement but Otherwise Living Paycheck to Paycheck

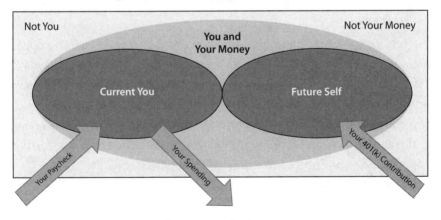

You: I tried that, payroll won't go for it.

Bummer, but possible at some companies. No problem. Time for Plan B.

You: Plan B?

Visit the bank where your check is deposited. Request the bank automatically (and at no charge to you) regularly transfer 10 percent of your pay from your checking account to your saving account. By doing so, you'll enjoy the universe displayed in Figure 11-4.

Figure 11-4

Your Universe of Money, If You're Saving But Your Company Doesn't Offer a Workplace Retirement Account

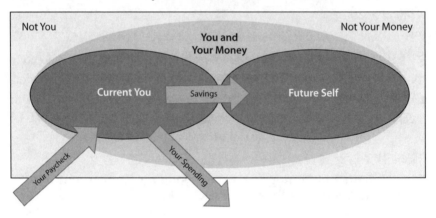

You: "Regularly" is rather vague.

It is. Ten percent of your net pay also needs to be translated into a dollar amount for the bank. As for the transfer date, choose the day after payday.[6] Tell the bank what that means for you (e.g., every other Friday, every Friday, on the 15th and 30th, etc.) Paying your Future Self in this manner (i.e., coinciding with each payday) is more sustainable and realistic than saving at the end of the month alone. Indeed, once you decide to make regular payments to your Future Self, you view each payday equally.

You: Not like now.

What do you mean?

You: Now I get two paychecks a month. The second one comes around the time my rent/mortgage is due, so it's like I don't have a second

---

[6] Use the day *after* payday just in case of a rare problem with your paycheck.

monthly paycheck. At least it feels that way, so it's really hard to save anything from my second check.

I want you to get away from that.

You: Me too!

Automatic saving means no paycheck is "matched" with a specific spending event (e.g, rent, mortgage, car payment) any more than you have a paycheck earmarked for saving. With automation, *part of every paycheck goes towards saving.*

You: That does sound better.

It is better. Plus, remember saving happens without any ongoing conscious effort on your part.

You: What do you mean?

You set up automation one time. Then it just happens—with every paycheck. Ideally you'll start with your workplace retirement account (e.g., 401(k), 403(b), 457). If not, you can choose an IRA, a Roth IRA, or a regular savings account. Soon, you will be living on the reduced net income flowing to Current You's checking account. With every paycheck You, Current You, and your Future Self grow wealthier as your saving is officially on the "I feel no pain" auto-pilot plan.

Figure 11-5

Your Ideal Universe of Money

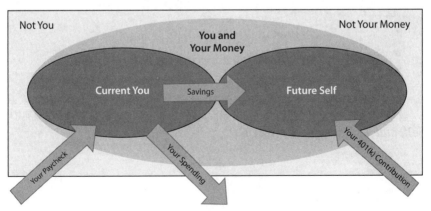

THE BEST BILL IN THE WORLD

You: Earlier, you noted paying my Future Self could actually increase my net worth. How?

If you can contribute to a workplace retirement plan such as a 401(k) or 403(b), you have an opportunity to instantly increase your net worth. Here's how it works.

Let's say your gross pay for a particular period is $3,000. It doesn't matter whether your paycheck covers a week, two weeks, or a month. Just imagine the pay period provides you with $3,000 of gross income.

You: Out of which comes a mountain of taxes.

Correct, and every penny of tax you pay is gone forever. But imagine you could keep some of the money you currently pay in taxes?

You: I'm pretty sure those taxes are required, Mr. Financial Guy.

Ah, but you can reduce your taxes.

You: Within your paycheck? I thought you could only get creative on your tax return.

You can save money in both places. I prefer saving from my paycheck because paychecks happen sooner and more often than tax returns.

Next is a list of the easy steps required to pay your Future Self *and reduce your income taxes at the same time.*

You: You've got my attention.

Good. It's simple. You're ready?

You: Go.

➤ Step 1: Enroll in your 401(k) plan.

➤ Step 2: There is no Step 2.

You: That's it?

That's it.

You: How does saving in my 401(k) plan lower my taxes, pay my Future Self, and increase my net worth?

Let's say instead of being paid the entirety of your $3,000 gross pay less taxes, you contribute 10 percent ($300), to your 401(k) plan. Assuming a 25 percent income tax rate, your paycheck looks like Figures 11-6, 11-7, and 11-8.

Figure 11-6

The Positive Effect of a 401(k) Contribution on Your Net Worth

No 401(k) Contribution		$300 401(k) Contribution	
Gross Pay	$ 3,000	Gross Pay	$ 3,000
		401(k) Contribution	$ (300)
		Revised Gross Pay	$ 2,700
Taxes @ 25%	− $ (750)	Taxes @ 25%	− $ (675)
Amount of paycheck	$ 2,250	Amount of paycheck	$ 2,025
401(k) contribution	+ $ −	401(k) contribution	+ $ 300
Increase to Net Worth	$ 2,250	Increase to Net Worth	$ 2,325

Difference: $ 75

If you don't contribute to your 401(k) plan, you receive $2,250 after taxes. By contributing $300 to your 401(k) plan, you receive a $2,025 paycheck.

You: So I lose $225 by signing up for the 401(k) plan?

No, not really. Current You loses $225, but your Future Self gains $300. You are up $75.

You: How come I'm up $75? And how come my net pay didn't go down by $300, only $225?

The answer to both of those questions is the same—your contribution to your 401(k) plan reduces your gross income. As such, the amount you owe in taxes is reduced. If you're in the 25 percent tax bracket, every dollar you contribute to your 401(k) saves you 25 cents of taxes.

You: So the tax savings increase my net worth?

Exactly. Your taxes decrease and Your net worth increases because your Future Self receives more than Current You gives up. A single 401(k) contribution does all of that. Sometimes, it does even more.

You: Do tell.

Figure 11-7

Universe of Money: Gross Income of $3,000 and no 401(k) Contibution

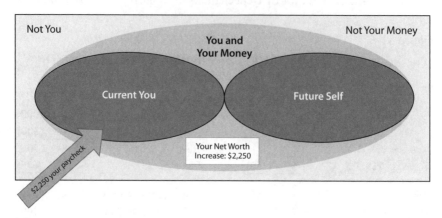

Figure 11-8

Universe of Money: Gross Income of $3,000 and $300 401(k) Contibution

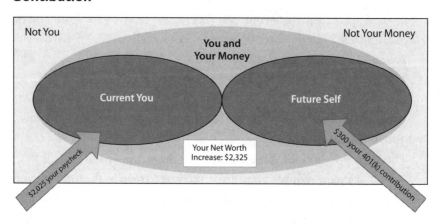

MATCHING PROGRAMS

When you pay your Future Self via a 401(k) contribution, your net worth increases by significantly more at some companies than at others.

You: I need to get a job at one of the first group of companies.

Not a bad idea.

You: But how can I find out if a company has a souped-up retirement plan?

Just ask.

You: Ask them what?

Ask, "Do you match an employee's retirement plan contributions?"

You: They'll tell me?

Of course! It's part of your compensation package. You wouldn't think of taking a new job without knowing the salary, would you?

You: You're right. No matter how bad the economy is, no matter how much I need a job, I always ask how much the job pays.

Good. Now just add the question about matching contributions. Imagine a company which matches your 401(k) contributions. See Figures 11-9 and 11-10.

Figure 11-9

The Ridiculously Positive Effect on Your Net Worth of a 401(k) Contribution With an Employer Match

No 401(k) Contribution			$300 401(k) Contribution		
Gross Pay	$	3,000	Gross Pay	$	3,000
			401(k) Contribution	– $	(300)
			Revised Gross Pay	$	2,700
Taxes @ 25%	– $	(750)	Taxes @ 25%	– $	(675)
Amount of paycheck	$	2,250	Amount of paycheck	$	2,025
			401(k) contribution	+ $	300
			Employer Matching Contribution	+ $	300
Increase to Net Worth	$	2,250	Increase to Net Worth	$	2,625

Difference: $ 375

Figure 11-10

Universe of Money: Gross Income of $3,000 and $300 401(k) Contibution With a 100% Employer Match

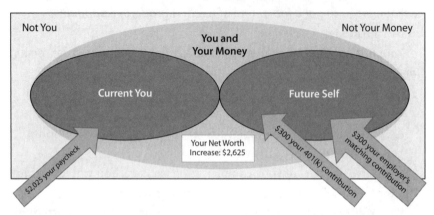

By making a one-time $225 sacrifice, Your net worth immediately goes up by $600.[7] This happens regardless of your investment performance. Heck, it happens regardless of your investment selection or even the existence of an investment advisor.

Gary: Here I am!

Somehow I just don't quite feel like saying "Hello!"

You: What are you doing here?

Gary: I'm ready to offer you some tips to maximize your investment performance.

You: But Michael just told me how to instantaneously more than double my money without any risk. Can you do that?

Gary: No.

You: So why are you here again?

Gary: I can help you with your IRA money.

You: How so?

Gary: Can you say "annuity?"

You: I don't think that's a good idea.

---

[7] Recall a typical company match is dollar for dollar. If you put in $300, your employer puts in $300. Read Chapter 7 of *Beyond Paycheck to Paycheck* for more information.

It's not.

You: You guys are making me uncomfortable.

Gary: Want to go golfing? Free dinner?

You: I'm outta here.

Gary: Me too. These books are a terrible place to do business.

Your kind of business, Gary.

You: I think he's gone.

Good. You're still hanging around though, right?

You: Sure. "I'm outta here" was just a line.

You will, of course, need to invest the money in your 401(k) plan. Since this is not an investing book, I'll limit the investment education to just one sentence:

> The greater the amount of time between now and when you expect to retire, the higher the percentage of your savings should be in stock-based mutual funds or exchange traded funds (ETFs).

But remember, you do not need to take any risk to instantly increase your net worth—just incorporate Saving Strategy 9 into your retirement plan.

IF YOU CAN'T AFFORD YOUR 401(K) PLAN

Whenever I hear someone say, "I can't afford to contribute to my 401(k) plan," I correct the person.

*You: Isn't it **possible** someone might not be able to afford to contribute to their 401(k) plan?*

No, not really. It *is* possible an individual might not be able to afford a 401(k) contribution *and* all his other expenses. However, if he chooses to cut his 401(k) contribution and not the other spending, he is cutting the wrong thing.

Total Candor: you can't afford NOT to contribute to the 401(k) plan. Add in a possible matching contribution, and it becomes an absolute no-brainer.

Not contributing to your 401(k) plan at least as much as your employer matches is a major mistake.

You: I'd rather not make major mistakes.

Me too.

THE BLINDNESS ADVANTAGE: YOU WON'T SPEND WHAT YOU CAN'T SEE

Would you like to know the best part of Saving Strategy 9?

You: That's easy. What can possibly beat an instantaneous no-risk increase in your net worth?

Fair enough. Would you like to know the second best part of Saving Strategy 9?

You: Sure.

No budgeting.

You: Did you just say, "No budgeting?"

I sure did.

You: Can you say that?

Too late now, isn't it?

You: This is a book about saving and cash-flow management. You'd better explain your "no budgeting" comment.

I have a whole chapter on that topic.

You: When?

Now.

CASE STUDIES

SAVING ON ONE INCOME

Adapted from the *Beyond Paycheck to Paycheck* blog, August 1, 2008

It's Friday, so it's time for this week's reader-submitted Q & A. If you'd like to submit a question, simply visit http://totalcandor.com/blog/q-a or send a question to questions@totalcandor.com

How can I possibly save on one income?
—Sue W., Clinton, NJ

STRAIGHTFORWARD ANSWER

You save on one income the same way you save on two incomes—spend less than you make.

More Detailed Explanation:
Saving is Simple

While not necessarily easy to accept, saving truly is simple. There are no tricks. There are no gimmicks. If you spend more than you make, you will always struggle. Period.

On the other hand, if you spend less than you make, you are—*by definition*—saving. Many people think the answer to their financial prayers is to make more money, be it via a second job, a spouse who begins to work for pay, or a big raise.

You: Or the lottery.

Also not a financial strategy.

Even those who successfully raise their incomes frequently fail to increase their savings.

You: Why?

Because just as soon as we make enough money to live comfortably, we want to live extravagantly. Many people I meet today make a lot more money than they did ten years earlier, yet continue to struggle financially. In order to take control of your finances, you must own *your* spending habits.

All or None? Don't Go There

Some people who feel they can't afford to save as much as they should—whatever that means—save nothing at all. Don't fall into that trap. You're familiar with the bathwater, right?

You: Yes. Dirty.

Absolutely, but you know not to throw the baby out with it. Everybody can find five bucks to save today. Five dollars. It's a start. Once you've found your five, keep at it. Save $5 a day for a few days or weeks. Then, look to save ten—it's only another five bucks. Soon enough, you'll be on your way.

ONCE-IN-A-LIFETIME SAVING OPPORTUNITY FOR NEW COLLEGE GRADUATES

Adapted from the *Beyond Paycheck to Paycheck* blog of July 28th, 2008

Congratulations! If you just graduated from college and got a job, you're going to make more money this year than you did last year.

You: That's what they tell me.

Furthermore, you're going to earn more next year than you will earn this year.

You: How did you hear about my raise before I did? And how much am I getting?

I don't know anything about your raise.

You: Then how do you know I'll make more money next year than this year?

Since you won't graduate until at least April, you'll work less than eight full-time months this calendar year. However, your income will be far higher next year when you work January through December.

You: That's cool, I guess. But where's the opportunity?

In tax planning.

You: Sounds boring.

It is boring. If you want excitement, go jump out of a plane.[8] If you want help saving, keep reading.

You: Okay. Go ahead, bore me.

The federal income tax withholding rules drive the strategy. Fortunately, the rules are quite simple.

You: Really?

No, but you can follow them.

You: I'll give it a shot.

In order to avoid interest and penalties when you file your income tax return, you must have withheld from your paychecks at least the *lower* of the following two amounts:

> ➤ 90 percent of your total federal income tax for the current year

> ➤ 100 percent of your total federal income tax from the prior year

You: Why is this so complicated?

Sing with me now: "535 members of Congress on the wall, 535 members of Congress, you take one down, pass around a lobbyist . . ."

As long as you withhold sufficiently, you will not owe any underpayment interest or penalties. That said, you can still owe a lot of income tax with your return next April *if* you chose to withhold based on last year's tax and your current year's income tax is much higher.

If you are a recent graduate who will make more each year than the previous year for the reasons outlined earlier, you have a major opportunity to **increase your net pay** right from the outset.

You: Increase my net pay? Maybe this isn't as boring as I thought.

Yeah, that phrase usually gets people's attention. Now, you don't want a big income tax refund next April, right?

---

[8] Okay, okay! "*. . . with a parachute.*" There, I wrote it. Satisfied? Jeez—freakin' lawyers are everywhere!

You: Huh? Of course I do.

No you don't.

You: I don't?

No, read *Beyond Paycheck to Paycheck.*

[One week pause]

You: Got it—no income tax refunds for me. Loved pages 73–74 and 125 on that topic.

Thanks.

You: Also, Gary's a riot.

Gary: Thanks!

Now look what you've done!

You: Is that all it takes for him to come around?

Gary: You bet!

Gary, we're talking about saving money on taxes.

Gary: Perfecto! Have I got a whole-life insurance policy for you!

We'll be back to you.

Gary: I'll be right over here.

You: Gary, I'll call you.

Really?

*You: No, but I find that line gets me a couple weeks. I should be done reading **The Savings Solution** by then.*

Clever. Anyway, if you, as a new college graduate complete Form W-4 without a strategy, you'll probably enter "1" for the number of allowances on line five. As a result, you'll wind up with a big refund, since the amount withheld from each paycheck assumes you'll earn your salary for 12 months. Since you'll only earn it for a few months this year, too much tax will be withheld. That's the first reason why you want to increase your allowances and lower your withholdings right away.

You: Is there a second reason to adjust my allowances?

<Game show voice-over man speaking:> In fact there is!

<Back to normal voice, whatever you think that might be:>

Since you need to withhold only the amount of your prior year's tax (virtually nothing as a full-time student), you can further increase your allowances and thereby reduce your withholdings.

Increasing your net pay in this manner allows you to receive more money when you need it most.

You: When is that?

Right away. You'll be facing all the start-up expenses of life including a security deposit, work clothes, and initial emergency fund savings. Get your money now. Although you might owe a small amount of taxes next year, adjusting your withholding gets you your money sooner—and it is **your** money. Remember, you don't want a big refund anyway. As long as you are prepared, adjusting your withholding is a good move.

To determine a level of allowances where you neither owe nor are refunded a large sum of money in April, you can use the handy withholding calculator on my web site.[9] Alternatively, you can spend four days using the calculator available at the IRS web site.

You: Is it really worth the effort?

Yes. During my first two years of working after school, I took 10 allowances and still received refunds each year. My refunds were not as big as they would have been without my withholding adjustment, but having the extra money in my initial paychecks allowed me to save far more aggressively than I would have been able to otherwise. I revised my allowances when my income stabilized, as should anyone who follows this strategy.

New graduates have an easy once-in-a-lifetime opportunity to develop good habits from the start. It's never too late to begin fiscal responsibility, but starting young sure makes achieving financial success much easier.

---

[9] http://www.totalcandor.com/resources.php

CHAPTER 12

Saving Strategy # 10: Constant Budgeting Isn't Required

"A man who both spends and saves money is the happiest man, because he has both enjoyments."
—SAMUEL JOHNSON

D id you skip ahead to this chapter?
  You: Maybe.
  I doubt you're the first. Saving without budgeting is an attractive concept. Unfortunately, Saving Strategy 10 is effective only when you buy into the other saving strategies we discuss previously. Still, as those who did not skip ahead already know, the word "budget" scarcely appears before this chapter.
  You: But so many personal finance gurus emphasize the importance of budgeting. Heck, even a few of my friends swear by it.
  Does budgeting work for you?
  You: Well, no.
  Do you like to budget?
  You: Definitely not.
  Are you careless?

You: No, carelessness is not the reason budgeting doesn't work for me.

But you did try it, right? You tried budgeting at some point?

You: Yes, I did. I absolutely tried it. It just didn't help me to save.

Budgeting doesn't help most people. It certainly never helped me.

You: Really?

Total Candor: I've never lived on a budget.

You: Because you're rich?

I'm comfortable—thanks to my saving strategies—but I am not rich. Remember, I'm the same guy who once withdrew $5 from an ATM—not because I was being cheap but because all I had in the bank was $8.38.

You: Explain to me how your no budgeting concept works.

Sure. It's an easy three-step process.

1. Determine your monthly income.
2. Subtract taxes.
3. Don't create a budget.

You: Oh, c'mon!

For real. To not do something, you must simply not do it!

You: So you really are advocating a no-budget lifestyle?

I have no problem with those who keep budgets. Truthfully, I am impressed by those who can do so. But I would never insist people do something a) I can't do, b) I don't feel is fundamentally necessary, and c) which can ultimately prevent their achievement of financial success.

You: So how do you handle your monthly cash-flow?

THE ONE RULE OF THE NO BUDGET LIFESTYLE

I never spend more money than I make.

*You: How do you do **that**?*

I make sure to spend less than I earn.

You: That response leaves me with the same question.

The most important part of the successful implementation of Saving Strategy 10 is a strict adherence to Saving Strategy 9.

You: You won't spend what you don't see.

Right. In Chapter 11 I share how I saved 19 percent of my gross pay in my 401(k) plan when I started my first job.

You: At that time, you had no family to support, an inexpensive car, and an inexpensive apartment.

Or, said another way, my girlfriend broke up with me, I drove a ~~slightly renovated go-cart~~ Plymouth Neon, and my homestead was a rather run-down bachelor pad in a place called Ypsilanti.

You: It sounded better when I said it.

You're right—marketing is important. Thank you.[1]

You: You're welcome.

Still, after saving 19 percent of my gross pay in my 401(k) plan, I had just a little money remaining in my checking account at the end of the month. Yet, even without any additional monthly savings, budgeting felt unnecessary.

You: Why not?

Because I was saving 19 percent of my gross pay and I was only 21 years old!

You: Right! You were on your way.

Who cares how you're spending 81 percent of your gross pay if you're already saving 19 percent? Budgeting is only critical if you find yourself unable to save a reasonable amount in the first place.

LIVING VS. LIVING ON A BUDGET

Most people find budgeting very difficult.

You: Why?

Living within the constraints of a budget is not fun. Furthermore, the process of setting up a budget alone is a drag.

You: I agree—I've done the "set-up" part.

Yet to me the least enjoyable part of living on a budget is the *living on a budget* part.

---

[1] Truth be known, things weren't that bad. I ultimately married the girlfriend who broke up with me, got nearly 100,000 miles out of the Neon, and learned my apartment looked like a dump primarily because I didn't have a clue how to decorate. Turns out houseplants and picture frames do more to fancy a place up than posters of Al Pacino in *The Godfather* and giant blue flags with a single letter "M" on them—who knew?

You: What do you mean?

Living on a budget removes much of the spontaneity that makes life what it can be. Living on a budget often means looking at a specific budget line and determining if you can "afford" to buy a specific item.

You: Why do you have "afford" in quotes up there?

You can see the quotes?

You: Even in a book, you talk with your hands.

Weird. "Afford" is in quotes because, although you may question a purchase's affordability when reviewing your budget, what you're really doing is comparing the line item category vs. some estimate you made previously.

You: What's wrong with that?

Your budget number is only an estimate. If you're realistic when you make your budget, you'll underestimate about half your budget categories and overestimate the other half. So why stress over getting each line precisely correct?

You: So you don't go over budget.

But you will. You can't predict everything. Say you budget $50 a month for medical expenses and need to visit the emergency room. Guess what? You're going over budget.

You: But isn't a budget necessary to keep spending in check?

Let me ask you this: Has budgeting worked so far?

You: Point taken.

If you're out to dinner with your significant other and the decision about dessert isn't based on how hungry you are, what looks good, or whether you *value* paying for dessert, but instead is based on what's left in your dining budget, that's not living! That's living on a budget.

BUDGET WHAT YOU SAVE, NOT WHAT YOU SPEND

Budget differently. Don't budget your spending, budget your saving.

You: What are you talking about?

Determine an amount you wish to save each month. Remember, the earlier in life you do this, the easier it is to succeed. Furthermore, the more you automate your savings, the better the odds you will stick with it. For both of those reasons, joining your 401(k) your first week at work is one of the best things you can do during your twenties or thirties.

You: That's a stretch!

Okay, it's one of the best things you can do, financially speaking.

HOW MUCH SHOULD YOU SAVE?

You: How much should I save?

You'd think that would be a straightforward question.

You: It is a straightforward question.

True enough. Unfortunately, the answer is less so. The amount you should save varies significantly. Here are just a few factors influencing your ideal savings percentage:

- ➤ Age
- ➤ Income level
- ➤ Marital status
- ➤ Children and their ages
- ➤ Whether you own a home
- ➤ Amount saved to date
- ➤ Current debt level and types of debt
- ➤ Anticipated retirement date
- ➤ Anticipated retirement lifestyle
- ➤ Expected inheritances
- ➤ Investment philosophy

You: So how much should I save?

Are you listening?

You: Reading a book right now. Bug me later.

Hello!

You: Yes? Oh. Sorry. Why won't you just answer my question?

No one-size-fits-all answer works. As a result, you must factor in the considerations from the list above and adjust accordingly. Still, here are some guidelines by age.

TWENTY-SOMETHINGS

If, as a twenty-something, you can save 10 percent of your gross pay from your very first paycheck, you might be off to a good start.

You: Why only "might be?"

I did 19 percent in my first job.

You: But you can't expect everyone to do so.

I don't. But some people can. Those who have no or limited school debt and get a job right upon graduation can save 19 percent of their gross pay or even more.

On the other hand, those who are unemployed can't save anything. Folks who have decent incomes but sizable student loans can save something but probably less than 19 percent. But if one of those people receives help from The Bank of Mom and Dad, than my expectations of what they can save go up—and so should yours.

THIRTY-SOMETHINGS

Those of you who are 35 years old, married with two kids, and own a home with a white picket fence out front might find saving as aggressively as you once did impossible today.

You: Why? More money is coming in.

Good to hear it. Yet your expenses have likely gone through the roof.

You: But the student loans are paid.

Hopefully so, yes. But now a big mortgage has replaced relatively cheap rent and the kids go through organic blueberries like they're Cheerios.[2]

For each of those reasons, you may find it more difficult to save in your thirties than you once expected. But everyone's circumstances are different. So if you just got a big promotion and your spouse's grandparents left you a bunch of money . . .

---

[2] I have personally observed both of my daughters each simultaneously swallowing over 90 cents worth of fruit in a single gulp.

FOLKS IN THEIR FORTIES AND FIFTIES

You: What if I'm 49?

Are you?

You: That's none of your business.

If you're 49, my answer to the question, "How much should I save?" is the same: It depends.

By the time you reach your forties or fifties, your necessary savings rate is largely determined by what you've already done—or not done—to prepare yourself for retirement. Those who have been saving since they were 21 should be in a good financial place. But people who have planned to start saving by January 13 of each of the last 24 years only to give up on their financial New Year's resolution at the same time as their "eat less and exercise more" commitments will be in quite another.

You: That's not exactly uplifting.

Total Candor: If you blow off saving for a couple of decades, you will eventually pay a real price. But you can still do a tremendous amount of good by saving aggressively from this point forward. You can still achieve nearly any reasonable retirement goal. You simply must commit to the discipline necessary to save—today. Don't come back to this book ten years from now in the same place as you are today.

IN YOUR SIXTIES

If you're 63 years old, rent an apartment, haven't saved a dime, make a middle class income, have no pension, and want to retire in a life of luxury, you need to make a couple of adjustments. First, to that non-existent savings level of yours. Second, to your expectations. That beach home in Florida isn't going to happen. When you start saving very late in life, it might be impossible to achieve such big dreams.

You: So just give up?

Far from it. Instead, start saving aggressively today to avoid entering the least anticipated kind of retirement: a working retirement.

PUT IT ALL TOGETHER

Because of all the variables, it's impossible to create a single savings rate benchmark. Comparing yourself to a friend isn't going to work either, because you never know his true financial situation. Setting an aggressive savings goal is critical. Automate the process, ideally through a retirement plan. Follow the other saving strategies to success. The *right* dollar amount will follow and it will be far higher than you expect.

You: And I don't have to budget to get there.

You don't have to budget your spending. You do have to budget your savings. Saving is your number one financial goal. It is your most important "expense."

Save first and save automatically. Follow this Saving Strategy and you'll never ponder if there's money left in the budget to buy something. Instead, save aggressively and spend the rest. No matter what you spend on, you'll already be saving and on your way to wealth.

*You: And en route to a life way **Beyond Paycheck to Paycheck**.*

Well said.

CASE STUDIES

TOP 10 EXCUSES FOR NOT SAVING

Adapted from the *Beyond Paycheck to Paycheck* blog, November 9, 2007

From the home office in Portsmouth, New Hampshire, here are the:

Top 10 Excuses For Not Saving
(followed by reasons those excuses are lame)

1. I'll save later, when I make **much** more money.
2. But I really do need **this**.
3. Life is too short.
4. What's another $X?
5. But I don't want to be cheap!
6. My friends don't save.
7. Mom and Dad help with all that.
8. I wouldn't have a clue what to do with any money I saved.
9. I have so much debt!
10. My spouse/partner/accountant/buddy Norm from the help desk/mailman/crazy roommate/barista/dog handles my household finances.

And now the matching reasons those excuses are lame:

1. Did you remember saying something similar two promotions ago?
2. When was the last time you used **it?** Okay, how about where you put **it?** Do you even own **it** anymore? Do you remember what **it** is?
3. Then your retirement may be too long.
4. Depends on how long it takes to pay it back. Could be many times $X.
5. Me neither. Instead, be fiscally responsible.

6. Do you really need me to respond to this? Didn't your mother tell you 1,000 times, "If all your friends jumped off the bridge, would you?"

7. Good for you. Count your blessings. When you're done, hit 'em up for something else, like a financial education.

8. That's what we call a good problem. Furthermore, the amount you save matters far more than how you invest.

9. Then you need to pay your debt off. Spending less than you make is the only way to do it. Kind of sounds like saving, no?

10. You can outsource love/tax prep/expertise/postal delivery/ loud music/a mean espresso/fetching. But you can never delegate basic financial knowledge and responsibility.

LESSONS FROM FLIGHT 1549

Adapted from a post on the *Beyond Paycheck to Paycheck* blog, January 16, 2009

Yesterday, a US Airways plane landed in the Hudson River. Beyond any simple explanation, all 155 people on board survived. A newspaper headline about a plane without power in either engine is supposed to be followed by words and phrases like "tragedy," "death," "much too soon," and "unfortunate victims." Although it's unlikely anyone on yesterday's flight will ever read this, their experiences provide us with several lessons.

Lessons From the Pilot, Chesley B. "Sully" Sullenberger

Lesson One: Be Realistic

Upon realizing both engines lacked power, the pilot momentarily considered returning to LaGuardia or proceeding to Teterboro, New Jersey on the other side of the river. But Sullenberger quickly eliminated an attempted airport landing as being more risky than putting down in the Hudson River. Rather than deny reality or try to force a full recovery, he chose to make the best of a particularly bad situation.

Financial lesson: If a previous financial decision is no longer attractive because facts have indisputably changed for the worse, be realistic. Don't try to make yourself whole. Instead, make the best of your current situation by proceeding with a plan you believe in now.

Lesson Two: Know What You're Doing

Sullenberger was no rookie. With 29 years of commercial aviation experience preceded by a fighter pilot career, he's a true veteran flier. Although he never landed a plane in a river, I bet he contemplated and simulated landing with no engine thrust. While he wouldn't have imagined doing so around New York City or into the Hudson River, his extensive experience and training gave him as much familiarity and relative comfort with powerless flight as anyone.

Still, he had to be shocked to lose power to both engines. (Had he expected to lose even one engine, he would have requested a new aircraft!) Nonetheless, he drew upon his far-reaching experience to make the best of the absurd situation. Thank goodness—no one wants a rookie pilot at the helm during that kind of episode.

Financial lesson: Before you take a substantial risk, understand what you're doing. If you can't wait to obtain the necessary experience, hire an expert, like a highly regarded financial advisor you've personally vetted, to help you.

What You Can Learn From The Passengers of Flight 1549

Lesson Three: Stay Calm

Once in the Hudson River, the plane began filling with water. Pushing and shoving did **not** happen next; a fact nearly as impressive as the pilot's actions. Less than two months earlier, a Wal-Mart employee was trampled **to death** by eager bargain hunters only 20 miles from the Hudson River. Yet with their plane taking on water and passengers facing a life or death situation ***not*** of their making, women and children somehow were the first ones out.

What a contrast.

When it became apparent little room remained on one wing for standing passengers, some passengers simply went to the other wing. All this rational behavior occurred despite bone chilling cold air, frigid water temperatures, and a six-minute flight from pure hell.

They stayed calm.

Fortunately, passengers listened to flight attendants' instructions and reasoning, not to their own fears and emotions.

Financial lesson: If you're in a really bad situation through no fault of your own, don't ask "Why?" Instead, ask "How can I get through this? What can I control?" Ask "Why?" later. Making important decisions while you're not thinking straight is a recipe for disaster. Find a way to take a deep breath and seek guidance from people trained to handle a situation like the one you face. Take one step at a time, be it out of debt, out from under a bad investment, or onto a financial life raft.

Lesson Four: Have Faith

While the majority of passengers couldn't have known why their plane was going down and where it was heading, most understood the situation as life-threatening. Some felt death was likely.

After the collision with the birds which caused the engines to lose power, three minutes passed before the plane made impact with the river. Other than staying calm and praying, passengers could do incredibly little to increase their odds of survival. How extraordinarily frustrated and powerless each must have felt. Yet their collective faith in the pilot and crew enabled them to survive not only the water landing, but also the aftermath.

Financial lesson: The Great Recession which began in 2008 was painful for nearly everyone. Little could be done to avoid being hit and hit hard.

Most of the passengers will fly again. My guess is some have already made it to Charlotte or beyond. Similarly, if you stopped saving, you must begin saving once again.

Like you can arrive in Charlotte without flying, you can arrive in retirement without saving. But attempting to walk 600 miles or denying your basic fiscal responsibilities will probably prevent you from reaching your destination. If you believe in what you do and stay the course during tough times, you will eventually arrive where you want to go, even if each day fails to demonstrate smooth sailing.

Lesson Five: The Unexpected Happens

Like many people, I learned only yesterday that birds take out jet engines fairly regularly. I suppose the FAA also knew it was theoretically possible, but highly improbable, that birds could take out both engines simultaneously. Yet with enough flights and enough years, my unfounded mathematical conclusion is such an event was likely to occur—eventually. Maybe not yesterday on a US Airways flight from New York City, but sometime, somewhere.

Financial lesson: Just because something is unlikely doesn't mean it won't happen. You could have your identity stolen—protect it. You could be laid off—save for an emergency. Stocks could go down further in value—diversify. You could become disabled or die early—have appropriate disability and life insurance policies, not to mention a will. If birds could take out two engines at one time, you could simply be unlucky. Are you ready for something unfortunate to happen? Sooner or later, it will. What's the downside of being prepared?

What a wonderfully happy ending to this absurdly unlucky flight crew and passengers. It would be a shame if we didn't learn from it. I'm sure it changed their lives.

Lucille Bayer:
A Woman With a Lesson

"It is better to live rich than to die rich."
—Samuel Johnson

M y first job after college was in Detroit, Michigan. Though worse
today, Detroit was already quite economically depressed when I
worked there in the mid 1990s. In fact, Detroit has been tied to a single
declining industry—automotive—for generations.

One client of the company I worked for was an auto supplier. Facing
significant financial difficulties, the supplier offered a VERP to a selected
group of its employees.

You: What's a VERP?

When I first heard the term bantered about the office, I didn't know
what a VERP was either. VERP was an acronym the auto supplier simply
created; it stood for Voluntary Early Retirement Program. VERP was a
euphemism, a nice way of saying, "Hey, we're laying off all the old people."

You: Can they do that?

Absolutely. Unfortunately, it happens all the time.

You: How does it work?

Early retirement programs vary, but at the client company I worked with,
employees were offered a trade. If they accepted the VERP, they received

an increased retirement benefit in exchange for retiring earlier than they would have otherwise.

In the midst of such a dispiriting environment, the client took the rare and positive step of offering all affected employees an opportunity to meet with a financial planner. At the company's expense, such individuals could receive professional one-on-one guidance as to their financial readiness to retire from the workforce.

I was one of those financial planners. Over the course of two weeks, I met with over twenty individuals who had been offered the VERP. These people were remarkably similar to one another. They were all between 58 and 62 years old, had been with the company a very long time, and made in the vicinity of $50,000 per year.

They were also alike in another regard: despite being days away from losing their jobs, none could afford to retire.

You: Why do you say they were "days away from losing their jobs?" Wasn't the Voluntary Early Retirement Program voluntary?

Technically, yes. But everyone knew the word voluntary was in quotes.

You: Huh?

In other words, the Voluntary Early Retirement Program wasn't voluntary; it was "voluntary." Employees knew if they did not accept the "voluntary" retirement program, they were likely to receive the less generous *involuntary* early retirement program (i.e., be laid off) in the very near future.

You: And I suppose firms can do that?

Yes. Yet, while most employees I met with were disappointed to confirm they could not yet afford to retire, the news surprised no one.

You: Why not?

The company employed classic blue-collar middle class workers. The people I met with fully expected to work until age 65. They knew the VERP would be helpful, but also suspected it wouldn't be generous enough to make up for the additional years they had anticipated working. Nevertheless, facing a near certain far less valuable lay-off, each chose to accept the VERP and began looking for work elsewhere.

Then, on my last day meeting with affected employees, I met Lucille Bayer. Like the other employees I spent time with, she had also been with the company for more than 10 years. Her income and age were similar to the others too, at $49,500 and 61 years old respectively. But, unlike all the other people I met those two weeks, Lucille *could* afford to retire. She had saved a ton of money.

You: How much?

So much that within 10 minutes I, a rookie financial planner, determined Lucille could afford to call it quits—permanently.

But I was only 21. I have since learned that I, like many young twenty-somethings, was not quite as professionally polished as I would have liked to believe.

So out of my mouth came something I was perhaps justified in thinking, but never should have actually said: "Wow, Lucille, that's great! How did you do that?" Combined with the excessive enthusiasm of my tone, the "How did you do that?" part was really over the top.

Nonetheless, she answered my inappropriate question. To this day, I don't know why. It may have been because she was old enough to be my grandmother. Perhaps she felt sorry for me because I demonstrated note-worthy inexperience by asking a question in such an awed way. Another possibility? Our meeting was scheduled for an hour and only ten minutes had passed. Why rush back to work, especially for a company that's about to eliminate your job?

Regardless, this is what Lucille told me.

"Michael, my husband Ralph and I have lived what you would probably call a very traditional life. We lived in the same house for 42 years. We raised our children in that home.

"When our first child was born, I quit my job and became a housewife. In fact, I stayed home to raise all three of our children. While we had everything we needed, we had to keep things simple. There was no money for extravagances. To the extent we took vacations, they were driving trips. We'd go to Chicago one year, maybe Toronto the next. We'd camp at the Ludington State Park every once in a while too. We certainly never took a *plane* to an island somewhere and the two of us *never* took a trip alone together.

"I'll tell you something else, Michael: We paid for all the college expenses of our three children."

Impressive, I thought to myself, and nodded for her to continue.

"When our youngest child—our daughter, Alissa—went off to school, I got a job here. And did I get a slew of paperwork my first day! I brought all the materials home so Ralph and I could go through them. The pile contained forms about health insurance, taxes, disability coverage, and more. Ralph completed most of the paperwork for me, but when we got to the 401(k) enrollment form, he paused.

"Gosh, Michael, I can remember this conversation—one that took place ten years ago—like it was yesterday. Ralph said:

"'Lucille, you know our whole lives have been about sacrifice—for the kids—and they've turned out great. I couldn't be happier with how we raised them. But when we get to retirement one day, I don't want to have to sacrifice anymore. I would like to know if we want a new car, we could get one. I would like to know if we want to go on vacation, we could go. Heck, I'd like to be able to move to Florida, if that's what we decide we'd like to do.

"'So we should do this 401(k) thing.

"'In fact, if you think about it, you haven't been paid for your work in more than 25 years, Lucille. You've been busting your hump all this time, but not for pay. Now you're going to be paid, but every dollar you collect from this work is going to be money we never received before. As we have lived on my income alone all these years, your income will truly be money we've never relied on. So let's save as much in the 401(k) plan as we are allowed.'

"So that's what we did, Michael," Lucille wrapped up.

I was rather impressed. I had recently read *The Millionaire Next Door* by Thomas J. Stanley and William D. Danko. In a nutshell, the book demonstrates most millionaires do not earn high incomes. Instead, many millionaires are people with middle class incomes who save consistently for a long time.

Lucille was the first person I met who had followed that formula. You looked at her income and you looked at her 401(k) balance and they just didn't go together.

So, once again, in my youthful exuberance I said something I should have only thought, declaring, "Wow, that's great. I am so excited for you. Congratulations!"

I was completely unprepared for Lucille's response.

A tear had suddenly formed underneath her right eye and she quickly looked down. When, a few moments later she looked back up at me, any trace of the tear was long gone. Indeed, she was ever the prideful sixty-something Midwestern woman she had been moments before. Lucille looked me straight in the eyes and said, "Well, the good Lord didn't see it that way."

"What do you mean?" I asked.

"Ralph died last year," she told me.

"I'm so sorry," was all I could muster.

"Our whole lives have been about sacrifice. First, for the children and, more recently, for retirement. Now I'm not an old fool, Michael. As a widow about to lose her job, I am very fortunate to have my little pot of gold here. It gives me comfort knowing I won't have to worry about making a mortgage payment or putting food on my table. But I will never have the retirement of my dreams, because the retirement of my dreams was to be spent with Ralph—and he's not here. And, obviously, Ralph won't get the retirement of his dreams either, since he's already passed away."

# # #

I was only 21 years old when I spent my only hour with Lucille Bayer, but it is an hour which has stayed with me ever since. I share it with you now because, while it's true most people could do a much better job saving, no one should swing so far the other way and become like Lucille.

If you had a crystal ball, you could spend your last dollar on your last meal.[1] But life doesn't work that way. Of the many people who read this book, some will unfortunately not live into their sixties. The vast majority will. Since you don't know which group you will be in, you have to plan for both possibilities.

Though few people save appropriately, not all save too little. The majority, regardless of income level, plan to save "soon," when things "calm down,"

---

[1] Kentucky Fried Chicken for me, thank you. Yes, it's not the healthiest thing in the world but, hello, I'm about to kick it in this scenario, so why exactly would I eat kale?

or become more "stable," but have been using similar words, phrases, and timelines for years, if not decades.

The comparably smaller group of inappropriate savers consists of excessive savers. They buy books and attend keynote presentations like mine because they seek creative ways to save *even more* than the already very high amounts they squirrel away.

Neither group has it right. Those who don't save face the high probability of being completely unprepared for old age. Those who save too much sacrifice endlessly for a benefit that might not ever arrive.

You are only young once. You may get only one shot at certain experiences. I'm not advocating frivolous spending for the sake of it, but if you are already an excessive saver, recall Lucille. She would be the first to tell you she was *not* the big winner among the people I met.

What would Lucille have done differently if she knew Ralph wasn't going to live to retirement? I'm not sure. By the time I thought to ask, I was determined to stop asking inappropriate questions. Nevertheless, I can guess. So can you. Think about it for a minute.

With knowledge of his shortened life expectancy, it is not hard to imagine Ralph urging Lucille to schedule an island vacation for the two of them—alone. Similarly, I can picture Lucille insisting Ralph buy the car she knows he really wants.

Now think about yourself and your family. Imagine learning you or someone you love will get cancer in a few years. What would you do differently? If you wait until it's too late, neither I nor Lucille has taught you anything.

True happiness, together with financial security, can happen only if you live for today while saving for tomorrow.

Bonus Chapter:
How to Buy a Car

THREE QUESTIONS BEFORE FOUR WHEELS

By the time you pay for *anything*, you have *already* answered three questions:

1. Do I need/want it?
2. Which one do I need or want?
3. Should I buy or rent it?

You make those decisions every day.

You: Every day?

Absolutely. When you write spaghetti sauce on your grocery list, you answer "Yes" to Question #1.[1] Selecting Ragú® Old World Style Sweet Tomato Basil Pasta Sauce answers Question #2. Finally, buying the sauce addresses Question #3.[2]

People typically begin with Question #2, skipping Question #1. Although insignificant when considering occasional grocery items, starting with "Which one?" instead of "Do I need it?" is costly when contemplating large purchases.

For example, most people believe the process of their last car purchase began with online research or test-drives.

You: Both seem like good places to start.

---

[1] While saying "No" to olive-based chopped liver with chives.
[2] Can you imagine *renting* spaghetti sauce? Things don't seem so bad now, huh?

Online research and test drives are good steps to take—*after* you decide to get a car. Such exploration helps determine *which* car to buy—not whether to buy a car.

You: So you're saying I have to decide to buy a car first?

Close. You have to decide *whether* to buy a car first.

You: Why does that matter?

Choosing to purchase a car is the most important decision in the entire car buying process. For hundreds or perhaps thousands of consecutive days, you don't buy a car. Then, for some reason, you do buy a car one day, requiring a major cash outlay and affecting your ability to save.

After a certain period of time, many people assume they need another car and start shopping. Don't do that. Instead, give the decision to buy another car conscious thought. Most importantly, consider the tradeoffs, including how your decision affects when you will reach the Promised Land of Savings, discussed later.

THE BEST CAR FOR YOUR MONEY

In the summer of 2006, Susan—a woman I worked with at my first job and had last seen in 1998—called out of the blue to say she and her family were passing through my town. Thrilled by the spontaneity of her potential visit and anticipating a nice time together, my wife and I immediately invited Susan and her family to our home.

Shortly after their arrival, one of my daughters came down with a low-grade fever. Out of the proper medicine,[3] I suddenly needed to visit the drugstore in the middle of Susan's family's brief visit. Generously, Susan's husband, Sam, offered to drive with me to the store and I accepted.

---

[3] Infant Tylenol® and Children's Tylenol are *not* the same.

As we drove to the drugstore, I learned more about Sam's occupation as district manager for a major car manufacturer. I knew Sam as an honest man who had worked for different car companies before his current job. Suddenly, my curiosity got the best of me and I asked him a pointed question.

"Sam, what's the best car to get for your money?"

"Strictly financially speaking?" he clarified.

"Yes, you've worked for different car companies. You've worked in dealerships throughout the country. You've seen the sales process from the other side of the table. You know what salespeople and their "managers" can and cannot do to make a deal. So, as of this moment in time, what's the best car out there to get, financially speaking?"

"Michael, that's an easy question," Sam said flatly.

"Really?" I said.

"The best car for your money is always the car you already own."

"Wow, Sam."

"You lose money when you walk through the door, Michael."

"What about my exhaustive research and negotiating skill?" I wondered.

"It'll help, but your best move, financially speaking, is to keep the car you own."

"Thanks, Sam."

"You're welcome. Just don't tell too many people," Sam winked.

"Only my biggest fans," I said, winking back.

Unfortunately, many people spend the majority of their shopping time answering Question #2.

You: Why is that unfortunate?

At the detail level, "Which one do I want or need?" is relatively unimportant.

You: I'm surprised to hear you say that. Choosing which car to buy would seem to be very important to my finances.

Choosing an $18,000 car instead of a $50,000 car *is* important (and wise). But most people don't spend time debating that type of "Which kind of car do I want?" decision. Instead, they go right to stressing over whether to get the car they have their heart set on in red or white, whether to get leather seats, and whether to go for other various upgrades.

You: That's true.

Because those decisions are relatively meaningless, we're not going to talk about Question #2 anymore. On the other hand, Question #3, "Should I buy or rent it?" is a key consideration in the car buying process.[4] Yet despite its significant effect on your financial affairs, most people do not spend sufficient time considering the question.

Sometimes, the choice is obvious. If you're traveling to Los Angeles for a long weekend, you'll need a car.[5] Obviously, it won't make sense to buy a car you plan to use for only two or three days. Renting is a superior financial option. The same thing goes for your housing: you'd reserve a hotel room for a couple of nights, you wouldn't buy a condo.[6] However, when contemplating a car or place to live for a period of years—not days—the choice between renting and owning is less clear.

While I discuss car leasing on page 272, let's now talk about the three negotiations of car buying.

You: I'll have three negotiations?

Yes.

You: In addition to the three questions I just answered?

Correct.

You: Just to buy a car?

Yes.

You: This is like work.

That depends on your occupation.

You: I suppose.

---

[4]   Think of a lease as a long-term rental.

[5]   L.A.'s public transportation ~~sucks~~ is rather poor.

[6]   Okay, *Entourage's* Johnny Drama might buy the condo, but a) your brother isn't Vince, and b) *Entourage* is fiction.

And job satisfaction.

You: Don't rub it in.

AND NOT A PENNY MORE: THE THREE NEGOTIATIONS OF EFFECTIVE CAR BUYING

To successfully buy a car, you must initiate and stand your ground through three consecutive negotiations.

You: What are the three negotiations?

1. The price of the car
2. The value of your trade-in
3. Your financing terms

You: I knew the first was negotiable and figured the second was, but the third? Are you sure you can negotiate financing?

Absolutely. Using my experience buying my first car, I'll show you how.

You: What kind of car did you get?

A red Plymouth Neon.

You: Nice.

Enough. When I bought my first car, I was looking to save money.

You: Right from the get-go, huh? How old were you when you bought your first car?

I was 21 years old.

You: Why were you so motivated to save at 21?

Because I didn't have any money when I was 21! I had just graduated college. Because my first job was 45 miles from my apartment and not commutable by public transportation,[7] I *needed* a car. Embarrassingly, I didn't use the Internet to help me with my car buying experience.

You: Why not?

When I graduated college in 1994, the Internet was still a geek thing. Most computers didn't have browsers.

You: I thought you were younger than that.

Me too. Anyway, I visited a few car dealers and ultimately decided the Plymouth Neon was the car I truly wanted.

---

[7] Detroit is known as the "Motor City" for more than one reason.

You: Really?

Of course not! I wanted a Ferrari.[8] But the Neon was my top choice among affordable cars. After deciding which car to pursue, I next sought the best price.

You: How did you do that?

I simply asked the salesman for the best price.

You: And he just gave it to you?

No.

You: So what did you do then?

I told him I was going to the other Chrysler dealership in town to "make sure" he had given me the best price.

You: Then what happened? Were you given the best price when you started to leave?

No, but I *was* given a better price. Still, I left for the other dealership.

You: Did you feel like you were being cold?

No. Although the salesman did try to make me feel guilty, I didn't. I was simply trying to get the most out of my very limited money.

Upon arriving at the second dealership, I informed the salesman I had already selected a car to buy and wanted his best price.

You: Did you get it?

Eventually.

You: How do you know?

After four hours of negotiating—

You: Four hours? Isn't your time worth money?

Now? Absolutely. Then? Not really.

After four hours, the sales manager wrote down a compelling number on a piece of paper and threw in a 10-disc CD player. Although I felt more than a little guilty for the indulgent stereo, I told him we had a deal.

You: Done.

So I thought.

You: You're kidding. You said it was your first car. You couldn't have had a car to trade-in.

---

[8] Blame Magnum, P.I.

Correct. In this instance I had no trade-in, so we skipped negotiation number two.

You: So what did you negotiate next?

Financing.

You: Financing is really negotiable, huh?

Everything is negotiable.

You: How did you know it was negotiable when you were 21?

I didn't.

You: But somehow you negotiated it anyway. This should be good. Go on.

I learned financing was negotiable in real time.

You: Real time?

In other words, I discovered financing was negotiable while I was at the dealership. When we finally had a deal on the price of the Neon, I was ushered into an office to meet with the business manager, Frank. After making me sit about 20 minutes, he returned to his office.

"Great news. It wasn't easy, but I was able to get you a loan," he declared.

"Glad to hear it," I replied.

"All you have to do is sign a bunch of papers," he told me as he started laying out multi-colored sheets of paper on the table in front of me and handed me a pen. "In just a few minutes, you'll have the keys to your own—"

"Excellent. Can you tell me about the loan? What's the interest rate?" I inquired.

"You want to know the interest rate? Okay. Hold on a second." Frank thumbed through his paperwork and told me, "Twelve percent."

"Twelve percent?" I asked.

"Yes."

"That seems kind of high."

"Look, Mr. Rubin, it was hard to get you a loan at any interest rate," Frank said.

"Why?" I asked, somewhat stunned.

"Because you have NO credit history. All you have is a job offer letter. You haven't started working. Heck, you could quit before you start the job.

Twelve percent is a pretty good rate for a guy in your shoes," Frank said, rather dismissively.

"But your top salesman, Jim over there, told me one reason to buy from this fine dealership was because you guys could get me good rates, like 8 percent," I told him.

"You're telling me Jim said we could get you an 8 percent rate?"

"Absolutely," I replied. It was true.

"I'm going to talk to Jim," Frank said in a rather exasperated tone and went off in a tiff.

Out of the office went Frank the business manager. For a long time. A very long time.

You: How long was he gone?

An hour.

You: An hour?! And you were just sitting there, waiting?

Yup.

You: Weren't you frustrated?

Candidly, I was more bored and puzzled than anything else. Besides, it was raining outside so I wasn't missing much.

Finally, Frank came back and said, in a *very* frustrated voice, "Well, I had to call a bunch of banks to get this to work out but I got you 8 percent."

"Great, thank you," I told him.

"You're welcome," he said.

Only two hours earlier, I didn't know financing was negotiable. But to me, the interest rate was part of the *package*. If the business manager had changed the sales price of the car from what the manager had scribbled on my paper, I would have had an obvious gripe. I merely viewed the sudden and random interest rate spike the same way. Accordingly, I asked the business manager to honor the salesman's promise. Consequently, I successfully negotiated my rate and saved nearly a thousand dollars of interest in the process.

I've since learned car dealerships have as many car loan rates as they have car prices. The difference is most people don't know about the various financing opportunities and therefore pay "sticker price" for their financing.

CONSIDERATIONS WHEN NEGOTIATING YOUR FINANCING

Always keep your negotiations separate.

You: Separate from what?

Separate from each other. In other words, don't fall for the, "What do you want your monthly payment to be?" trap.

You: Why is that question a trap?

Because the salesman and manager can make the monthly payment equal to almost anything simply by adjusting the term of your loan.

You: Meaning?

They can give you a lousy price for the car, a lousy interest rate for your loan, yet still meet your monthly payment requirements by merely stretching out your car loan.

You: Stretching out?

Sure, instead of a three or four year car loan, they might lengthen it to seven years.

You: Seven years?

Yes. Not good.

Keep the car price and financing negotiations separate. First, come to an agreement on the price of the car. Then—and only then—discuss financing.

COME PREPARED

When it's time to talk financing, it'll help if you already have a deal in your back pocket.

You: Back pocket?

In other words, it's to your advantage to arrive at the dealership with financing already in place.

You: How do I do that?

Visit a bank or two and ask about their car loans. Get their best rate for the car you are about to buy and obtain a written loan offer.

When you get to the dealer, you know not to accept any loan with worse terms than those provided by your bank. You may be able to do much better, however.

You: Sounds good. How?

Very low interest rates are frequently available for certain cars and—

You: Yes?

To qualified buyers.

You: I've heard the "for qualified buyers" disclaimer before. How do I know if I will qualify?

If you have good credit, you typically qualify.

You: Otherwise?

You might not qualify. Keep in mind dealer-advertised rates like 0 percent and 2.9 percent won't be available directly from a bank.

You: Then how do I take advantage of such low rates?

You must do three things: 1) have good credit, 2) pick a car which qualifies for a low rate, and 3) arrange financing through the dealer. If you choose to go this route—as I did when I received 0.9 percent financing on the purchase of my second car—you skip financing negotiations entirely and instead focus on the other two negotiations.

YOUR TRADE IS A NEGOTIATION TOO

I was unexpectedly thrust into heated negotiations when I bought my second car, a Saturn®.

You: I thought Saturn had a no negotiation policy.

They did.

You: What happened?

They went out of business.

You: Did your negotiation have anything to do with it?

I doubt it.

You: If you couldn't negotiate the price of the car and you had already locked in 0.9 percent financing, what did you negotiate?

My trade-in.

You: What were you trading in?

My red Plymouth Neon. When I went to trade the little guy in, Mr. Neon had more than 93,000 miles on him and no transmission.

You: No transmission?

Correct. The Neon could go from zero to sixty in no time.

You: Huh?

No matter how much time you gave it, the poor guy simply could not get to 60 miles per hour.

*You: So you truly needed a **new** car.*

At least on highways, yes. The complete transmission failure of my first car led me to buy my second car. As I advise Genevive in Chapter 5, it does not make sense to put more money into a car than it will be worth after the contemplated work is completed.

You: How did you negotiate the trade-in value of your Neon? It doesn't seem as if you would have had any leverage.

I agree.

You: You do?

Sort of. After the sales manager drove my Neon around the parking lot, the salesman came back to his desk where I waited. The salesman then chuckled and said, "Do you want tens or twenties?"

"Excuse me?" I responded.

"We'll give you a hundred bucks for your Neon."

"It's worth far more than that," I pleaded.

"It's got 93,500 miles on it and a few dents. It's worth $100," he insisted.

Now *I knew* it wasn't worth even $100. But the guy didn't say anything about the transmission. He only focused on the high mileage and minor dents. Like with every negotiation, car or otherwise, preparation is key. My previous research showed me—absent the transmission issue—the Blue Book[9] value was $1,800.

You: Even with the high mileage and dents?

Yes, or it would have been worth more than $1,800. By assuming I didn't know what my car was worth, the dealership was clearly trying to take advantage of my perceived ignorance. Consequently, I felt completely justified—even compelled—in my attempt to take advantage of theirs.

"Not according to Blue Book," I said, in response to their $100 offer.

"What do you want for it?" the salesman asked.

---

[9] The Kelly Blue Book value of virtually any car in any condition is available free at kbb.com.

"Blue Book says it's worth $1,800," I replied.

"Man, there's no way you're getting $1,800 for it."

"Well, I guess we're done then," I said and started to walk out.

"Jeez, Michael, don't blame me because of what my manager said your car is worth. I thought you wanted your new Saturn. It's right here. I want to see you in this car," the salesman pleaded.

"Then it's on you to get your manager to talk reasonably to me," I said sternly. My blood pressure was somewhat elevated.

"Just don't go," he asked

"You have two minutes," I told him.

He left.

He came back with the manager three minutes later.

"$500—that's it. The AC works, but c'mon, it's a 1994 Neon with a ton of mileage," said the sales manager.

"No, Blue Book says I'd be a fool to give this to you for just $500," I told him.

"The 0.9 percent financing offer expires tonight. You're going to throw that away?" he scolded. (The dealer was trying to merge two negotiations into one, a suboptimal approach for a buyer. I needed to change the direction he was heading.)

"One thing has nothing to do with the other," I insisted.

"If you walk away, you lose the financing deal, which would save you far more than the $1,300 difference in the trade if I give you $500 for your Neon," he said.

It was though he was trying to teach me.

"I wasn't born yesterday. You—and other dealers—will have new financing deals out by the weekend," I told him and stood up, preparing to leave once again.

"One thousand dollars. But I am going to lose money on this," he lamented.

"$1,500," I countered, showing some flexibility.

"I can't do $1,500," he said.

"Let's split the difference. How about $1,250?" I said.

"Done," he retorted and he walked away.

I never saw him again.

You: Really?

Really. Even if I took his initial $100 offer, I would have never seen him again. Don't think about any "relationship" when you're negotiating in a car dealership. There is none.

You: So why did you agree to accept only $1,250 when the Blue Book value of your car was $1,800?

Blue Book said it was worth $1,800 *if* it was in the condition the dealer thought it was in. But without a working transmission, it was actually worth close to nothing. Consequently, $1,250 for something worthless seemed like a good deal. If I went somewhere else and tried to trade-in the Neon, the manager at the other dealership might have actually tried to take the Neon out of the parking lot and onto a highway. If that happened, I'd get virtually nothing for the car. During any negotiation, consider: pigs get fat, hogs get slaughtered.

In total, the deal was compelling. I got a new car at a fair price, a great value for my trade, and a ridiculous 0.9 percent interest rate on my car loan.

Remember, every time you buy a car you will have three negotiations. If you take each negotiation consecutively and seriously, you will save significant dollars *every month* with only a minimal change to your lifestyle.

Alternatively, think about how often you'd have to cut out vending machines, doughnuts, or lattes to save $50 a month. Those are decisions you'd have to get right *every day* for years. Spending the time to get the car buying process right is far easier. After all, for most people, buying a car happens only two to three times a decade.

ADDITIONAL CAR BUYING CONSIDERATIONS

After you've answered the three questions and mastered the three negotiations, you're almost ready to buy a car.

You: Excellent.

But not quite. Two more things to think about first are:

➤ buying used vs. new
➤ leasing vs. buying

CHOOSING BETWEEN USED AND NEW CARS

Your net worth takes a huge hit whenever you buy a car.

You: Why?

Because you pay for much more than what you receive.

You: You mean like overpriced floor mats?

The mats are one potential reason, but their impact to your net worth is minimal. On the other hand, more costly expenses with *no real value* include sales tax, delivery, license, and several other miscellaneous fees you should negotiate to zero.

You: Easier said than done.

Not really. Just make sure you are always negotiating the "out the door" price. Make it clear you want a price which includes *everything.* Then, call the bluff and threaten to walk away if either the salesman or business manager tries to add anything later.

You: Okay.

Yet you're still going to pay more for the car than it's worth.

You: Argh! Why?

At least two reasons. The first is sales tax. To keep the math easy, say you buy a car for $20,000 in a state with a 5 percent sales tax. Since 5 percent of $20,000 is $1,000, you pay $21,000.[10] How much do you now owe, not including interest?

You: $21,000.

Exactly. What's the car worth?

You: $20,000.

Let's say you're right.[11] Let's review what happened as a result of your car purchase.

You: Let's.

Assuming you financed the whole thing, your assets—the car you now own—have increased by $20,000. Yet your debts—the car loan you now owe—have increased by $21,000. Consequently, your net worth decreases by $1,000.

---

[10] Ideally, you negotiated sales tax into the "out the door" price. Still, you effectively paid sales tax—it's just the sales tax was included in the amount you paid.

[11] You're not.

You: Just because of the sales tax?

Yes.

You: Jeez. What if I made a down payment?

Say you put $1,000 down for the car. As a result, your new debt is $20,000—not $21,000. However, your assets increase by only $19,000—not $20,000.

You: Why?

To make the down payment, you removed $1,000 from savings. This reduces your assets. Consequently, after factoring in the new $20,000 car, your total assets increase by only $19,000. Regardless of how much you finance, your net worth will decrease by $1,000 as soon as you purchase the car.

You: @$ %#$!

It's actually far worse.

You: Why?

Because your car isn't worth $20,000.

You: Why not? I thought you told me everything I needed to know to get a good deal.

Hopefully, you did a ton of research. Ideally, you negotiated like a maven. In a perfect world, you sent emails to several dealers asking for their best "out the door" price inclusive of all silly fees like delivery, license, registration, destination, organization, and fascination. Even if you did all those things and knew $20,000 was the absolute lowest price anyone could pay for a car such as the one you bought, *your* car isn't worth $20,000.

You: WHY NOT?!

You turned right out of the parking lot.

You: But I live that way! I should have taken the long way home?

Hardly. Once you exit the dealer's parking lot—in any direction—your car suffers massive and immediate depreciation.

You: Meaning?

It's not worth what you paid for it.

You: Why not?

Let me ask you a question.

You: Okay.

Which of the following two identical make and model cars would you pay more money for?

1. A dealer's brand new car. The odometer reads 002.
2. Some random guy's car with an odometer reading of 014.

You: The dealer's brand new car.

Why?

You: The random guy's car isn't new. I don't know what's happened to it. Maybe someone smoked in it or it was in an accident. Why would he sell a car with so few miles on it anyway?

I agree. So does everyone else. Consequently, a new car suffers from massive depreciation (i.e., decline in value) the moment you drive it away.

You: How much do you lose?

It depends on the car, but 25 percent ($5,000 on a $20,000 car) is not unreasonable. A car you negotiate to a $20,000 sales price is probably worth only $15,000 by the time you get home from the dealership. You now owe $21,000 (remember the $1,000 in sales tax) for a car worth about $15,000.

You: So my net worth just went down by $6,000?

Assuming you got a good deal and drove home safely, yes. Car transactions are very costly.

You: What can I do to minimize the impact?

Two strategies can dramatically reduce the effects. First, consider buying a high-quality low-mileage used car with a dealer warranty, which will experience a far lower percentage drop in value due to immediate depreciation.

You: Makes sense. Someone else already suffered the new car depreciation.

Exactly. Second, choose to get a car less often.

You: What do you mean?

Keep your cars longer. Doing so means bearing the massive depreciation, sales tax, and interest expense less often over your lifetime.

LEASING VS. BUYING YOUR CAR

An easy way to suffer both financially and repeatedly is to go for one of the car salesman's favorite opportunities.

You: What opportunity is that?

The one where he offers you a great lease payment.

You: Why is that not a good thing? A lower monthly car payment ought to enable me to save more, no?

Beware, a lease is a trap!

You: A trap? With an explanation point? My goodness, why?

Leasing is a reasonable option only if you are a "car person." A "car person" is someone who considers the kind of car they drive *very* important. Car people are willing to give up other things in exchange for always driving a nice and relatively new car.

You: What kinds of things do "car people" have to give up?

It depends on the financial circumstances of the individual of course, but such sacrifices might include anything from fewer dinners out to a smaller home to a later retirement. Still, nothing is wrong with choosing to be a "car person."

You: There isn't?

No. However, plenty is wrong with being a "car person" but denying it. No one can afford to prioritize everything as most important. If a nice new car is at the top of your priorities list, knock yourself out. But if you're seeking to lower your expenses and increase your ability to save, your car represents a huge opportunity.

WHAT IS A CAR LEASE, REALLY?

When you lease a car, you effectively rent it, typically for a multi-year lease term. Like with any rental, your payments cease when the term ends. *However, you must also give back the car.* Anticipating they will need another car upon turning in their leased vehicle, most people make arrangements to lease another car. The result is an endless series of car payments.

You: Endless?

If you always lease cars, you always have car payments.

You: Right. But if I buy a car and finance it, I would have monthly payments too.

Yes, but not *endless* payments.

Rather than lease a car, a better strategy is to buy your car. Then, keep it well beyond the length of the car loan. Unless you drive excessively or recklessly, your car will last far longer than the typical five-year financing term. At that point, you reach the Promised Land of Savings™.

THE PROMISED LAND OF SAVINGS

You: What's the Promised Land of Savings?

You reach the Promised Land of Savings when you have a car but no car payment. Once a several-hundred-dollars a month bill disappears, saving is suddenly much easier. In fact, you can periodically splurge when your car payments cease yet still save far more than before.

Unless you are a "car person" willing to forgo other expenses, buying—not leasing—a low mileage used—not new—car and keeping it for a long time—well beyond the term of your car loan—is one of the easiest and most significant ways to increase your ability to save. It is only a minor change to your life, yet by tweaking your approach to cars, you start down the road to significant savings. This is true even if you make no other changes to your financial life.

Doesn't the Promised Land of Savings sound exactly like the silver bullet you're looking for? Or are you still looking for the new silver DX? Your call—you're the one behind the wheel now.

Bonus Chapter:
When and How to Buy a House

THE MOST EXPENSIVE PURCHASE OF YOUR LIFE (SO FAR)

I bought my first home just a few months before I wrote this chapter.

You: You bought a home just so you could write this chapter more effectively?

Although I am dedicated to my readers, other factors caused my wife and me to buy a home.

You: Aren't you kind of old to be a first time home buyer?

You could say that.

You: I did say it. Am I right?

It depends on what your definition of "old" is.

You: Bubba?

No, it's still Michael.

You: Why are you suddenly mincing words?

I find my definition of "old" changes as I age. For example, 40 is now a lot younger than it was when I was in high school. Regardless of your definition of "old," it is true that I was just about the last of my friends to buy a home.

You: Why?

I waited until the time was right.

You: Does that mean you lived with your parents until you were in your thirties?

No. I left Salt Meadow Lane after high school and never returned to live with my family.

You: So you rented your own place all those years?

Yes.

You: Isn't renting like throwing money away?

No, it's not.

You: I've heard more than one expert say renting is the same as throwing money away.

I've heard them say that too.

You: But?

I disagree.

You: Why?

Because throwing your money away means you don't get anything for your money, like when a Rangers fan buys a ticket to a game at Madison Square Garden and they get shutout by the New York Islanders.

You: What did you get for your rent money?

A place to live, of course.

You: Got it.

As you'll see, home ownership and renting each have advantages. Which one makes the most sense for you largely depends on where you are in life.

You: So why did you buy a home when you did?

My wife and I reached the point where the advantages of home ownership outweighed the advantages of renting. Until that point, we benefited from the principal advantage of renting.

You: Which is?

FLEXIBLE LIVING

Compared to buying a home, renting one is typically a quick, clean, and simple process. It's also short-term in nature. For each of those reasons, renting provides you with tremendous flexibility.

You: Do I need such flexibility?

How's your life?

You: Excuse me? What are you getting at?

When you're ready to settle down, flexibility loses its importance. But as a young person, flexibility is critical—even if you're pretty stable.

You: Why?

Stable is a relative term, especially to people in their twenties. Should you wish to move to a different city because of a job, romantic, or educational opportunity, you'll be glad you're not tied down to a house you own. Similarly, should you wish to take a year to travel or to "start over" in Cabo San Lucas, New York, or Fond du Lac,[1] the absence of a financial albatross you can't sell can mean the difference between dreaming your dreams and living them.

Until you know you don't need flexibility, you're better off renting. But when you're ready, it's critical to understand the advantages and disadvantages of home buying.

ADVANTAGES OF BUYING A HOME

YOU'RE ACTUALLY SAVING WITH PART OF EVERY MORTGAGE PAYMENT

When you rent a home, your monthly payment is called rent. When you buy a home, your monthly payment is called a mortgage.

You: Why do I need a mortgage?

Unless you are independently wealthy (or the son or daughter of one of the aforementioned), you will need to borrow money in order to buy your first home.

You: Why?

Because homes are very expensive.

You: How expensive?

According to the U.S. Census, the average sales price of an American home during October 2010 was $248,200.[2]

You: I don't have that kind of money.

---

[1] It's possible (and in Wisconsin).

[2] In some parts of the country, especially the pricier east and west coasts, average home prices are higher still—even after the housing correction.

Neither do most people. Consequently, most people need to borrow money to buy a first or second home.

You: Why is it called a mortgage instead of a home loan?

As Kramer once pondered in *Seinfeld*, "Why does Radio Shack™ ask for your phone number when you buy batteries? I don't know."

You: What's so special about a mortgage?

A mortgage is a loan secured by your home.

You: Great. Now in English, please.

If you don't pay (i.e., default on) the loan, the bank can take your home.

You: That I understood.

Still, they make you sign 347 pages to that effect when you get your mortgage.

You: Which bank takes my home if I default? The bank which loaned me the money?

Possibly, but probably not.[3] Instead, the financial institution which owns your mortgage, if and when you default, takes your home via a foreclosure process.

You: Figures. Getting back to the headline of this section, why does part of every mortgage payment go to me? Doesn't it all go to the bank?

Technically, yes—but let's dig deeper. Every mortgage payment contains at least two distinct components. The first is interest.

You: Why is there interest?

The bank charges you interest in exchange for the enormous sum of money it lent you so you could buy your home.

You: Right. What's the other portion of the payment?

The other portion of the payment is a partial repayment of your loan.

You: But that piece also goes to the bank.

Sort of.

You: Sort of?

While the money leaves your checking account and goes to the bank, the portion of your payment which represents debt repayment increases *your* net worth.

---

[3] A snide remark based on your political persuasion *could* be appropriate at this time.

You: Even though I'm basically paying a bill?

Yes.

You: How so?

Because, upon paying your monthly mortgage payment, you owe less on your home.

You: So?

Paying down debt increases your net worth. Said another way, part of each mortgage payment represents savings. Even better, it's money you can't spend.

You: Why not?

Because the money is tied up in the value of your home. You can't spend your second bedroom at the Apple Store.

You: Money and savings I can't spend? That sounds like Saving Strategy 9: You won't spend what you don't see!

Right on.

YOUR MORTGAGE INTEREST IS TAX DEDUCTIBLE (AND SO ARE YOUR REAL ESTATE TAXES)

Long ago, the government of the United States decided to encourage home ownership.[4] Consequently, home mortgage interest and real estate taxes reduce your income tax.

You: Cool, I like tax deductions.

You should, but keep in mind a tax deduction doesn't make your mortgage free.

You: Why not? I'll just write it off and get my money back.

No you won't.

You: Pretty sure that's how it works for me.

Good for you. Here's how it really works:

Say you spend $1,000 in property taxes and $3,000 in mortgage interest during a year.

You: Meaning I've spent $4,000 in monthly housing payments during the year?

---

[4] A snide remark based on your political persuasion *could* be appropriate at this time.

No.

You: Why not?

Remember, part of each mortgage payment is interest and part is debt repayment. You can only deduct the interest portion.

You: How will I know how much is interest?

The bank will figure it out and let you know.

You: Why would they do that?

The government requires they tell you (and the IRS) on Form 1098.[5]

You: So although I would have paid more, $4,000 is the amount I can deduct?

Right. Furthermore, let's assume you are in the 25 percent tax bracket.

You: Consider it assumed.

Your tax savings as a result of the deductions are $1,000.

You: Why $1,000?

The value of the deduction is calculated by multiplying the $4,000 in deductions by your 25 percent tax rate. The result is $1,000.

You: A thousand bucks is a thousand bucks.

It certainly is—which is why the deductibility of your mortgage interest and property taxes is a major advantage of home ownership.

You: What are some other advantages?

YOU CAN BENEFIT FROM PRICE APPRECIATION

Over the long term, home prices tend to increase.

You: Define long term.

That's a moving target.

You: What's a moving target?

The definition of long term.

You: What do you mean?

During the mid 2000's, long term for home ownership was about the length of time it took to get a haircut.

You: A woman's haircut experience or a guy's chop at the barber shop?

---

[5] A snide remark based on your political persuasion *could* be appropriate at this time.

Does it matter?

You: I suppose not.

Home prices, especially in markets like Miami, Phoenix, and Las Vegas increased rapidly, causing many poor decisions to be made.[6] Furthermore, expectations became unrealistic.

Rationally, long term means many years—not many minutes. If you buy a home and hold onto it for many years, you have a reasonable chance of it being worth more than you paid for it. Consequently, you can—but are not assured—of making money by owning and properly maintaining your home over the long term.

PRIDE

When you own a home, you grow roots.

You: A foot fungus?

No! Where do you live? By growing roots, I mean taking ownership in your community. Homeowners frequently become involved locally because their neighbors and neighborhood will be part of their lives for many years to come. Homeowners make improvements to their yards and their homes because they can—they own them.

While you can't quantify the value of pride in home ownership, it is undeniably real (or at least my wife has convinced me of it).

But home ownership isn't all roses.

DISADVANTAGES OF BUYING A HOME

The mere title above was enough to generate great scorn (if not rotten tomatoes) thrown in my general direction when I used it in presentations several years ago. Alas.

A LARGE DOWN PAYMENT IS "REQUIRED"

You: What is a down payment?

A down payment is the large sum of money required to obtain a mortgage.

---

[6] A snide remark based on your political persuasion *could* be appropriate at this time.

You: Why does the bank require a large sum of money from me? Aren't they giving me money?

A large down payment ensures you have skin in the game.

You: First fungus and now this. What skin?

The bank wants to be reasonably confident you'll pay back the money they lend you. The prospect of losing your down payment represents your skin in the game, giving you a great incentive to pay back your loan.

You: Makes sense. I felt the same way with Charlie in fourth grade when I loaned him my Trivial Pursuit™—I got his Stratego™. But how does my down payment make the bank more comfortable with my loan?

Let's say you're going to buy a $250,000 home. If you put nothing down—

You: Is that possible?

Not anymore.

*You: It **was** possible?*

At one time.

You: That sounds crazy.

It was crazy.

You: What happened?

People went crazy.

You: Why? How?

Well,[7]

You: I see.

Regardless, you pretty much can't buy a home today without a down payment.

You: Why do you say "pretty much?"

Because doing so is still possible, just much harder.

You: OMG.[8]

I totally agree—great point.

Anyway, if you borrowed the entire $250,000 purchase price to buy your home and subsequently hit a very rough patch financially, you wouldn't have a great incentive to keep paying the mortgage.

You: Why not?

---

[7] A snide remark based on your political persuasion *could* be appropriate at this time.

[8] A snide remark based on your political persuasion *could* be appropriate at this time.

Because none of your money would be at stake if you stopped paying the mortgage.

You: But my house would be.

Indeed, so you might pay the mortgage for a while. But let's say, in addition to your financial difficulties, your home decreased in value by $25,000 to $225,000. How hard would you try to pay back your loan now?

You: Not quite as hard.

Probably not. That's the problem with lending money to a person with no skin in the game. Too often, he would walk away if the going got a little tough.

Now imagine instead of putting no money down on your $250,000 home purchase, you made a down payment of 20 percent, or $50,000. As a result, your mortgage is only $200,000. Your home equity (the amount your home is worth less the amount you owe on it) is $50,000. Keep in mind: your home equity is *your money*. You can't get at it easily, but it is your money so long as you own the home. If you were to hit a rough financial patch, how hard would you try to pay your mortgage?

You: Very hard.

Why?

You: Because I wouldn't want to lose my equity—my $50,000 down payment.

Nor your home. Even if your home decreased in value to $225,000, you would still have skin in the game—your home equity would be $25,000 ($225,000 home value—$200,000 mortgage).

Banks know a sizable down payment reduces the odds a buyer will default on their loan. Furthermore, banks make money when borrowers pay back their loans. Consequently, banks provide big incentives to consumers who make large down payments.

You: What are the incentives I'll get if I make a large down payment?

You'll get a better interest rate on your loan.

You: Big deal.

Actually, it's a huge deal as I discuss beginning on page 301.

You: Fine. What else? Do I get an extra home buyer tax credit for putting down more money on my home?

No.

You: Why not?

The first time home buyer tax credit[9] expired in early 2010. Furthermore, the credit was not based on how much or whether you made a down payment.[10]

You: Okay. Besides a low interest rate, what incentives do I receive by making a large down payment on my home purchase?

None. However, the banks do provide a large disincentive to people who do not make a significant down payment. Said another way, putting a substantial down payment on your home purchase allows you to avoid a nasty penalty.

You: What nasty penalty?

PMI.

You: What is PMI?

PMI is private mortgage insurance.

You: What is private mortgage insurance?

You are typically required to purchase private mortgage insurance if you borrow more than 80 percent of the value of your home. Said another way, if you do not make a down payment of at least 20 percent of the purchase price, you will be required to purchase PMI.

You: Why is that so terrible?

PMI is an additional cost.

You: Yes, but then I get insurance.

No, you don't.

You: You just said I'd be required to buy private mortgage insurance.

Indeed I did.

You: So why are you now saying I don't get the insurance.

Because you don't.

You: You're not making any sense.

Welcome to the wonderful world of home mortgages.

You: Doesn't seem so wonderful so far.

Just wait. The reason you don't get the insurance but do have to pay for it is because the insurance doesn't protect you.

---

[9] A snide remark based on your political persuasion *could* be appropriate at this time.
[10] A snide remark based on your political persuasion *could* be appropriate at this time.

You: Who does my PMI protect?

The bank.

You: What bank?

The bank lending you the money so you can buy the home.

You: Then why do I have to buy the insurance?

You don't.

You: You just told me I had to buy the insurance!

You only have to buy the insurance if you can't or don't put down at least 20 percent of the purchase price. If you put down 20 percent or more, you don't have to purchase or pay for PMI.

You: How expensive is PMI?

Not surprisingly, the cost varies.

You: Based on?

How little of a percentage you put down and the total amount of the loan. But $75 to $100 a month—or even more—is not uncommon.

You: That doesn't seem too expensive.

Remember you're not getting anything for this money.

You: So paying PMI is sort of like throwing money away.

That's one way to put it.

You: I guess you can throw housing money away whether you rent or own.

Yes—if you're not careful.

Each dollar you pay for PMI represents money you could have used to more aggressively pay down your mortgage, buy furniture, or save. No matter how you would choose to otherwise use those funds, you need to first avoid PMI.

You: And to do that, I need to make a larger down payment.

Correct. At least 20 percent of the purchase price of the home.

You: Twenty percent of the home I want to buy is a LOT of money.

An appropriate down payment is a major hit to most first time home buyer's savings accounts. That's why a large down payment is a disadvantage of home ownership. Most people have to save for a very long time to obtain such a large sum. Then, to intelligently buy a home, they must use most of their large savings account as a down payment. Afterwards, they can't get to their money easily—only by selling the home or borrowing against their home equity.

You: What if I can't afford the 20 percent down payment on the home I want to buy right now? What I am I supposed to do?

You have three choices.

You: I like options. What are they?

1. You can choose to put down a lower down payment and therefore pay PMI.

2. You can choose to buy a less expensive home so you can afford to put down 20 percent.

3. You can wait to buy a home until you can put down 20 percent on a home similar to the one you want to buy right now.

You: What should I do?

I don't know.

You: That's not helpful.

But it is Total Candor. I'm not a fan of option number one. I think the need for PMI is an indicator (not 100 percent foolproof, but pretty reliable) someone is about to stick their neck out too far. You usually won't get into financial trouble by being too conservative.

Both of the other two options are good ones. Which is best for you depends on your specific situation and how you fare on the other advantages and disadvantages of home ownership.

You: What are those?

MAINTENANCE

As a renter, it's the landlord's problem when something major in your home breaks. From plumbing problems to leaky roofs, the landlord pays to keep your home in satisfactory condition.

As a homeowner, those same issues are on your dime. As many new homeowners learn quickly, such expenses can add up.

You: How much are we talking?

Expect maintenance spending to cost about one percent of your purchase price every year.

You: Every year?

Every year.

You: Wow.

If you buy the previously mentioned average American $250,000 home, you can reasonably expect to spend about $2,500 each year, or $200 every month, on maintenance.

Of course, reality is often much different. During your years of homeownership, you're unlikely to incur expenses of $200 each month. What's more likely? A few dollars here and there and then—boom!—January 13 and you suddenly find yourself staring at a $4,000 home repair bill. I hope you had money set aside.

You: Me too.

Maintenance's nature as an unpredictable yet potentially significant expense makes it a key disadvantage of home ownership.

You: I see why.

HOMEOWNER'S INSURANCE

When you rent, you should purchase renter's insurance. Fortunately, it's very inexpensive.

You: How inexpensive?

Renter's insurance is often just a couple of hundred dollars a year.

You: Why is it so cheap?

Because you're renting, you do not need to insure the building you live in—that's insurance your landlord should purchase. Instead, you should insure only what could go wrong to the things and people inside. Consequently, renter's insurance is cheap.

When you own a home with a mortgage, you're required to have homeowner's insurance. Since you're not only insuring what's inside the home but also the structure itself, homeowner's insurance will be more expensive than a renter's policy. Plus, if you're in a high risk area, homeowner's insurance could be very expensive.

You: What do you mean by a high-risk area? Kabul? Baghdad? Pyongyang?

Those are higher risk than I am thinking.

You: Where are you thinking?

When I refer to high-risk, I mean places which are flood or hurricane-prone. Getting separate flood insurance—often required—can be a substantial expense. Be sure to get a flood policy quoted before committing to buy a home in a flood-prone area.

PROPERTY TAXES

As a homeowner, you'll be blessed with new taxes to pay—real estate (i.e, property) taxes. In the past, your landlord paid the property taxes on the building you lived in, using part of your rent money to do so. As a homeowner, property taxes are a direct burden to you. Although, as discussed on page 279, real estate taxes are deductible, you should evaluate the property taxes on any home you consider before buying it.

Even within the same state, real estate taxes can vary dramatically from community to community. Sometimes the additional expense can be easily explained and worth it (e.g. a reputation for better schools). Other times, there is no rational way to explain it.[11]

SHORT-TERM PRICE DEPRECIATION POTENTIAL

It can happen.
You: What can happen?
Home prices can go down.
You: I know that.
You do now.
You: No, I knew it before you told me.
Did you know it in 2005?
You: I don't think I thought about it in 2005.

Neither did anyone else. While I have always insisted home prices had to eventually cool off—as my father used to say, "Trees don't grow straight to the sky"—through much of the mid-2000s people reacted as though I was a crazy person.
You: Were you?

---

[11] A snide remark based on your political persuasion *could* be appropriate at this time.

Was I what?

You: A crazy person.

No—but I was wrong. It took until the very late 2000s before things started to change. Like everyone else, I had no idea when the change—a decline—in home prices would occur. But it was bound to happen.

People can lose money on their homes. You are a person. Therefore, you can lose money on your home.

You: That was the most logical and irrefutable paragraph of the entire book.

Thank you. Here's the good news: the longer you live in your home, the less likely your home price will decrease dramatically. However, there is always a risk prices could decline—especially if everyone tells you it can't possibly happen.

TRANSACTION COSTS

Buying a home is expensive. Selling a home is also expensive.

You: I understand why buying a home is expensive, especially since you told me an average American house costs a quarter of a million dollars. But why is selling a home expensive? Wouldn't I get $250,000 if I sold an average house?

No.

You: Why not?

Transaction costs.

You: What are transaction costs?

Every time you buy or sell a home you incur transaction costs such as sales commissions, recording fees, attorney fees, appraisal fees, and Port-a-potty relocation fees.

You: Really?

All except the last one. Usually. But I've seen some crazy fees and they add up. Take, for example, the real estate agent's sales commission.

You: What is that?

The real estate commission is what you pay to the selling agent who sells your home.

You: How much is that?

Typically, six percent.

You: Of what? The purchase price?

Yes. If an agent sells your home for $250,000, you'll pay a six percent, or $15,000, sales commission.

You: That sounds like a lot of money.

Fifteen thousand dollars is a lot of money.

You: Do I have to pay it?

If you use an agent and don't successfully negotiate the rate charged, you'll absolutely pay it. The overwhelming majority of homes sell with an agent involved.

Real estate agent commissions are only one of several transaction costs. Since transaction costs make it very expensive to buy and sell a home, you have a financial incentive not to move around frequently. Even if your home increases modestly in value, the transaction costs alone could cause you to lose money when you sell a few years later. Consider how long you expect to live in a home before you buy it.

BIG MONTHLY PAYMENT

As a homeowner with a mortgage, you must pay not only principal and interest on a sizable loan, but also real estate taxes, homeowner's insurance, and potentially PMI. Still, the amount due each and every month might or might not exceed the cost of your alternative—renting.

Many financial articles and web sites compare the cost to rent vs. the cost to own by metropolitan area. In certain places, it will appear cheaper to rent than to own. In other towns, the opposite is true. But every such analysis I've seen assumes you'd rent the same place as you'd buy.

You: Makes for a reasonable comparison.

And a simple one too. But such comparisons don't reflect your true choices.

You: What do you mean?

Who's to say you'd rent the same place as you'd buy?

You: What?

You could evaluate the situation differently. When my wife and I began looking for places to buy in Chicago in 1999, we considered very nice 1BR condos in very nice buildings with very nice neighbors who drove very nice cars going past very nice restaurants. When we ultimately decided not to immediately buy, we didn't choose to rent a similar place with all the niceties, though we could have afforded to do so.

We took an entirely different approach. If we were going to rent, we decided, we'd rather save more money. In doing so, we'd have more funds available as a down payment for a nicer place down the road, as well as increased retirement savings.

When contemplating your next home, don't solely compare buying and renting two very similar housing options, for you can always rent a lesser home and save more money. If the stars aren't aligned for you to buy a home yet, why not save as much as you can to speed up the time in which they do?

WHEN IS THE RIGHT TIME TO BUY A HOME?

The right time to buy a home is when you are ready.

You: How will I know when I am ready?

When you can afford the home you want to buy. Can you?

You: I think so, but could I know for sure?

When you can answer "Yes" to each of the following five questions, you're ready to buy a home in my book.[12]

1. Will you be able to make a down payment of at least 20 percent of the purchase price?

If so, you not only avoid the previously discussed unnecessary and unhelpful expense of PMI, but you also demonstrate evidence you are not about to over-extend yourself financially.

2. Upon buying the home, will your monthly housing expense be less than 30 percent of your gross monthly income?

Add your projected monthly mortgage payment, your monthly real estate taxes, and your monthly homeowner's insurance premium. That sum

---

[12] Literally.

is your total monthly housing expense. Now consider your gross monthly income. For most middle-class people, nearly all of this income comes from what they are paid—before taxes—each month by their employer(s). If you are married *and* you and your spouse expect to work for the foreseeable future, add the two gross incomes together.

If you project your total home expenses will exceed 30 percent of your gross monthly income, you're in danger of purchasing a home you can't actually afford—notwithstanding a bank's willingness to loan you money assuming a higher percentage of your income being consumed by your basic housing expenses. Just remember, a bank is not concerned if you can afford cable or, for that matter, furniture, in your house. A bank's sole concern is your ability to pay back the loan, not your ability to enjoy the house while doing so.

3. Upon buying the home, will your total debt exceed 36 percent of your monthly income?

Take your total monthly housing cost you calculated while answering question two and add to it your existing monthly debt payments. Such payments include, but are not limited to:

➤ Car loans or car leases
➤ Student loans
➤ Credit card monthly payments on balances you carry
➤ What you owe Vinny every month because of the bad bet on the stupid %#^$&*@ Jets

If the new total, when divided by your gross monthly income, exceeds 36 percent, you're beginning to enter the "stretched" category. When you get over 40 percent, you're playing with fire. When you approach 50 percent, you're being just plain irresponsible. Again, that's not to say a bank wouldn't lend you the money anyway. But remember, they're not the ones who have to live in a home where the owner can't afford to put out bath mats, or for that matter, have toilet paper in both bathrooms at the same time.

4. After paying the down payment and closing costs, will you still have a few thousand dollars in savings to deal with all the unplanned and unexpected miscellaneous housing related expenses you will undoubtedly incur in your new home?

Ideally, even after making your sizable down payment, you'd still have at least three months of living expenses squirreled away for an emergency. While I realize a 20 percent down payment and a 3-month emergency fund is a lot of money, some unfortunate people do get fired or very sick shortly after they buy their home.

Don't put every last penny into your new home. After you move in, you will need money to pay for many new expenses. You're not going to want to go into credit card debt for the repeated visits to Home Depot™ or Lowe's™. Those visits are going to happen—even if you buy new construction.

Those are the first four key home affordability questions. When you can answer yes to each of them, you're in good shape to buy a home. But, even then, it still might not make sense to buy a home.

You: Why not?

You still have one more question to answer "Yes" to before you can be confident it's a good idea to buy a home.

You: What is the question?

5. Do you expect to stay in this home for at least five (preferably at least seven) years?

You: Why does that matter?

The longer you expect to live in your home, the lower your risk of losing money on it. I don't want you to lose money on your home.

You: Me neither. In fact, I'd like to make money on my home.

Me too. But the shorter the amount of time you own your home, the more likely you could suffer from a price decline and the more likely your transaction costs could wipe out the small gain you might have had otherwise. In addition, home ownership means losing a tremendous amount of flexibility—as discussed on page 276—to pursue dreams which might require relocation. So if you think five years in one place is a stretch, you value flexibility greatly—stay in your current place or rent another.

But when you're ready to buy a home, you're ready to begin the journey of home buying. Approach it methodically and keep your emotions out of it. Or, at least try to keep your emotions out of it.

WHEN YOU KNOW YOU'RE READY TO BUY A HOME

The first and most important thing to do once you know you're ready to buy a home is to get pre-approved.

PRE-APPROVAL VS. PRE-QUALIFICATION

You: What does pre-approval mean?

It means the bank has researched you and your finances and, upon doing so, is potentially prepared to make a commitment to you.

You: Do I need to make a commitment to the bank?

No.

You: Good, I am not much of a commitment person.

This is a different kind of commitment.

You: I knew that. How?

When you are pre-approved, the bank tells you, in writing, how much you can borrow to buy a home. You should take your pre-approval letter with you when you interview buyer's agents (discussed later).

A pre-approved buyer is taken much more seriously than one who is not. Remember when, after her transformation at a competing dress shop, Julia Roberts in *Pretty Woman* walks into the dress shop where she had been snubbed previously and says, "I was in here yesterday, you wouldn't wait on me. You work on commission right? Big mistake. Big! Huge!"

When you're pre-approved, you don't need to say anything. Just like Julia Roberts, everyone knows you're for real.

You: I don't look as good as she does.

Me neither—and this is getting weird, I admit. With a pre-approval letter, you will be taken seriously.

You: Because I have a bank's commitment.

Indeed, pre-approval shows your agent, the selling agent, and the seller you can afford the home. You're a player now.

You: What do I have to do to become pre-approved?

Go through the pre-approval process with one bank. Use a bank where you already have an existing relationship.

You: A relationship?

Yes, like a checking or savings account. To gain pre-approval, you need to provide information to your bank/mortgage lender. Such documentation will probably include:

- Pay stubs
- Recent W-2s
- Bank account statements
- Retirement account statements
- Recent tax returns

Depending on your history, the bank might require additional information. Since the bank will do a credit check, you'll also need to provide your social security number. If you plan to buy a home with someone else, such as a spouse or partner, he or she will also need to provide the information above.

A short time after reviewing your documents, your bank notifies you of your pre-approval amount. You're almost ready to look at homes!

You: What about pre-qualification?

Pre-qualification is a less-involved process which is, not coincidentally, also much less meaningful. If you are wondering how much home you could afford, but are not yet serious about actually buying one, pre-qualification is a good option. Pre-qualification typically does not require a credit check but consequently doesn't do much to assure agents and owners you are a serious and qualified buyer. That's because the bank isn't putting its neck on the line in terms of approving you for a loan.

You: So what's a pre-qualification worth?

It's as if you're Julia Roberts and you walk into the fancy dress shop and instead of looking all fine with your new multi-thousand dollar wardrobe, you come in wearing an outfit your older sister gave you last year and tauntingly flash a debit card from a local credit union.

You: Huh?

You'll be taken more seriously than someone who looked like Miss Roberts did the first time she went into the shop, but no one's going to lose any sleep they didn't get a chance to sell to you. A pre-qualified buyer is not half the player a pre-approved buyer is.

Get pre-approved.

BUYER'S AGENTS

After you get pre-approved, it's time to find a qualified agent.

You: To sell my home?

Yes, unless you think you can sell it by yourself.

You: What if I don't own a home? Do I need an agent if I am buying, but not selling, a home?

Yes, in that case you should work with a buyer's agent.

You: Do I have to pay a buyer's agent?

It depends on your perspective. Here are my thoughts on the matter, plus some advantages of working with a buyer's agent and how to find the right one for you.

HOW AND WHY TO CHOOSE A BUYER'S AGENT

Adapted from a post to the *Beyond Paycheck to Paycheck* blog, July 15, 2009

After my wife and I were pre-approved, we began to look for a buyer's agent.

You: Why a buyer's agent?

Although you can shop for a home without a buyer's agent, a buyer's agent's assistance can be critical, especially for first time home buyers like my wife and me. I understand many things about home buying, particularly on the financial side. But there are also a lot of intricacies I don't understand including roofs, heating systems, and septic concerns. With other parts of the home buying process, I don't even know what I don't know.

You: Unconscious incompetence.

Yes—the scariest kind.

The Cost of a Buyer's Agent

You: So how much does a buyer's agent cost?

Anywhere from nothing to 3 percent to 6 percent of the sales price of the home you buy.

You: So on a $300,000 home, a buyer's agent could cost me $18,000?

Yup.

You: That's a lot of money—why would you pay $18,000 if you could get a buyer's agent for free?

You can't get a buyer's agent for free.

You: But you just said I could get a buyer's agent for as little as nothing.

I did.

You: So what are you talking about?

Who Pays the Buyer's Agent?

It's a matter of perspective. Some people claim a home buyer doesn't pay for the services of a buyer's agent because the payment isn't actually taken from the buyer's funds at closing.

You: ¿Qué significa eso, en Inglés?

Pardon me?

You: What does that mean, in English?

Right.

Closing is when the sale actually occurs and the money and the house deed are exchanged. When you close on a home, a typical seller pays a 6 percent commission to the seller's agency. This 6 percent fee is subsequently split, usually evenly, between the buyer's agency and the seller's agency. If the buyers don't have an agency representing them, the seller's agency keeps the whole commission.

You: Your explanation makes it sound as if my buyer's agency is free to me, since the seller pays a 6 percent commission and I don't make any payment. What's the argument I'm really paying a 3 percent or 6 percent commission as a buyer?

Let me answer your question with a question of my own.

You: It's your book.

Think about the money the seller pays to the selling agency from his funds at closing.

You: Okay.

Where does that money come from?

You: From the seller's funds at closing—you just said so!

Fine. Where did the seller get those funds just a few seconds earlier?

You: From the buyer.

Right. It's a matter of perspective. I liken it to the half of the Social Security tax your employer pays on your behalf. Sure, the employer writes the check to the government, but its money which could have otherwise been paid to you. You feel the pain of the tax payment even though you don't actually write the check. Likewise with a buyer's agent, the agency commission costs you even if you don't write a check.

Wisely selecting a buyer's agent is a worthwhile exercise; besides, you're paying for one anyway!

How to Choose a Buyer's Agent

You: How did you choose your buyer's agent?

Deliberately. Just as you shouldn't choose a surgeon from a phone book, you shouldn't pick a buyer's agent based solely on who hosted a recent open house or who introduced herself at the grocery store last week while you were both pondering the sorry state of the organic kiwi selection.

My wife and I have learned a few things about buyer's agents during our years scouting homes together in the various states in which we lived. One of the most important rules of buyer agent selection is recognizing the best agents won't be in the office when you call or randomly stop by.

You: Where will they be?

Selling homes.

You: Even in a down market?

Especially in a down market. In fact, in a lousy market they may be the only ones selling homes. Some of the less effective agents are eliminated from the profession entirely when the economic downturn removes the easy sales.

You: So how do you find the best buyer's agents?

Your referral network. Talk to your friends and colleagues. Find out who they've used and are excited to recommend. Those who have had good buyer's agents will be eager to share his or her name. But don't just ask your friends, "Do you know a real estate agent?"

You: Why?

Because everyone knows a real estate agent. Heck, some of your friends may be real estate agents themselves—not that there's anything wrong with that. But you want an agent who comes recommended based on the *experience* of someone you trust.

We found two excellent buyer's agents using this approach and, quite honestly, liked them both. However, you can only work with one agent at a time.

You: Why?

Because that's how it works.

You: Not helpful.

Sorry. In order to get the best efforts of your buyer's agent, he or she is going to want an exclusive right to work with you for a period of time. To me, a time period of a few months is a reasonable request—especially if you've thoroughly vetted the candidate.

You: So how did you choose between the two agents you liked?

It wasn't easy, but it came down to their referral networks. One simply had been in the business longer and knew more people. Such extensive experience is worthy of your consideration too. Plus, if you have multiple qualified candidates, you can also evaluate their "intangibles."

You: Like fit? Personality?

Certainly, but not simply because you like one more than the other. Rather, base your decision on whose style you think will be most effective at landing you the right house at the right price. Choose someone who not only knows their stuff but also has the confidence to call you out if you're about to do something you shouldn't do or to not do something you ought to.

You: What if I don't know anyone who can make a trustworthy referral?

Then find out who sold the most properties in your area last year and make an appointment with that person.

You: For real?

Yup. That guarantees you're not going to get Buddy.

You: Buddy?

Buddy is the new guy. You don't want the new guy.

You: How do I find out who sold the most properties?

Go into a local real estate office and find the sales awards plaques in the lobby. See who has his or her name on the wall the most times. Tell the receptionist you have or would like to make an appointment with that person.

You: That will work?

Buddy might not like it—since he's sitting around the office waiting for a new client—and the top agent might find it a bit odd, but he or she will be thrilled to have a new client, especially one that's pre-approved.

You: What else should I consider when buying a home?

It's a great question you should pose to your new buyer's agent. As he or she would tell you, schools are important.

You: But I don't have any kids.

You might have kids one day.

You: What if I feel pretty strongly I won't?

Even if you don't want kids, aren't married, don't want to be married, are allergic to children, or are already in your seventies, schools still matter.

You: Why?

Because one day you will try to sell your home.

You: And?

And the people who might buy it from you are going to care about the schools.

You: But the home is an over 55 community.

Schools still matter.

You: Really?

Even in a retirement community, schools play a role in the resale value of your home, since some old folks like to have grandchildren somewhat nearby.

You: What else should I consider when buying a home?

As the saying goes, the three most important things in real estate are:

1. Location
2. Location
3. Location

You: But you said schools were critical.

I did. But think about it—the schools are based solely on the location of the property.

You: Right.

Furthermore, there are many other reasons why location is the most important consideration.

You: You mean top three considerations.

Correct.

You: What else matters when shopping for a home?

FINANCING MATTERS!

SHOP AROUND

When it comes to financing, don't say yes to the first offer.

You: What?

In the previous chapter about car buying, we discuss keeping car sales-people honest by ensuring they know you could walk away from the deal at any moment. The same strategy is required with home mortgage lenders.

You: But I've never heard a banker say, "What would it take to get you in this 30 year mortgage today?"

Me neither. Still, car and mortgage salesman have more in common than their attempted sale of expensive products and a plentiful supply of breath mints.

You: What else do they have in common?

Flexibility.

You: How do you mean?

In the same way cars have many prices, banks have many rates. Furthermore, different banks have different rates. When the seller has accepted your offer, it's time to shop around to obtain the absolute best rate you can find.

You: Why does it matter? How much could I possibly save shopping around? A quarter of a percentage point? A half of a point?

Perhaps.

You: Is that really a big deal?

It's a huge deal! So many people carefully watch their minor expenses only to fail miserably on their mortgage decisions—their most major of major expenses. Remember Saving Strategy 5: Major on the major, minor on the minor. A mortgage is an area where you must focus. Do not simply take the first offer or talk solely to the one mortgage banker who your real estate agent recommended.

Figure A-1 shows the amount of interest you pay over 30 years assuming various fixed interest rates and home prices. If you live in the Northeast, an average home cost $234,100 during early 2011. If you make a 20% ($46,820) down payment to avoid PMI, your mortgage is $187,280. Every quarter of a point (0.25%) you save on the interest rate of your mortgage means a reduction of approximately $10,000 of interest you pay. Save a half a point and expect to save about $20,000.

Figure A-1

Grand Total of Mortgage Interest Paid Over 30 Years

U.S. Region	Northeast	Midwest	South	West
Average Home Price	$ 234,100	$ 124,400	$ 141,800	$ 197,400
Mortgage with 20% down payment	187,280	99,520	113,440	157,920
Interest Rate:		Total Interest Paid:		
4.50%	154,331	82,011	93,482	130,137
4.75%	164,419	87,372	99,592	138,643
5.00%	174,649	92,808	105,789	147,270
5.25%	185,020	98,319	112,071	156,014
5.50%	195,528	103,903	118,436	164,875
5.75%	206,169	109,558	124,882	173,848
6.00%	216,942	115,282	131,407	182,932

All mortgages are assumed to be 30-year fixed mortgages.

Let that sink in: You can potentially save $20,000 by merely being more attentive to your home financing than the Average Joe out there. Same house. Same neighborhood. Same schools. Twenty-thousand dollars saved.

You: That's a lot of money.

You can buy a bunch of lattes for $20,000. Major on the major.

UNDERSTANDING THE DIFFERENT LOAN OPTIONS

Shopping for a mortgage is like visiting an ice cream shop.

You: I've heard bankers can be cold.

While that's true, especially to those with poor credit, the analogy has less to do with temperature and more to do with flavors. When you visit a Baskin Robins™, Carvel™, Friendly's™ or Stucci's™, you can choose vanilla. You can even choose chocolate. But you'll also have dozens of other flavors to choose from. Some of those other flavors were created just last week and, after a disappointing consumer response to Orange Passion Provolone Fruitcake, are never manufactured again.

You: That sounds disgusting.

It was.

You: I thought you made that flavor up.

No comment.

VANILLA—THE THIRTY YEAR FIXED

The most traditional kind of home mortgage loan is a thirty-year fixed rate mortgage. If you use this type of mortgage, you will make 360 (30 years multiplied by 12 months) equal payments. At the end of 360 payments, you will own your home free and clear. This is the best option for the vast majority of people.

You: Why?

The fixed rate means the interest rate charged on your loan never changes. As a result, your payment never changes. This gives you, as a buyer, a great deal of predictability in planning your cash-flow. Furthermore, should your earnings increase, the mortgage becomes easier to pay since your payment is fixed.

You: What other mortgage options are there?

Plenty!

You: Like flavors at the ice cream shop.

Yup. Another common mortgage is an adjustable rate mortgage, often called an "ARM."

You: And to think I was embarrassed to ask what an ARM was.

Why?

You: It sounded like something I should have already known. After all, I have two arms myself.

You should ask any questions you have as you go through the home buying and mortgage processes. It might be cliché, but you shouldn't buy or sign anything you don't understand. A good mortgage banker and a good agent are the first to agree—and to explain anything you don't understand.

An adjustable rate mortgage, like it sounds, features a mortgage interest rate which can change over the term of the loan. ARMs are often 30 years long as well—meaning you make 360 payments—and the rate is often locked-in for a period of years. Common ARMs are 5/1 and 7/1.

You: What do 5/1 and 7/1 mean?

A 5/1 ARM has a guaranteed rate for five years. After five years, the rate can change, but only once per year. With a 7/1 ARM, your rate won't change for at least seven years. Subsequently, it too can change once per year.

You: So the number before the slash is the number of years for which the rate is fixed and the number after the slash is how many times per year the rate can increase after the lock expires?

Well-said.

You: I guess I can do this.

Yes, you can.

You: So if the rate can change with an ARM, why would anyone choose an ARM instead of a fixed rate mortgage?

Because the initial rate on an ARM will be less than the rate on a fixed rate mortgage. Consequently, people who are certain they will move during the first five or seven years of homeownership will pay less in interest choosing an ARM.

You: But?

But you already have my thoughts on buying a home if you intend to move in less than five years.

You: Right—I shouldn't.

Unless you love risk and/or are already very sound financially. Besides, people tend to be pretty lousy at making long term predictions.

We all know folks who fully expected to live in their dream house forever only to pick up and leave two years later due to a family issue or job relocation. Similarly, we have friends who were just going to "get into the neighborhood first" and then "trade up," yet they're still sitting there six years later and the very thought of having to pack the attic or basement creates instant and lasting fear.

You: The bottom line?

Be careful about predicting how long you'll be in a home. The older you get the faster time passes.

You: What other loans do I need to know about?

Although there are many other creative types of mortgage loans, none are any good for you. Consequently, I am not going to discuss interest-only loans which, incidentally, are exactly what they sound like and should never have been widely available.

You: So if you only pay the interest on the loan and not the principal, how exactly does the loan ever get paid back?

Great question. Funny—banks stopped asking it for a while.

You: I'm not sure if it's "funny."

Me neither. Payment-option loans are a real hoot too.

You: Are those for real?

Sadly. Regardless of which loan you take, don't choose a mortgage because it's the only way you can afford the home you like. If the only way you can afford the home is to purchase it using creative financing, guess what?

You: What?

You can't afford the home. It's just no one has told you because they don't think you want to hear it. As an author with thick skin who won't see your reaction, I can be more honest:

You can't afford THAT home. Buy a different, less expensive home or wait until you can afford it. Life will go on and you will sleep much better. Come to think of it, so will I.

Thanks, I feel better now.

You: Me too.

Good.

You: What else should I know about financing?

TERMS

While most loans feature thirty year terms, other terms exist. Besides the 30 year home loan, the most commonly advertised mortgage is a 15 year note.

You: What's a 15 year note?

A mortgage whereby you make 180 (15 years multiplied by 12 months) monthly payments before your debt is paid.

You: So if you only have to make half as many payments as a 30 year note, why wouldn't everyone chose the 15 year option?

Because you have to pay more every month.

You: Right. Twice as much.

Wrong.

You: Wrong?

Sort of. You're right that a person who takes a 15 year note has to pay more than if he took a 30 year note. However, the payment required does not double. In fact, it doesn't come close to doubling.

You: Really?

Really. The payment required on a 15 year mortgage is far less than twice the payment required on a 30 year mortgage.

You: So you'd pay far less in total if you chose a 15 year mortgage vs. a 30 year mortgage?

Absolutely.

You: So, again, why wouldn't everyone choose a 15 year mortgage instead of a 30 year mortgage?

Simple: the combination of expensive home prices and people's expectations precludes the majority from taking advantage of a 15 year note.

You: That doesn't sound simple.

Most people can't afford what they want unless they take out a 30 year mortgage. A 15 year note, despite the incredible amount of money it saves is—quite ironically—out of reach for most people.

You: Why is that ironic?

Something about people feeling they can't afford to spend less strikes me as ironic.

You: I see.

Especially when it's their choice to spend more and their decision results in their reduced ability to save for their future.

You: Ugh.

But *you* can choose to be different. With a substantial down payment and some candid soul-searching before you start looking at houses, *you can choose* to limit your home search to places you can afford with a 15 year mortgage.

If your finances make such a goal impossible as a first time home buyer, consider trying it with the next home you buy. Remember, a 50-year old signing up for a new thirty-year mortgage should expect to be making mortgage payments until he turns 80 (good luck with that when you're on Social Security) or selling his home long before. Sooner or later, you do have to pay back the loan.

Personally, I prefer sooner.

The best motivation for a shorter mortgage is math. Take a look at the charts nearby which compare 30-year and 15-year mortgages of $150,000, $250,000, and $500,000. To my special friends in California or the east coast, I included a $750,000 loan for shock value too.

Figures A-2

Comparison of Total Interest Paid on a 15 vs. 30 year Fixed $150,000 Mortgage

Length of Mortgage	30 years	15 years	Comparison
Monthly Payment	$ 760	$ 1,147	At 4.5%, the 15-yr mortgage has a $388 higher monthly payment.
Total Interest (4.5%)	123,610	56,548	At 4.5%, the 15-yr mortgage saves $67,062 in interest charges.
Monthly Payment	852	1,226	At 5.5%, the 15-yr mortgage has a $374 higher monthly payment.
Total Interest (5.5%)	156,606	70,613	At 5.5%, the 15-yr mortgage saves $85,994 in interest charges.
Monthly Payment	948	1,307	At 6.5%, the 15-yr mortgage has a $359 higher monthly payment.
Total Interest (6.5%)	191,317	85,199	At 6.5%, the 15-yr mortgage saves $106,118 in interest charges.

Figure A-3

Comparison of Total Interest Paid on a 15 vs. 30 year Fixed $250,000 Mortgage

Length of Mortgage	30 years	15 years	Comparison
Monthly Payment	$ 1,267	$ 1,912	At 4.5%, the 15-yr mortgage has a $646 higher monthly payment.
Total Interest (4.5%)	206,017	94,247	At 4.5%, the 15-yr mortgage saves $111,770 in interest charges.
Monthly Payment	1,419	2,043	At 5.5%, the 15-yr mortgage has a $623 higher monthly payment.
Total Interest (5.5%)	261,010	117,688	At 5.5%, the 15-yr mortgage saves $143,323 in interest charges.
Monthly Payment	1,580	2,178	At 6.5%, the 15-yr mortgage has a $598 higher monthly payment.
Total Interest (6.5%)	318,861	141,998	At 6.5%, the 15-yr mortgage saves $176,863 in interest charges.

Figure A-4

Comparison of Total Interest Paid on a 15 vs. 30 year Fixed $500,000 Mortgage

Length of Mortgage	30 years	15 years	Comparison
Monthly Payment	$ 2,533	$ 3,825	At 4.5%, the 15-yr mortgage has a $1,292 higher monthly payment.
Total Interest (4.5%)	412,034	188,494	At 4.5%, the 15-yr mortgage saves $223,540 in interest charges.
Monthly Payment	2,839	4,085	At 5.5%, the 15-yr mortgage has a $1,247 higher monthly payment.
Total Interest (5.5%)	522,020	235,375	At 5.5%, the 15-yr mortgage saves $286,645 in interest charges.
Monthly Payment	3,160	4,356	At 6.5%, the 15-yr mortgage has a $1,195 higher monthly payment.
Total Interest (6.5%)	637,722	283,997	At 6.5%, the 15-yr mortgage saves $353,726 in interest charges.

Figure A-5

Comparison of Total Interest Paid on a 15 vs. 30 year Fixed $750,000 Mortgage

Length of Mortgage	30 years	15 years	Comparison
Monthly Payment	$ 3,800	$ 5,737	At 4.5%, the 15-yr mortgage has a $1,937 higher monthly payment.
Total Interest (4.5%)	618,050	282,741	At 4.5%, the 15-yr mortgage saves $335,309 in interest charges.
Monthly Payment	4,258	6,128	At 5.5%, the 15-yr mortgage has a $1,870 higher monthly payment.
Total Interest (5.5%)	783,030	353,063	At 5.5%, the 15-yr mortgage saves $429,968 in interest charges.
Monthly Payment	4,741	6,533	At 6.5%, the 15-yr mortgage has a $1,793 higher monthly payment.
Total Interest (6.5%)	956,584	425,995	At 6.5%, the 15-yr mortgage saves $530,589 in interest charges.

You: Some of this seems hard to believe. Do I understand it correctly?
Probably.

You: Walk me through an example anyway.

Look at the middle column in Figure A-3. Assuming a 5.5% interest rate and a $250,000 loan, a standard 30-year fixed mortgage requires a $1,419 monthly payment. A 15-year mortgage entails a $2,043 monthly payment, which is $623, or 44%, higher. However, if you were to select the 15-year note you would pay $143,323 LESS in interest.

You: Wow.

Of course, this assumes the interest rate for the 15-year mortgage is the same as the rate charged for the 30-year mortgage.

You: Is that realistic?

Actually, since banks consider 15-year mortgages less risky, the rate on a 15-year mortgage will be lower than on the 30-year note.

You: So a shorter mortgage is even better than it first appears?

Figures A-6

Comparison of Total Interest Paid on a 15 vs. 30 year Fixed $250,000 Mortgage

Length of Mortgage	30 years @ 5.5%	15 years @ 4.75%	Comparison
Monthly Payment	$ 1,419	$ 1,945	Because of the lower rate, the monthly payment on the 15-year mortgage increases by $526 (not by $624, as before)
Total Interest	261,010	100,024	Furthermore, the total interest saved is an enormous $160,986 or 62%!

Yes. In the hypothetical example shown in Figure A-6, the 15-year interest rate is 0.75% less than the rate charged on the 30-year note.[13] Due to that interest rate difference, a 15-year note is a) less painful than originally shown in the middle column of Figure A-3, and b) probably the largest saving opportunity you will ever consider. That a 15-year mortgage is a tough pill to swallow is indisputable. Before you conclude you can't afford it, consider how your life will change—at least from a wealth creation perspective—if you can somehow pull it off.

POINTS

One last choice you'll be given by the mortgage lender is the option to pay points.

You: What are points?

A point is a percentage point.

You: What does it mean in this context, Einstein?

For a $250,000 loan, one percent is $2,500.

You: So if it's optional to pay $2,500, why would I do so? Why would anyone?

---

[13] While the exact amount of the differential changes all the time and varies by bank, 0.75% is a reasonable difference.

Paying points can lower your mortgage rate. Once again, math dictates whether paying points is a good or bad idea.

You: Do tell.

The longer you expect to be in your home, the more likely prepaying interest, which is what a point represents, makes sense.

You: Why?

Because you'll pay the reduced interest rate for a longer period of time.

You: How do I know if I'll be in my home long enough for paying points to make sense?

You won't know, but you can make an educated guess.

You: How?

Figure out how much the points cost. In the example above, it is $2,500. Next, compute how much you would save in monthly interest. The lender can help you with this calculation. Say you'd save $25 each month. Since $2,500 divided by $25 equals 100, 100 months is the break-even point.

You: Meaning?

Meaning if you expect to say in the home more than 100 months (8 years and 4 months), you'd be better off paying the point. However, if you felt such a long stay was unlikely, you'd be better off saving your cash and paying the slightly higher interest rate.

Points, like most housing decisions, are pure mathematical decisions with far-reaching impact on your overall financial affairs. Fortunately, the calculations are few and not overly difficult.

Spend a few minutes today to figure out your best strategies to save thousands of dollars, perhaps tens of thousands of dollars, tomorrow. You'll never be able to save so much more by sacrificing so little. After all, you still get your house—it'll just be less expensive. What does this approach cost you? Only a bit of time and a little patience.

Enjoy your journey over the threshold. Live the life you really want.

CASE STUDIES

FRIDAY Q & A: WHERE TO PUT YOUR FUTURE HOUSE DOWN PAYMENT MONEY TODAY

Adapted from a post to the *Beyond Paycheck to Paycheck* blog, June 12, 2009

Coincidentally, I received the following two emails less than five minutes apart from one another:

*You signed my copy of **Beyond Paycheck to Paycheck** sometime ago. In it, you refer to a hypothetical 8 percent rate of return in several places. Where or how does one get this rate? I have $60,000 I should be able to grow with little or no risk. I'd like to buy my first home in six months—with most of this money as a down payment. What options do I have to safely grow this money?*

—Becky B., Chicago, Illinois

I'm thinking of buying my first house sometime in the next four to five years and I know I should start saving now. But what is the best way of saving? Should I put my money in a high-interest savings account, in a 3-year CD, or invest in a mutual fund? How do I choose the best option? Thank you.

—Diana C., Los Angeles, California

Straightforward Answer: Your investment choices must match your time horizon.

More Detailed Explanation:

Whenever you save money, you *must* invest it.

You: No, I could put it in the bank.

Putting your money in the bank is an investment. It's called investing in "cash." Broadly speaking, your investment choices are:

- ➤ Cash (includes savings accounts, checking accounts, money in your wallet, and change in the couch).
- ➤ Fixed Income (includes savings bonds, municipal bonds, corporate bonds, and the stable value option in your retirement plan)

➤ Equities (includes stocks)

You: What about mutual funds?

Mutual funds can fall into any of the three categories above.

You: Even cash?

Absolutely. A money market fund is actually a mutual fund invested in ultra-safe assets such as "cash and cash equivalents." Furthermore, some mutual funds invest in more than one category.

You: They can do that?

Sure. A balanced fund, for example, often has a large percentage invested in both fixed income and equities.

Your Risk Tolerance, Time Horizon, and Investment Choices

As covered in depth in the investing chapter of *Beyond Paycheck to Paycheck*, your risk tolerance should drive your investment choices. Unfortunately, that's often not how it's done, since people frequently make choices:

➤ Out of fear of losing their funds. Therefore, they keep all their money in the bank; this is known as a "Depression Mentality"

➤ Out of fear of missing out on the next good thing. Therefore, they purchase 17 condos in Miami, putting $1,000 down per unit; this is known as the "Greed Mentality"

But that's a post for another day.

Your risk tolerance is based on your personality and time horizon. Both Becky and Diana have shared their time horizons as six months and four to five years respectively. Let's first address Becky's conundrum.

Becky wants an 8 percent return and has a 6-month time horizon

Becky won't be happy.

You: Why not?

Because she has two mutually exclusive objectives. The first is to earn an 8 percent rate of return on her money. The second is extreme safety for her money since she needs it for a home down payment in just 6 months.

You: Why can't she achieve both of her two goals?

She can—just not at the same time on the same money. In order to *expect* to earn about 8 percent, she'll need to invest her funds in the stock market.[14]

You: So?

There's a ton of volatility in the stock market.

You: Well, there's a newsflash.

To some people it is. Secondly, when times are good—which they will be again—many people forget about risk. Or, more precisely, they redefine risk as "not making as much money as someone else did." All along, in good markets and in bad, you can make money and you can lose money investing in stocks.

No matter how aggressive Becky feels, she must keep her down payment money in cash. Doing so is the only way to ensure she will absolutely have her money available to her when she needs it six months from now.

Only with her cash in a savings account or a money market fund can she be certain she won't lose her principal. Furthermore, only cash affords her the ability to avoid timing the market. Where will the stock market be in six months?

You: I don't know.

---

[14] If you are skeptical an 8 percent rate of return is remotely achievable or feel it dramatically understates today's opportunity, I say only: I don't know what's going to happen to any specific investment or group of investments. By the way, neither do you.

Eight percent is the long-term historical return of the stock market. Since 1900, the rate exceeds nine percent. Since 1990, it's more than seven percent. Consequently, eight percent is a reasonable estimate for long-term stock market performance.

Me neither. You wouldn't want Becky to be forced to sell if we're back down at Dow Jones 6,500 six months from now, would you?

You: No. Will it go back to 6,500 again?

I don't know.

You: Me neither.

I think you see my point.

You: Right. So Becky can't get 8 percent without risking her principal?

Correct—and please don't comment about the sure thing in soybeans.

Gary: It's actually frozen orange juice.

Whatever. There's no "sure thing" in any commodity investment.

Becky, just keep your money in a high-interest savings account and you'll be fine. If you're absolutely certain you won't need it for six months and you can get a better rate with a 6-month CD, feel free.

Diana Has More Time—Can She Take More Risk?

Diana's four to five year time horizon is a bit longer. But her risk of missing her goal is less from a potential loss of principal than from a lack of sufficient savings. Diana needs to aggressively begin saving to achieve her goal of buying a home. It takes a long time to obtain a down payment of 20 percent of the price of the home to avoid costly and utterly unnecessary PMI—especially in California.

You: Why is PMI unnecessary? I thought it was required if you put down less than 20 percent.

It is required. It's unnecessary because no one forces you to buy a home on which you can't afford to put 20 percent down.

You: But—

But nothing. Save longer or buy a less expensive home. Or, like Diana and Becky, start saving well before you actually go home shopping.

You: When Diana starts saving, where should she put her money she has earmarked for a home?

In the bank.

You: She shouldn't invest in stocks?

Probably not.

You: Why not?

Because the risk of principal loss is still too great.

You: But if the next three years prove to be stellar for the stock market, this would prove to be the wrong advice.

No, it would prove to be unlucky advice. It's the right advice for that very reason: we simply don't know what stocks will do over the short-term. Many people advocate investing in stocks for your long-term objectives like retirement. Count me among them. From my vantage point, stocks make sense for my retirement plan as much today as they did 15 years ago when I started investing. I still felt that way earlier this year when the Dow was down in the mid 6,000s.

Don't get me wrong, the market trauma may have periodically caused some lower intestinal distress, but it was, and still is, the best way to go—for the long-term.

You: What's long-term?

At least 10 years. Four or five years is just too short. Diana, put your money in something much safer than stocks. A CD (or more than one CD) could be attractive, but you shouldn't be investing your home money in anything where you could actually lose your principal.

More aggressive and sophisticated investors could consider bonds or other fixed income investing—but given where we are with interest rates at the moment, even those may prove to be overly risky—especially for someone new to the investing game.

> **Good News**
>
> All of this leads to a wonderful conclusion: saving is the primary factor for when and what kind of home you buy someday. When a person calls his bank, shares his impeccable credit history, and tells the lender he's going to put down 20 percent, he gets the maximum borrowing power at the lowest rates available. This is the future for Becky and Diana.
>
> *You: And me?*
>
> It's up to you.

BIDDING ON A HOME

Adapted from a post to the *Beyond Paycheck to Paycheck* blog, July 27, 2009

> My wife and I bid on a house last weekend.
> *You: Did you get it?*
> You have to hear the story first.
> *You: But I'm excited! Did you get the house? Where is it?*
>
> # # #
>
> My wife and I have had several discussions about the trade-offs between a great location and a great home.
> *You: How would you categorize the home you bid on?*
> While the home had some curb appeal, it was all about location.
> *You: How so?*
> Great neighborhood. Side street. Excellent schools. Walkable community. But the home itself is dated and small, especially for a family of four. In addition, some significant non-cosmetic updates, like windows and the septic, need to be immediately addressed.
> *You: Changing the windows sounds like a cosmetic upgrade, no?*
> Ordinarily, yes. But the big problem with the windows in this home is their age. Since they haven't been addressed in a couple of

generations, they were filled with unabated lead paint. You can argu-
ably get away with that if you don't have kids in your house, but I'm
planning on taking my kids with me to my next home.

You: I should hope so. Did you get the home?

Wait a minute. We had a second showing of the home last weekend. In the days leading up to the showing, we learned a bid on the
home had been verbally accepted. But because the agreement wasn't
signed and the sellers didn't know if or how we'd bid, they wanted us
to see the home anyway.

As a result, this was the most intense property viewing we've
had to date. We knew if this were a home we wanted to buy, we'd
need to bid on it that day. Because of the verbally accepted offer,
there would be no tomorrow for this property—it would be sold.
We went through the home with our buyer's agent, trying to notice
each of the various advantages and disadvantages of the home.

Then our time was up. We had to make a decision.

You: So you decided to bid? That is the title of the post, after all.

Yes, sort of.

*You: I don't think you can sort of bid. You either bid or you
don't bid.*

We told the selling agent we were going to bid but didn't throw
out a number.

*You: The number is the most important part of the bid. Without a
number, anyone can bid. Bid, bid, bid, bid.*

This is starting to remind me of the *Seinfeld* car rental scene
where Jerry discusses the important elements of taking a car rental
reservation. Because our agent had a busy day ahead of her with
other clients, she told the seller's agent we would make an offer, but
not until the evening when she would have time for us to reconvene,
run comps (i.e., research similar recent home sales) and come up
with a number to offer.

The seller's agent agreed, noting our offer would need to be strong.

Over the next several hours we stressed over whether to bid.

You: But you already said you were going to bid.

We were, but then we had time to think about it.

You: So you reconsidered?

Absolutely. This was a major decision. Not only because of the financial implications, but also because the decision to put our family in a small, older home weighed on us. At about 6:30 PM, I met our agent at her office. She offered to start pulling up comp numbers.

I told her she needed to take off her agent hat for a minute and be a psychologist first. She graciously agreed. I then—and I am not making this up—had the most indecisive hour of my life. I couldn't decide whether to make a move on this home. I was trying to reconcile all the pro's and con's in my head and wound up arguing with myself. It wasn't pretty. Finally, the agent attempted to put an end to my madness by saying, "You have to decide."

You: So what did you do?

What any man would do in such a situation.

You: Punt?

No. I called my wife.

You: She wasn't there?

She was getting the kids down to bed and waiting for the babysitter to arrive. (We had planned on going out to dinner that evening.)

You: What did your wife say?

She repeated what she had told me all day. Specifically, she told me she would be very happy to live in the home, but also that she didn't **need** to live there and saw herself being very content in a number of other homes.

You: Did that help?

Not really. I told her the vote was one to one between me and myself and she needed to break the tie. We spoke for another few minutes and it suddenly became evident where we were, at least emotionally.

You: Emotionally?

You bet. There are a ton of emotions during the home buying process. I try to stay aware of my feelings, but there's no denying them.

You: So what were you feeling?

While we were excited about the prospect of living in the home because of its location and charm, we were not overly enthusiastic given the high price, small size, and work (and additional money) required getting it into the shape we'd need. Finally, we came to a conclusion: we would bid on the home but only to the point where we would be enthusiastic to have purchased the house.

You: Did you get it?

Wait! Once we decided we would bid, we needed to decide how much. Our agent suggested we each come up with a number we'd feel comfortable bidding. So I came up with one number, my wife another. The numbers were different, but not dramatically so.

You: Did you average them?

We thought about doing so, but decided against it. Instead, we agreed to use the lower of the two numbers.

You: Saving you some money.

And also decreasing the chance of landing the home. Remember, another party had already placed an offer on the home.

You: So why did you use the lower number?

Because the lower number represented the highest one of us was willing to pay. By definition, going above that number would have caused one of us to go out of his/her comfort zone.

Then we signed our name a few dozen times, initialed our names 349 additional times, and left the agent's office. As we walked to dinner, we were nervous. We still weren't sure if we had done the right thing. Much of the stress was caused by the speed at which we felt compelled to make a decision in this, a supposed buyer's market.

Then, rather suddenly, I was at ease.

You: Why? A glass of wine before dinner?

No—I simply realized something. Just allowing a few minutes to pass enabled me to appreciate that my wife and I had done the right thing.

You: How so?

While our offer was a good offer, it wasn't a particularly "strong" offer. The only way we were likely to get the home was if the seller's agent had been bluffing. Since I didn't think she was bluffing, we most likely wouldn't get the home, leaving us disappointed. On the other hand, our bid ensured we would not overpay, which was a relief.

If we did get the home, we'd get it at a price where we would be excited. The reduction from asking price would allow us, from a financial perspective, to comfortably replace the windows and update the septic. Instead of being stressed at the price we bid, we'd be enthusiastic.

Ultimately, I was comfortable because we came to the same conclusion in one stressful day we would have arrived at had we had several days to consider the purchase. I was happy. We had a nice dinner. By the time we got home, we already had an email from our agent.

You: What did she say?

The sellers were going with the other, stronger, offer.

You: How do you feel?

Just as I thought—relieved and disappointed. But I now know this home wasn't meant to be. The search goes on . . . but I know we'll find a great home.

Post-script: Indeed we did get a great home. Our home is less than one mile from the one discussed in this post. We got it at a better price with far fewer issues. It just took another few months.